CUBA'S REPRESSIVE MACHINERY
Human Rights Forty Years After the Revolution

Human Rights Watch
New York·Washington·London·Brussels

ISBN 1-56432-234-3
Library of Congress Catalog Card Number: 99-63561

Addresses for Human Rights Watch
350 Fifth Avenue, 34th Floor, New York, NY 10118-3299
Tel: (212) 290-4700, Fax: (212) 736-1300, E-mail: hrwnyc@hrw.org

1630 Connecticut Avenue, NW, Suite 500, Washington, DC 20009
Tel: (202) 612-4321, Fax: (202) 612-4333, E-mail: hrwdc@hrw.org

33 Islington High Street, N1 9LH London, UK
Tel: (171) 713-1995, Fax: (171) 713-1800, E-mail: hrwatchuk@gn.apc.org

15 Rue Van Campenhout, 1000 Brussels, Belgium
Tel: (2) 732-2009, Fax: (2) 732-0471, E-mail: hrwatcheu@skynet.be

Web Site Address: http://www.hrw.org

Listserv address: To subscribe to the list, send an e-mail message to majordomo@igc.apc.org with "subscribe hrw-news" in the body of the message (leave subject line blank).

Human Rights Watch is dedicated to protecting the human rights of people around the world.

We stand with victims and activists to bring offenders to justice, to prevent discrimination, to uphold political freedom and to protect people from inhumane conduct in wartime.

We investigate and expose human rights violations and hold abusers accountable.

We challenge governments and those holding power to end abusive practices and respect international human rights law.

We enlist the public and the international community to support the cause of human rights for all.

HUMAN RIGHTS WATCH

Human Rights Watch conducts regular, systematic investigations of human rights abuses in some seventy countries around the world. Our reputation for timely, reliable disclosures has made us an essential source of information for those concerned with human rights. We address the human rights practices of governments of all political stripes, of all geopolitical alignments, and of all ethnic and religious persuasions. Human Rights Watch defends freedom of thought and expression, due process and equal protection of the law, and a vigorous civil society; we document and denounce murders, disappearances, torture, arbitrary imprisonment, discrimination, and other abuses of internationally recognized human rights. Our goal is to hold governments accountable if they transgress the rights of their people.

Human Rights Watch began in 1978 with the founding of its Europe and Central Asia division (then known as Helsinki Watch). Today, it also includes divisions covering Africa, the Americas, Asia, and the Middle East. In addition, it includes three thematic divisions on arms, children's rights, and women's rights. It maintains offices in New York, Washington, Los Angeles, London, Brussels, Moscow, Dushanbe, Rio de Janeiro, and Hong Kong. Human Rights Watch is an independent, nongovernmental organization, supported by contributions from private individuals and foundations worldwide. It accepts no government funds, directly or indirectly.

The staff includes Kenneth Roth, executive director; Michele Alexander, development director; Reed Brody, advocacy director; Carroll Bogert, communications director; Cynthia Brown, program director; Barbara Guglielmo, finance and administration director; Jeri Laber special advisor; Lotte Leicht, Brussels office director; Patrick Minges, publications director; Susan Osnos, associate director; Jemera Rone, counsel; Wilder Tayler, general counsel; and Joanna Weschler, United Nations representative. Jonathan Fanton is the chair of the board. Robert L. Bernstein is the founding chair.

The regional directors of Human Rights Watch are Peter Takirambudde, Africa; José Miguel Vivanco, Americas; Sidney Jones, Asia; Holly Cartner, Europe and Central Asia; and Hanny Megally, Middle East and North Africa. The thematic division directors are Joost R. Hiltermann, arms; Lois Whitman, children's; and Regan Ralph, women's.

CONTENTS

ACKNOWLEDGMENTS

This report was written by Sarah A. DeCosse, researcher with the Americas division of Human Rights Watch, on the basis of research she carried out between 1997 and 1999. Anne Manuel, deputy director of the Americas division, contributed research and writing to the chapter on international policy and edited the report. José Miguel Vivanco, executive director of the Americas division, Joanne Mariner, associate counsel at Human Rights Watch, and Jeri Laber, senior advisor to Human Rights Watch, also edited the report. We received help with the research and production of this report from Megan Himan, Jessica Galería, and Monisha Bajaj, associates with the Americas division, as well as several interns, including Amanda Sussman, Ariana Grebe, Loren Becker, Shadi Aryabod, Carina Cristovão, Jessica Baumgarten, and Sarah Carey. Special thanks to Steven Lee Austin for his assistance in the production of this report.

We are indebted to all of the Cuban former political prisoners, family members of political prisoners, human rights activists, independent journalists, labor rights activists, and others interviewed for this report. We especially appreciate the willingness of those living in Cuba to speak to us. We also are grateful to Giselda Hidalgo and Amado J. Rodríguez of Human Rights in Cuba for their valuable assistance. We would like to thank David Nachman, board member of the Americas division of Human Rights Watch, who interviewed Cuban Justice Minister Roberto Díaz Sotolongo for this report.

The J.M. Kaplan Fund provided generous support for the translation of this report into Spanish. The report was translated by Juan Luis Guillén.

I. SUMMARY AND RECOMMENDATIONS

Summary

Over the past forty years, Cuba has developed a highly effective machinery of repression. The denial of basic civil and political rights is written into Cuban law. In the name of legality, armed security forces, aided by state-controlled mass organizations, silence dissent with heavy prison terms, threats of prosecution, harassment, or exile. Cuba uses these tools to restrict severely the exercise of fundamental human rights of expression, association, and assembly. The conditions in Cuba's prisons are inhuman, and political prisoners suffer additional degrading treatment and torture. In recent years, Cuba has added new repressive laws and continued prosecuting nonviolent dissidents while shrugging off international appeals for reform and placating visiting dignitaries with occasional releases of political prisoners.

This report documents Cuba's failures to respect the civil and political rights enumerated in the Universal Declaration of Human Rights (UDHR) as well as the international human rights and labor rights treaties it has ratified. It shows that neither Cuban law nor practice guarantees the fundamental rights enshrined in the Universal Declaration. Cuba's obligation to respect the declaration arises from its incorporation into the United Nations Charter, rendering all member states, including Cuba, subject to its provisions. The UDHR is widely recognized as customary international law. It is a basic yardstick to measure any country's human rights performance. Unfortunately, Cuba does not measure up.

Repression of Dissidents

Cuban authorities continue to treat as criminal offenses nonviolent activities such as meeting to discuss the economy or elections, writing letters to the government, reporting on political or economic developments, speaking to international reporters, or advocating the release of political prisoners. While the number of political prosecutions has diminished in the past few years, Cuban courts continue to try and imprison human rights activists, independent journalists, economists, doctors, and others for the peaceful expression of their views, subjecting them to the Cuban prison system's extremely poor conditions. Even as Cuba released some political prisoners early in 1998—most of whom had completed most of their sentences—continuing trials replenished their numbers. Prison remained a plausible threat to any Cubans considering nonviolent opposition. In the case of four dissident leaders arrested in July 1997 and only tried—for inciting sedition—in March 1999, receiving sentences ranging from three and one-half to five years, the arbitrariness of Cuban repression was starkly on display.

In the past two years, Cuban prosecutors have relied heavily on criminal code provisions against enemy propaganda and contempt for authority (*desacato*) to silence dissent. During this period, prosecutors also have tried dissidents for defamation, resisting authority, association to commit criminal acts (*asociación para delinquir*), failure to comply with the duty to denounce (*incumplimiento del deber de denunciar*), and the catch-all charge "other acts against state security" (*otras actas contra la seguridad del estado*). Cuba's prisons also hold nonviolent political prisoners tried for crimes against state security, such as enemy propaganda, rebellion, sabotage, and revealing secrets concerning state security. Individuals convicted of state security crimes often are serving long sentences of ten to twenty years. In addition, Cuba continues to imprison, for "dangerousness," scores of citizens who have not committed a criminal act and also confines persons for "illegal exit" for attempting to exercise their right to leave Cuba.

Cuban Laws Restrict Human Rights

While Cuba's domestic legislation includes broad statements of fundamental rights, other provisions grant the state extraordinary authority to penalize individuals who attempt to enjoy their rights to free expression, opinion, press, association, and assembly. In recent years, rather than modify its laws to conform to international human rights standards, Cuba has approved legislation further restricting fundamental rights. A notable exception to this trend is the partial restoration of religious freedom. But Cuba has consistently refused to reform the most objectionable elements of its laws. Cuba's concurrent refusal to amnesty political prisoners and its continued prosecution of nonviolent activists highlight the critical role that Cuba's laws play in its machinery of repression.

The Cuban Criminal Code lies at the core of Cuba's repressive machinery, unabashedly prohibiting nonviolent dissent. With the Criminal Code in hand, Cuban officials have broad authority to repress peaceful government opponents at home. Cuban law tightly restricts the freedoms of speech, association, assembly, press, and movement. In an extraordinary June 1998 statement, Cuban Justice Minister Roberto Díaz Sotolongo justified Cuba's restrictions on dissent by explaining that, as Spain had instituted laws to protect the monarch from criticism, Cuba was justified in protecting Fidel Castro from criticism, since he served a similar function as Cuba's "king."

Cuban authorities go through strained circumlocutions to deny the existence of political prisoners in Cuba. Despite his admission that Cuban law bars vocal opposition to Castro and other officials, Díaz Sotolongo claimed that Cuba has no political prisoners. He said that Cuban criminal laws only penalize conduct, but not thought, and, as an example, distinguished between the illegality of committing an overt act in the furtherance of a murder versus the legality of merely thinking about it. Numerous Cuban laws explicitly penalize the exercise of fundamental freedoms while others, which are so vaguely defined as to offer Cuban officials broad discretion in their interpretation, are often invoked to silence the government's critics. Díaz Sotolongo's statement also is at odds with Cuba's penalizing the propensity to commit a criminal act, under the Criminal Code's "dangerousness" and "official warning" provisions.

Cuban authorities often refer to peaceful anti-government activists as "counter-revolutionaries." But Cuba's invocation of a state security interest to control nonviolent dissent—for acts as innocuous as handing out "Down with Fidel" flyers—represents a clear abuse of authority. Under Article 29 of the Universal Declaration of Human Rights, restrictions of fundamental rights are only permissible "for the purpose of securing due recognition and respect for the rights and freedoms of others and of meeting the just requirements of morality, public order and the general welfare in a democratic society." Cuba's efforts to silence critics fall well outside these limits.

Cuba frequently denies its citizens internationally recognized due process guarantees. Cuban legislation undercuts the right to a fair trial by allowing the country's highest political authorities to control the courts and prosecutors, granting broad authority for warrantless arrests and pretrial detentions, and restricting the right to a defense. Unfortunately, Cuban courts have failed to observe the few due process rights available to defendants under the law.

The Constitution of the Republic of Cuba explicitly states that the courts are "subordinate in the line of authority to the National Assembly... and the Council of State," a supreme executive branch body, and that the Council of State may issue the courts instructions. This structure robs Cuban courts of even the semblance of independence and impartiality. Cuba permits civilians to be tried in military courts, the independence and impartiality of which are also in question. Cuban judges occasionally choose to try nonviolent government opponents behind closed doors, violating the right to a public trial.

Cuba's criminal procedure allows the police and prosecutorial authorities to hold a suspect for a week before any court reviews the legality of the detention. This clearly violates international norms requiring that a court review any detention without delay. Equally troubling, authorities are not required to notify the accused of his or her right to an attorney until after the court decides on the legality of the detention, which may take up to seventy-two additional hours. Failing to notify the accused of this right until up to ten days after an arrest denies legal assistance to detainees during a critical period and enables authorities to put undue pressure on the detainee through interrogations or intimidation. In practice, Cuban authorities do not comply even with the narrow provisions of this law. The Criminal Procedure Code grants judges broad latitude in determining whether to hold suspects in pretrial detention. Judges often abuse this authority with respect to government critics.

The Cuban constitution states that citizens have the right to a defense, but Cuba's procedural laws, the banning of an independent bar association, and powerful, politicized judicial and prosecutorial authorities seriously debilitate this right. Legally permitting ten-day detentions without any requirement that detainees be notified of their right to an attorney, much less appointed an attorney, violates the right to a defense. The government's close ties with judges, prosecutors and state-appointed or approved attorneys leave many defendants with little hope that their attorneys can or will do anything but request a slightly shorter sentence. In 1973, Cuba eliminated private law firms and required all attorneys who did not work directly for the state to join "collective law firms" (*bufetes colectivos*). Several independent attorneys who had represented dissidents were refused membership in the collective firms.

Although Cuba's Associations Law (*Ley de Asociaciones y Su Reglamento*, hereafter, Associations Law) claims to guarantee the right of association, the law effectively bars the legalization of any genuinely independent organization. The law requires organizations to "coordinate" and "collaborate" with a counterpart state entity. Fulfilling this condition necessitates the group's subjugation to the government organization, by allowing a representative of the state entity to attend and speak at any planned or unplanned meetings; requiring the group to notify the government entity in advance of any publications; coordinating with the government entity regarding participation in any national or international event; regularly reporting to the government entity on its activities; and providing prior notice of the date and hour of any meetings or other activities.

Far from relinquishing control over freedom of expression, association, press, and movement, in recent years the Cuban government has created new mechanisms to strengthen its repressive authority. In February 1999 Cuba's National Assembly approved the Law for the Protection of the National Independence and the Cuban Economy (*Ley de Protección de la Independencia Nacional y la Economía de Cuba*), which took effect in March 1999. The law created harsh penalties of up to twenty years for any actions that could be interpreted as support for the U.S. embargo on Cuba. The new law served as the implementing legislation for a law passed in late December 1996, the Law Reaffirming Cuban Dignity and Sovereignty (*Ley de Reafirmación de la Dignidad y Soberanía Cubanas*), which Cuba described as "a response to the Helms-Burton Law." The March 1996 Cuban Liberty and Democratic Solidarity Act (also known as Helms-Burton) solidified the U.S. trade embargo on Cuba. In response, Cuba created broad restrictions on free expression, criminalizing even the appearance of support for U.S. policies. In February 1997, Foreign Minister Roberto Robaina signed a ministerial resolution creating regulations governing foreign media reporting from Cuba. The regulations require that foreign correspondents demonstrate "objectivity, adhering strictly to the facts and in consonance with the professional ethics that govern journalism," or face reprimand or the withdrawal of credentials. An April 1997 decree restricted internal movement as a purported response to public health, welfare, and public order concerns. While these concerns may be legitimate under international human rights norms, President Castro's statements highlighting the government's interest in minimizing "indiscipline" and maintaining tight control over citizens' movement for security reasons suggest that one motive for the decree may have been political control. While the law did not result in massive round-ups and deportations, Cuban migrants to Havana expressed frustration that they could not choose where to live and that police demands for their personal papers and proof of "legal" residency had increased.

Cuba retains the death penalty for several crimes and adopted it for two additional crimes in early 1999. Human Rights Watch opposes capital punishment as an inherently cruel practice often carried out in a discriminatory manner. Furthermore, the fallibility of all criminal justice systems creates the risk that innocent persons will be executed even when full due process of law is respected. The Cuban legal system's serious procedural failings and lack of judicial independence practically guarantee miscarriages of justice. Cuban law affords convicts sentenced to death minimal opportunities to appeal their sentences. Cuba's reliance on the Council of State—an entity presided over by President Castro, selected by the Cuban National Assembly, and considered the "supreme representation of the Cuban State" under national law—as the ultimate arbiter in death penalty cases denies defendants a meaningful avenue of appeal.

Cuban minors risk being forced to serve as soldiers. The Cuban armed forces conscript minors as young as sixteen.

Cuba's Prisons

Cuba confines its sizable prison population under substandard and unhealthy conditions, where prisoners face physical and sexual abuse. Cuban prison practices fail in numerous respects to comply with the United Nations Standard Minimum Rules for the Treatment of Prisoners, which provide authoritative guidance on prison conditions. In preparation for this report, Human Rights Watch interviewed dozens of former Cuban prisoners, family members of current and former prisoners, and human rights activists within Cuba, many of whom are former political prisoners. These interviews provided us with information on twenty-four of Cuba's maximum security prisons and numerous other detention centers, such as police stations and state security offices.

Most prisoners suffer malnourishment from an insufficient prison diet and languish in overcrowded cells without appropriate medical attention. Some endure physical and sexual abuse, typically by other inmates with the acquiescence of guards, or long periods in isolation cells. Prison authorities insist that all detainees participate in politically oriented "re-education" sessions or face punitive measures. In many prisons, authorities fail to separate all of the pretrial detainees from the convicts and minors from adults. Minors risk indefinite detention in juvenile facilities, without benefit of due process guarantees or a fixed sentence.

The Cuban Interior Ministry runs the prison system, with soldiers often serving as prison guards and labor camp overseers. Each prison's staff includes a re-educator, usually a military official, assigned to direct the prison population's political indoctrination. Prison guards in men's facilities name prisoners to powerful positions as members of "prisoners' councils" *(consejos de reclusos)* and rely on these prisoners to maintain internal discipline. The council members commit some of Cuba's worst prison abuses, including beating fellow prisoners as a disciplinary measure and sexually abusing prisoners, under direct orders from or with the acquiescence of prison officials.

Cuba's political prisoners, held for exercising their fundamental rights of free association, free expression, free opinion, or freedom of movement, provide the government's repressive machinery with credibility, demonstrating that opposition to the government engenders the genuine risk of serving time in prison. Scores of Cuban activists who suffer short-term detentions and who receive official warnings that they will face prosecutions for political crimes take the risk of prosecution and imprisonment in Cuba's jails seriously. While the existence of hundreds of political prisoners cows potential opponents at home, Cuba also uses occasional prisoner releases to maximize political capital abroad. Cuba's deprivation of these individuals' liberty represents a shocking disregard for their fundamental rights. The inhumane conditions and the punitive measures taken against prisoners have been, in several instances researched by Human Rights Watch, so cruel as to rise to the level of torture.

Beyond suffering the difficulties that all Cuban prisoners face, Cuba's political prisoners encounter problems unique to their status as nonviolent activists, often for holding views contrary to the government's or for criticizing human rights violations in the prisons. Prison authorities refuse to acknowledge political prisoners' distinct status and punish them for refusing to participate in political re-education, not wearing prison uniforms, or denouncing human rights abuses in the prisons. Guards restrict political prisoners' visits with family members and subject relatives to harassment. Prisoners' relatives also face government intimidation outside the prison walls. Moreover, Cuba's confinement of nonviolent prisoners with inmates convicted for violent crimes, often in maximum-security facilities with Cuba's most hardened criminals, is degrading and dangerous.

Many Cuban political prisoners spend several months to more than a year in pretrial detention, often in isolation cells. Following conviction, they face additional punitive periods in solitary confinement. The government also crushes free expression inside the prison walls with criminal charges and prosecution of previously convicted prisoners who speak out about inhumane prison conditions and treatment.

Cuban police or prison guards often heighten the punitive nature of solitary confinement with additional sensory deprivation, such as blocking light or ventilation from a cell, removing beds or mattresses, seizing prisoners' clothes and belongings, forbidding prisoners to communicate with one another, or restricting food and water beyond the already meager prison rations. Prison and police officials also disorient prisoners by leaving lights on in cells for twenty-four hours a day, incorrectly setting the time on clocks, or incessantly playing loud music. Experts in treating torture survivors recognize these as methods for imposing physical and psychological torture.

Cuba's treatment of political prisoners violates its obligations under the Convention against Torture and Other Cruel, Inhuman or Degrading Treatment or Punishment, which it ratified on May 17, 1995. Prolonged periods of incommunicado pretrial and post-conviction detention, beatings, and prosecutions of previously tried political prisoners—where those practices result in severe pain or suffering—constitute torture under the convention. Moreover, the Convention against Torture clearly prohibits retaliation against individuals who denounce torture.

When prominent international figures appeal for Cuban political prisoners' freedom, Cuba occasionally releases prisoners prior to the conclusion of their sentence often on the condition that they leave their country forever. In an October 1998 interview, President Fidel Castro frankly discussed Cuba's approach to prisoner releases, emphasizing the "spirit" in which requests for prisoner releases are made, rather than on the rightness or wrongness of Cuba's having prosecuted and imprisoned these persons. Castro's comments reveal the calculated, political nature of Cuba's response to requests for prisoner releases.

Routine Repression

Short of sentencing activists to prison terms or detaining them for lengthy periods without trial, Cuba employs additional tactics to impede individuals and organizations from undertaking activities that are, or that appear to be, in opposition to its policies or practices. The range of repressive measures includes short-term arbitrary detentions, official warnings (*advertencias oficiales*), removal from jobs and housing, surveillance, harassment, intimidation, and forced exile. Government actions against dissidents appear to occur in waves, with lulls followed by periods of intense harassment, often in response to heightened opposition activity. Although Pope John Paul's January 1998 visit to Cuba marked a period of relative calm, government pressures increased as the year went on. In early 1999, the government tried several dissidents and arrested dozens of independent journalists and activists. Dissidents willing to criticize the government publicly risk serious consequences, from the trauma of wrongful arrests and potential prosecutions to the loss of their homes and sources of income, as well as the significant emotional costs wrought by individual and group repudiations or the deprivation of contact with family, community, and culture through forced exile.

Human rights activists and independent journalists are among the government's most frequent targets, along with independent labor organizers. The Cuban government maintains a firm stance against independent journalism, relying not only on mass organizations but also on its security forces and courts to threaten, intimidate, detain, and prosecute journalists who do not espouse the government's views. Cuba also persists in prosecutions, short-term detentions, surveillance, phone interruption, and other intimidations of human rights activists. Prisoners who speak out against abuses face physical violence and other punishments in Cuba's detention centers. Others subjected to government harassment include members of independent political parties, organizations of independent academics, teachers, medical professionals, artists, and environmental activists. The government's denial of legal recognition to opposition groups leaves all members of unauthorized groups at risk of arrest and prosecution.

Cuba routinely bars international media and human rights investigators access to the country in an effort to avoid negative publicity. In an October 1998 interview, President Castro explained the conditions under which he would grant visas to reporters with U.S. news bureaus: "If I were certain objective reporters would come to Cuba and not be biased beforehand, we would...." Cuba's restrictions on press coverage and human rights reporting are among the most severe in the Western Hemisphere.

Labor Rights in Cuba

Wielding its position as virtually the only source of jobs in the state-controlled economy, the Cuban government exercises strict control over labor rights. Cuba not only bans independent labor groups and harasses persons attempting to form them but also factors criticism of the government into hiring and firing decisions. Official control over labor rights extends to the booming foreign investment sector, where foreign companies can only hire Cuban employees through government-controlled employment agencies. And Cuba's extensive prison labor program, meanwhile, fails to observe basic principles for the humane treatment of prisoners and violates an international ban on forced labor, by requiring political prisoners to work.

Ironically, these labor rights abuses occur despite the Cuban governments' claims of protecting the rights to association, assembly, expression, and the right to work. The government's assertions that it guarantees these rights are seriously undermined by the constitutional proviso that government-backed "mass and social organizations have all the facilities for carrying out [these rights], in which their members enjoy the most extensive freedom of speech and opinion." Cuba only permits one confederation of state-controlled unions, the Workers' Central of Cuba (Central de Trabajadores de Cuba, CTC), which is run by a member of Cuba's Communist Party Political Bureau (*politburo*). Cuba has not legalized any independent union, whether in the broader national economy or in the foreign investment sector, and the restrictive measures of the Associations Law all but preclude such a step. Independent labor activists regularly risk detentions, harassment, threats of prosecution, and pressure to go into exile.

Cuba impedes union formation in the international investment sector by mandating that all hiring be conducted by state-controlled employment agencies. Cuba's refusal to allow workers to organize or bargain collectively makes foreign investors complicit in the government's human rights violations.

Religious Freedom in Cuba

Pope John Paul II's January 1998 visit to Cuba fostered hope that the government would ease its repressive tactics and allow greater religious freedom. The papal visit provided a unique opportunity for public demonstrations of faith in a country that had imposed tight restrictions on religious expression in 1960 and was officially atheist until 1992. Although Cuba refused visas to some foreign journalists and pressured some domestic critics during the visit, the pope's calls for freedom of religion, conscience, and expression created an unprecedented air of openness. But while Cuba permits greater opportunities for religious expression than it did in past years, and has allowed several religious-run humanitarian groups to operate, the government still maintains tight control on religious institutions, affiliated groups, and individual believers. On a positive note, in November 1998 Cuba approved visas for nineteen foreign priests to take up residence in Cuba.

Cuba's Bar on International Human Rights Monitoring

The Cuban government often welcomes visits from international organizations providing humanitarian aid, particularly those that have publicly opposed the U.S. embargo. But it routinely bans international human rights and humanitarian agencies that may be critical of its human rights record. The Cuban government has not allowed Human Rights Watch to return to Cuba since 1995. Cuba never allowed the U.N. Special Rapporteur on Human Rights in Cuba to enter the country. The U.N. High Commissioner for Human Rights José Ayala Lasso visited Cuba in November 1994. Unfortunately, he failed to make a public comment about the country's human rights situation.

The Cuban government bars regular access to its prisons by domestic and international human rights and humanitarian monitors. Cuba barred the International Committee for the Red Cross (ICRC), which visits prisoners in custody for political and security offenses all over the world, from conducting prison visits in 1989. Cuba's refusal to allow human rights and humanitarian groups access to its prisons represents a failure to demonstrate minimal transparency. Moreover, the government's barring of the ICRC, which works behind the scenes to protect the rights of political prisoners and does not publicize its findings, shows a profound lack of concern for those prisoners' welfare.

Impunity

Cuba has failed to enforce constitutional provisions that demand accountability for state officials who commit abuses. Cuba routinely denies human rights abuses, fails to investigate or punish those who commit them, and retaliates against those who denounce them, particularly prisoners. The persistence of human rights violations in Cuba is undoubtedly due, in part, to the fact that Cuban officials have faced virtually no consequences for the thousands of human rights violations committed in the past forty years. Yet, Cuba has clear obligations under international law to offer effective remedies to victims of human rights abuses.

The Role of the International Community

After the demise of the Soviet Union, Cuba suddenly found itself in need of trading partners, foreign investment, and humanitarian assistance the outside world. Havana saw a need to repair relations with countries that had formerly treated it as a pariah. The international community thus has new opportunities to press for human rights reforms in Cuba. Unfortunately, the huge divide between U.S. policy and that of Cuba's major trading and investment partners has prevented the development of an effective, unified policy that could bring about change in Cuba.

The United States

Washington's approach to Havana remains defined by its decades-old trade embargo. The 1996 passage of the Cuban Liberty and Democratic Solidarity Act, also known as the Helms-Burton law, removed from the U.S. president's authority any possibility of modifying the embargo without passing new legislation. The embargo has not only failed to bring about human rights improvements in Cuba but has become counterproductive, providing a pretext for Castro's repression while alienating Washington's erstwhile allies. Indeed the U.S. policy of unrelenting confrontation with Cuba has been condemned in unequivocal terms by the United Nations General Assembly, Pope John Paul II, and governments of every political stripe around the world.

Moreover, the embargo restricts the rights to free expression and association and the freedom to travel between the U.S. and Cuba, thus violating Article 19 of the International Covenant on Civil and Political Rights, a treaty ratified by the United States. In 1998, only diplomats or members of intergovernmental organizations such as the U.N. could travel from the U.S. to Cuba without a special license. Following the pope's January 1998 visit to Cuba, President Clinton took the limited step of restoring direct charter flights from the U.S. to Cuba, which the U.S. had banned in 1996.

Criticism of the embargo's harsh impact on the Cuban population has spurred U.S. congressional efforts to ease its indiscriminate effects. Legislation was introduced in both houses of the U.S. Congress in 1997 to lift restrictions on the sale of food and medicines. In early 1998, Sen. Jesse Helms called for humanitarian assistance to "undermine the policies of Fidel Castro." The intended distributor of Helms's assistance, Cuba's Catholic church, made clear it would not play that role should the bill become law. In October 1998, fifteen senators, led by Republican Sen. John Warner, and several prominent foreign policy experts, including former Secretaries of State Lawrence Eagleburger and Henry Kissinger, called on President Clinton to establish a bipartisan commission to reexamine U.S. policy toward Cuba. The Clinton administration rejected this proposal in January 1999, instead opting for a package of limited measures intended to increase contacts between U.S. and Cuban citizens.

The European Union

In recent years, European trade and investment has surged in Cuba. The European Union (E.U.) has expressed strong opposition to the U.S. trade embargo while promoting political and economic openings with Cuba. But Havana has rebuffed efforts to use European aid as a carrot to induce Castro to implement human rights reforms. The "common position," which the E.U. adopted in December 1996 and has renewed at six-month intervals, makes full economic cooperation conditional on "improvements in human rights and political freedom...." In particular, the "Common Position" calls for "reform of internal legislation concerning political and civil rights, including the Cuban criminal code, and... the abolition of all political offences, the release of all political prisoners and the ending of the harassment and punishment of dissidents...." In June 1998 the

E.U. permitted the Castro government to participate as an observer in the negotiations of the Lomé Treaty, which offered preferential trade status to less developed countries. Yet full integration into the group remains conditioned on substantial progress in human rights and political freedom, terms that have been rebuffed by Havana, leaving European policy at a stalemate. The E.U. member states continue to provide economic cooperation and humanitarian aid on an *ad hoc* basis through nongovernmental organizations.

Canada

The Canadian government has sustained bilateral dialogue with Cuba about human rights in the past few years, terming its approach "constructive engagement." The January 1997 accord between Ottawa and Havana addressed investment, taxation, banking, and other issues, as well as calling on Canada to hold seminars and train Cuban judges on human rights issues. Since then, several seminars have been held on women's and children's rights, but the Cuban government does not appear to have changed its human rights practices as a result of the program. In 1998 Canada offered humanitarian assistance to seventeen political prisoners Cuba forced into exile following the pope's plea for prisoner releases. But Prime Minister Jean Chrétien's April 1998 mission to Cuba focused little attention on political and civil rights, and President Castro dismissed Chrétien's appeal for the release of the four leaders of the Internal Dissidents' Working Group. Canada, like the E.U., has aggressively pursued trade and investment opportunities in Cuba.

The United Nations

From 1991 through 1997, the U.N. Human Rights Commission approved annual U.S.-backed resolutions condemning human rights violations in Cuba. The resolutions renewed the mandate of a special rapporteur, Swedish diplomat Carl-Johan Groth, who produced several well-documented reports on the Cuban human rights situation. However, on April 21, 1998, the commission defeated the annual Cuba resolution, ending the special rapporteur's mandate without Cuba ever having granted him permission to enter the country. International resistance to U.S. policy toward Cuba doomed the vote, resulting in an unwarranted lifting of U.N. human rights monitoring. But Cuba's glaring actions in early 1999, trying prominent dissidents and passing repressive legal reforms, appear to have galvanized international support to renew pressure on Cuba. At the April 1999 commission meeting, a resolution condemning Cuban human rights practices, which did not include a provision for a rapporteur, passed by a narrow margin.

In October 1998, the General Assembly voted to condemn the U.S. embargo against Cuba for the seventh time.

Ibero-American Nations

Since the papal visit to Cuba, Latin American and Caribbean nations have intensified diplomatic contact with Cuba; some restored normal relations for the first time in decades. With some notable exceptions, however, these nations have failed to use their renewed dialogue with Cuba to press for human rights protection. In November 1999, the heads of state of all Ibero-American nations will hold their annual summit meeting in Havana.

Recommendations

To the Cuban Government

Legal Reforms, Prosecutions, and Harassment

- The Cuban government should undertake legal reforms to ensure its compliance with international human rights and labor rights treaties to which it is a party. In particular, Cuba should implement the Convention against Torture and Other Cruel, Inhuman or Degrading Treatment or Punishment, by making torture a crime and investigating, prosecuting, and punishing all government officials who employ torture. Such a measure should also penalize any official who retaliates against an individual alleging torture.

- The Cuban government should cease all prosecutions based on the individual's exercise of fundamental rights to free expression, association, and movement. The authorities also should cease repressive actions against human rights activists, independent journalists, members of independent political parties, organizations of independent academics, teachers, religious activists, medical professionals, artists, environmental activists, family members of political prisoners, and others based on their actual or imputed criticisms of the Cuban government or its policies. Such measures include short-term arbitrary detentions, official warnings (*advertencias oficiales*), removal from jobs and housing, surveillance, harassment, intimidation, and forced exile.

- The Cuban government should reform its Criminal Code, repealing or narrowing the definition of all crimes that are in violation of established international human rights norms and practices. Among the "crimes" that should be repealed are: contempt for authority (*desacato*), clandestine printing, illegal exit, defamation of institutions and mass organizations, insulting the nation's symbols, abuse of the freedom of religion, failure to comply with the Associations Law, and failure to comply with the duty to denounce. Cuba also should repeal its "dangerousness" and "official warning" provisions, which are unduly vague and subject to arbitrary enforcement.

- Cuba should cease application of the Criminal Code's state security crimes, including enemy propaganda, rebellion, revealing secrets concerning state security, sedition, sabotage, and other acts against state security (*otros actos contra la seguridad del estado*), against nonviolent dissidents for the exercise of their fundamental rights. These provisions should be repealed or reformed to eliminate vague language permitting their application against such persons.

- The Cuban government should halt the politically punitive use of other legal provisions that, while not explicitly targeting the exercise of legitimate political and civil rights, are so ambiguously and broadly defined that they may be employed to prevent Cubans from exercising those rights. Cuba should narrow the scope of several crimes including: criminal association, disobedience, resistance, insult, calumny, defamation, and illegal entry.

- The Cuban government should restructure its court system to establish judicial and prosecutorial independence.

- The Cuban government should reform the Criminal Procedure Code to provide due process guarantees for all criminal defendants. In particular, the Criminal Procedure Code should afford swift judicial review of all detentions and defendants' prompt access to lawyers. The Cuban government should permit lawyers to practice without joining collective law firms.

- The Cuban government should reform its Associations Law to allow for the legalization of independent groups that are not subservient to state-controlled organizations. The Criminal Code provision penalizing organizations not recognized under the current Associations Law should be repealed.

- The Cuban government should abolish the death penalty. Until such a step is taken, the death sentences of all persons currently on death row should be commuted to life sentences.

- The Cuban government should lift restrictions on foreign journalists working in Cuba, granting visas to journalists despite the content of any prior Cuba coverage.

- The Cuban government should cease the conscription of minors for service in its armed forces.

Prisons and Political Prisoners

- The Cuban government should immediately and unconditionally release all individuals currently imprisoned for having exercised their fundamental rights to free expression, association, assembly, or movement, including all those imprisoned for human rights monitoring and advocacy.

- The Cuban government should take immediate steps to improve prison conditions, particularly ensuring that no resources currently available in the prisons are arbitrarily denied to prisoners based on their political opinions. The government should ensure that all prisoners receive a sufficient daily minimal caloric intake, appropriate medical attention, and adequate housing and sanitary conditions. Cuba should encourage family visits and cease the arbitrary refusal of family provisions of supplies for prisoners, such as food and medicine. The government should address persistent physical abuse by prison guards with investigations and disciplinary measures against the responsible authorities and not by prosecuting prisoners who denounce such abuses.

- Until Cuba releases all its political prisoners, it should segregate political prisoners from common prisoners.

- The Cuban government should cease punishing political prisoners for expressing their views, including for failing to participate in political indoctrination sessions, refusing to wear prison uniforms, or criticizing prison abuses. In particular, Cuban authorities should immediately cease the use of pretrial isolation cells and solitary confinement, the effect of which is worsened by its use for long periods and by sensory deprivation.

- The Cuban government should cease harassment of political prisoners' family members, during visits and outside the prison grounds.

- The Cuban government should cease mandatory political indoctrination in its prisons.

- The Cuban government should permit pastoral visits by clergy, without subjecting prisoners to intense review of their justifications for such visits.

- To increase transparency, the Cuban government should make public detailed information on its prison system. Such materials should include: statistics on the number of prisoners held in preventive detention and those convicted of crimes; persons sentenced to death; the numbers of male and female prisoners; the numbers of prisoners assigned to maximum-security prisons, minimum-security prisons, and work camps; the number of minors held in prisons or other detention centers; and the charges against each detainee.

Human Rights Monitoring

- The Cuban government should permit domestic and international human rights monitoring. The government should officially recognize Cuban human rights organizations, other nongovernmental organizations, and political opposition groups. The Cuban government should grant regular access to its prisons by domestic and international human rights and humanitarian monitors. Cuba should allow the International Committee of the Red Cross to resume prison visits. The Cuban authorities also should permit international human rights organizations, including Human Rights Watch, to conduct human rights investigations in Cuba.

Labor Rights

- The Cuban government should comply with its obligations under international labor rights treaties that it has ratified.

- The Cuban government should ensure that prisoners participating in prison work programs are sufficiently nourished, physically fit, and receive adequate compensation. Cuba should cease compelling political prisoners to participate in prison work programs.

- The Cuban government should demonstrate respect for the freedom of association by ceasing repression of independent labor organizers. Cuba should allow independent labor unions to operate legally.

- The Cuban government should revise its foreign investment laws to eliminate reliance on state-controlled employment agencies and other impediments to labor activism.

Impunity

- The Cuban government should investigate, prosecute, and punish officials responsible for human rights violations and should provide victims of abuses with effective remedies. Any official retaliating against a person alleging human rights abuses should face severe disciplinary measures.

To the United States Government

- The U.S. government should terminate the economic embargo on Cuba. The embargo is not a calibrated policy intended to produce human rights reforms, but a sledgehammer approach aimed at nothing short of overthrowing the government. While failing at its central objective, the embargo's indiscriminate nature has hurt the population as a whole, and provided the government with a justification for its repressive policies. The embargo's restrictions on the free exchange of ideas through travel violate human rights. Finally, the embargo has made enemies of all of Washington's potential allies, dividing those nations that ought to act in concert to press for change in Cuba. Until such a step is taken, the U.S. should repeal those provisions of the Helms-Burton law that restrict the rights to free expression and the freedom to travel between the U.S. and Cuba, in violation of Article 19 of the International Covenant on Civil and Political Rights.

To the European Union

- The European Union's Common Position elaborates clear criteria for human rights gains in Cuba, making full economic cooperation with Cuba conditional on human rights improvements including reform of the Criminal Code, the release of political prisoners, an end to harassment of dissidents, the ratification of international human rights conventions, and respect for the freedoms of speech and association. Yet Cuba has not budged on these issues since the Common Position was adopted in 1996. European governments should redouble their efforts to press Castro for reforms.

To the Canadian Government

- The Canadian government has pursued a policy of constructive engagement with Cuba since signing a January 1997 accord on investment issues that also opened a dialogue on human rights. But Ottawa has little to show for its engagement with Havana and must now use its leverage to push for reforms.

To the Ibero-American Nations

- The Ibero-American countries should use the occasion of the next Ibero-American summit meeting in Havana, scheduled for 1999, to exert meaningful pressure for human rights reforms in Cuba. During the 1996 summit meeting, Castro signed the so-called Viña del Mar Declaration, which committed signatories to respect democracy and political and civil rights. Yet he has taken no steps to fulfill that promise. Nations attending this year's summit should hold President Castro to account for this failure and seek firm commitments, rather than empty promises.

To Foreign Investors in Cuba

- Foreign investors in Cuba should use their influence with the Cuban government to press for Cuban compliance with the international human rights and labor rights treaties that it is committed to uphold. Foreign investors should encourage and protect freedom of association and assembly in the workplace and endorse policies opposing political discrimination in hiring. Investors should strongly discourage Cuba from requiring reliance on state-controlled employment agencies for hiring employees. Companies also should take steps to avoid the inadvertent use of goods produced in whole or in part by prison labor programs that wrongfully require political prisoners' participation or require prisoners to work in abysmal conditions.

II. CUBA'S INTERNATIONAL HUMAN RIGHTS OBLIGATIONS

This report documents Cuba's failure to respect the civil and political rights enumerated in the Universal Declaration of Human Rights (UDHR) and international human rights treaties ratified by Cuba.[1] Cuba has stated that its domestic legislation complies with the UDHR,[2] but this report shows that neither Cuban law nor practices guarantee the fundamental rights enshrined in the declaration. Cuba's international obligation to respect the Universal Declaration arises from the fact that it is incorporated into the United Nations Charter, rendering all member states, including Cuba, subject to its provisions. Also, the UDHR is widely recognized as customary international law. The Universal Declaration constitutes a basic yardstick to measure any country's human rights performance.

Cuba is also bound to uphold numerous international human rights and labor rights conventions it has ratified. In doing so, Cuba assumed responsibility for complying with the treaties' provisions and for incorporating the treaties into Cuban domestic legislation. This report details how Cuban legislation and practices fall far short of compliance with these treaties and in many respects blatantly violate their provisions. The key international labor and human rights agreements ratified by Cuba include the Convention against Torture and Other Cruel, Inhuman or Degrading Treatment or Punishment (hereinafter Convention against Torture), ratified in May 1995; the Convention on the Rights of the Child, ratified in August 1991; the Convention on the Elimination of All Forms of Discrimination against Women (CEDAW), ratified in June 1980; and various International Labor Organization Conventions such as Convention 87, the Freedom of Association and Protection of the Right to Organize, ratified in June 1952; Convention 98, the Right to Organize and Collective Bargaining Convention, ratified April 1952; Convention 105, the Abolition of Forced Labour Convention, ratified June 1958; and Convention 141, the Rural Workers' Organizations, ratified in April 1977. Furthermore, Cuba has publicly stated that it is willing to comply with the provisions of the United Nations Standard Minimum Rules for the Treatment of

---

[1] The Universal Declaration on Human Rights, adopted by the United Nations on December 10, 1948, is included as an appendix to this report.

[2] Cuban report to the United Nations regarding International Human Rights Instruments, June 1997 (HRI/CORE/1/Add. 84), October 13, 1997.

Prisoners, which provide authoritative guidance on the treatment of prisoners.[3] Cuba's stated willingness to abide by these international human rights standards is laudable, although its failure to live up to these commitments is troubling.

Cuba has not ratified one of the key human rights treaties providing specific guarantees of civil and political rights, the International Covenant on Civil and Political Rights (ICCPR), and thus has not ratified the Optional Protocol to the ICCPR, which would allow individual victims of human rights abuse to present claims before the United Nations Human Rights Committee. Cuba also is notably absent among those countries that have signed or ratified the International Covenant on Economic, Social and Cultural Rights (ICESCR), which guarantees trade union rights among others.

When faced with criticism of its civil and political rights record, Cuba often defends its human rights practices by pointing to improvements in economic and social rights and blames any failings on the economic impact of the U.S. trade embargo against Cuba. But, as this report shows, Cuba's restrictions of civil and political rights directly impede Cubans' progress on economic and social rights. For example, Cuba's ban on independent labor unions severely limits workers' ability to improve working conditions and pay scales. Similarly, firing, evicting, or jailing nonviolent anti-government activists violate those individuals' rights to a job, a roof over their heads, and participation in the society. Cuba's denial of sufficient food to political prisoners, based on their political opinion, violates the right to adequate food. On a positive note, Cuba appears to have made significant strides toward compliance with its obligations under the International Convention on the Elimination of All Forms of Racial Discrimination, which it ratified in February 1972.

Cuba routinely insists that its laws guarantee fundamental human rights. But Cuba's constitution, which makes broad assertions of guaranteeing fundamental freedoms, including those of association, expression, and religion, simultaneously undermines these basic human rights, as do other Cuban laws. For example, the constitution nullifies freedoms when they are contrary to "the goals of the socialist State," "socialist legality," or the "people's decision to construct socialism and

---

[3] "Informe de la Fiscalía General de la República de Cuba," presented by Blanca Gutiérrez, Cuba's Attorney General for the Control of Legality in Penitentiary Establishments at the Instituto Latinoamericano de las Naciones Unidas para la Prevención del Delito y el Tratamiento del Delincuente conference, San José, Costa Rica, February 1997, p. 5.

Standard Minimum Rules for the Treatment of Prisoners, approved by the U.N. Economic and Social Council by resolutions 663 C, July 31, 1957 and 2076, May 13, 1997. The Standard Minimum Rules are included as an appendix to this report.

communism."[4] The constitution also has been used to negate the impact of human rights treaties ratified by Cuba by providing that any treaty, pact, or concession that disregards or diminishes Cuba's "territorial sovereignty" is illegal and void.[5] In international fora for the protection of human rights, Cuba often invokes sovereignty as a justification for non-compliance and non-cooperation.

Cuba has a mixed record on questions of international arms control. Cuba ratified the Chemical Weapons Ban Treaty in April 1997. However, at this writing Cuba had not signed the Mine Ban Treaty, which bans the production, use, and sale of anti-personnel landmines. As of September 1997, Cuba's Union of Military Industries (Unión de las Industrias Militares, UIM) still was producing landmines, along with other weapons and military technology.[6]

Torture

This report shows that Cuba's treatment of political prisoners in some cases rises to the level of torture, violating Cuba's obligations under the Convention against Torture and under the Universal Declaration.[7] The convention bars torture and "acts of cruel, inhuman or degrading treatment or punishment" and the Universal Declaration states that "no one shall be subjected to torture." [8] Cuba's imposition of prolonged periods of incommunicado pretrial and post-conviction detention, beatings, and prosecutions of previously-tried political prisoners—where those practices result in severe physical or psychological pain or

---

[4] Constitution of the Republic of Cuba (1992), Articles 10 and 62. Translation by Human Rights Watch. The Constitution and other legal provisions inhibiting the full exercise of human rights are discussed below, at *Impediments to Human Rights in Cuban Law.*

[5] Ibid., Article 11. Translation by Human Rights Watch.

[6] Octavio La Vastida, "Industrias Militares en la Senda de la Eficiencia," *Granma Internacional*, September 3, 1997.

[7] UDHR, Article 5. Torture in Cuban prisons is discussed below, at *Treatment of Political Prisoners: Torture*. The Convention against Torture is included as an appendix to this report.

[8] Convention against Torture and Other Cruel, Inhuman or Degrading Treatment or Punishment, U.N. Doc. A/39/51 (1984), entered into force June 26, 1987, Article 16(1). UDHR, Article 5.

suffering—constitute torture under the convention.[9] Cuba also has failed to comply with its obligations under the convention to "take effective legislative, administrative, judicial or other measures to prevent acts of torture in any territory under its jurisdiction" and to "ensure that all acts of torture are offenses under its criminal law."[10]

Arbitrary Arrest, Detention, and Exile

Cuba frequently subjects nonviolent dissidents to arbitrary arrests and detentions. Human rights activists and independent journalists are among the government's most frequent targets, along with independent labor organizers, religious believers, members of independent political parties, organizations of independent academics and medical professionals, environmental activists, and others. These improper arrests and detentions, which serve as intimidating measures designed to silence dissent, violate Article 9 of the Universal Declaration of Human Rights. Cuba often ratchets up pressure on government opponents by subjecting them to repeated arrests, short-or long-term detentions, or criminal prosecutions. In many cases, the government then presents activists with the "choice" to go to prison, or continue serving a prison term, or be exiled from their homeland. This practice violates the UDHR, which explicitly prohibits governments from exiling citizens from their own country.[11]

Detention Conditions

Cuba confines its sizable prison population in substandard and unhealthy conditions, where prisoners face isolation and physical and sexual abuse. Prison guards also commit abuses against prisoners that rise to the level of torture. Cuba's practices fail to comply with numerous provisions of the Standard Minimum Rules for the Treatment of Prisoners, including the rules governing food, health care, internal prison security, punitive measures, and prison work programs.[12] Short-term detainees usually are held in degrading and inhuman conditions in police stations.

---

[9] These practices are detailed below, at *Treatment of Political Prisoners: Punitive Measures Against Political Prisoners.*

[10] Convention against Torture, Arts. 2(1) and 4(1).

[11] Article 9.

[12] These practices are detailed below, at *General Prison Conditions*, *Treatment of Political Prisoners*, and *Labor Rights: Prison Labor.*

Cuba's integration of political prisoners into its prison labor programs violates a prohibition on forced labor performed by detainees held for their political opinion. This practice is banned under the International Labor Organization's Convention 105, regarding the Abolition of Forced Labor, a treaty ratified by Cuba.

Freedom of Expression and Opinion

Cuba exerts strict control over freedom of expression and opinion, both in law and practice, in violation of the UDHR's Articles 18 and 19. The Criminal Code grants officials extraordinary authority to crush dissent. Among the numerous criminal provisions restricting free expression and opinion, the government frequently employs those against enemy propaganda and contempt for authority (*desacato*) to penalize outspoken activists.[13] The government continues to prosecute its citizens for these and other crimes solely on the basis of their criticism of the government, as well as subjecting independent activists to arrests, detentions, and harassment. The government treats independent journalists and human rights activists with notable harshness. Prison indoctrination programs, where prisoners are forced to participate in pro-government sloganeering, and punishment of prisoners who criticize prison abuses also violate the freedoms of expression and opinion. In a remarkable statement, Cuban Justice Minister Roberto Díaz Sotolongo justified Cuba's restrictions on dissent by explaining that, as Spaniards had instituted laws to protect the monarch from criticism, Cuba was justified in protecting Fidel Castro, Cuba's "king," from criticism.[14]

Cuban authorities often refer to peaceful government opponents as "counter-revolutionaries." But Cuba invokes state security interests to restrict nonviolent dissent, for acts as innocuous as handing out "Down with Fidel" flyers. Under the Universal Declaration of Human Rights, restrictions of fundamental rights are only permissible:

---

[13] These and numerous other offensive provisions are detailed below, at *Impediments to Human Rights in Cuban Law: Codifying Repression*, while several recent prosecutions are discussed at *Political Prosecutions*.

[14] Díaz Sotolongo was referring to the crime of contempt for authority (*desacato*). In the course of the interview, Sotolongo twice referred to Castro with the term "king." Human Rights Watch interview with Roberto Díaz Sotolongo, New York, June 11, 1998. Translation by Human Rights Watch.

> for the purpose of securing due recognition and respect for the rights and freedoms of others and of meeting the just requirements of morality, public order and the general welfare in a democratic society.[15]

Cuba's efforts to silence critics fall well outside these limits.

Freedom of Association

Despite Cuba's assurances that it protects freedom of association, this report details how Cuban legal measures and actions stifle this fundamental freedom for independent labor unions, human rights groups, professional associations, and others.[16] Cuba does not allow any independent labor union to operate legally.[17] Cuba's Associations Law effectively bars the legalization of any genuinely independent organization, requiring associations to accept broad state interference in their activities and arbitrary state authority to shut them down. The government's denial of legal recognition to opposition groups leaves the members of unauthorized groups at risk of arrest and prosecution. Cuba also subjects members of independent organizations to frequent harassment, arrests, and detentions. Cuba's failure to guarantee freedom of association violates Article 20 of the UDHR. The government's infringement of labor rights violates Article 23(4) of the UDHR, as well as several International Labor Organization treaties ratified by Cuba, including Convention 87, the Freedom of Association and Protection of the Right to Organize; Convention 98, the Right to Organize and Collective Bargaining; and Convention 141, the Rural Workers' Organizations.

Religious Freedom

While Cuba permits greater opportunities for religious expression than it did in past years, the government still maintains tight control on religious institutions, affiliated groups, and individual believers.[18] Inside Cuba's prison walls, officials

---

[15] Article 29(2).

[16] Cuban restrictions on the freedom of association are discussed below, at *Impediments to Human Rights in Cuban Law: Codifying Repression* and *Associations Law, Political Prosecutions, Routine Repression, Labor Rights,* and *Limits on Religious Freedom.*

[17] Cuba's multiple pressures on labor activists and legal restrictions on labor organizing are detailed below, at *Labor Rights.*

[18] These restrictions are detailed below, at *Limits on Religious Freedom.*

restrict prisoners' access to pastoral care.[19] Since the exercise of religious freedom—guaranteed in Article 18 of the Universal Declaration—is closely linked to other freedoms, including those of expression and association, Cuba's laws and practices create direct and indirect impediments to religious expression.

Freedom of Movement

Cuba continues to criminalize unauthorized attempts to leave the island as "illegal exit." Cuba's failure to revoke this law calls into question its willingness to legitimize the basic right of its citizens to leave their country. Cuba also maintains its crime of "illegal entry," which has been used to penalize Cuban citizens returning to their homeland. Article 13 of the Universal Declaration of Human Rights guarantees the right of all citizens to leave their country and to return to their country. Cuba's pressuring nonviolent opponents to go into exile, often with threats of prison terms or as a condition of release from prison, violates Article 9's prohibition on exile.

Due Process Protections

Cuban legislation undercuts the right to a fair trial by allowing political figures to control the courts and prosecutors, granting broad authority for warrantless arrests and pretrial detentions, and restricting the right to a defense.[20] Unfortunately, Cuban courts have failed to observe the few legal guarantees of due process rights available to defendants under the law.
These laws and practices violate the due process protections under Articles 10 and 11 of the UDHR, which ensure the right to a fair and public hearing by an independent and impartial tribunal, the right to be presumed innocent until proven guilty, and the right to "all guarantees necessary" for a defense.

Children's Rights

The abuse of minors in Cuban detention centers represents a government failure to comply with the Convention on the Rights of the Child.[21] While Cuba's

---

[19] Prisoners access to religious attention is detailed below, at *General Prison Conditions: Restrictions of Religious Visits.*

[20] Cuba's violations of due process rights are discussed below, at *Impediments to Human Rights in Cuban Law: Due Process Denied, Political Prosecutions,* and *Treatment of Political Prisoners: Abusive Pretrial Detentions.*

[21] Convention on the Rights of the Child, Article 40. The treatment of minors in Cuban detention centers is discussed below, at *General Prison Conditions: Juvenile Justice.*

conscription of sixteen year olds for service in the armed forces satisfies the convention's age limit for child soldiers, Human Rights Watch and other members of the international Coalition to Stop the Use of Child Soldiers urge Cuba to raise the minimum recruitment age to eighteen.[22]

Impunity

This report documents extensive human rights violations committed by the Cuban government that remain unpunished.[23] Under the Universal Declaration and the Convention against Torture, Cuba has an obligation to provide an effective remedy for the violations of fundamental rights, particularly torture.[24] The UDHR states that "Everyone has the right to an effective remedy by the competent national tribunal for acts violating the fundamental rights granted him by the constitution or by law."[25] Beyond failing to take sufficient remedial measures for human rights violations, this report also details numerous retaliatory measures taken against Cubans who complain of governmental human rights violations.[26]

---

[22] Article 38(2) establishes the minimum age for child soldiers as fifteen. Coalition to Stop the Use of Child Soldiers, "Stop Using Child Soldiers!" *International Save the Children Alliance*, 1998, p. 22. The coalition is now leading an effort to create an optional protocol to the convention that would raise the minimum age for military recruitment to eighteen.

[23] The question of impunity for human rights abuses in Cuba is discussed below, at *Impunity*.

[24] UDHR, Article 8 and Convention against Torture, Articles 2(1) and 4(1).

[25] UDHR, Article 8.

[26] Repressive actions against human rights activists and human rights victims complaining of abuses are discussed below, at *Political Prosecutions*, *Treatment of Political Prisoners: Punitive Measures Against Political Prisoners*, and *Routine Repression: Human Rights Activists*.

III. IMPEDIMENTS TO HUMAN RIGHTS IN CUBAN LAW

The rights enshrined in the Universal Declaration on Human Rights are formulated in and protected by current legislation in Cuba. In particular, the Constitution of the Republic endorses each of those rights and specifies the essential guarantees of their exercise. Furthermore, all the rights and freedoms enunciated in the Constitution are duly elaborated in various legal provisions that make up our domestic substantive law.

Cuban report to the United Nations regarding International Human Rights Instruments, June 1997

When the world looks at this with objectivity.... it will see that we have judged these people in accordance with Cuban law.

Ricardo Alarcón de Quesada, Cuban National Assembly President and Politburo Member, regarding the conviction of four prominent dissidents, March 1999

The denial of basic civil and political rights is written into Cuban law. While Cuba's domestic legislation includes broad statements of fundamental rights, other provisions grant the state extraordinary authority to penalize individuals who attempt to enjoy their rights to free expression, opinion, association, and assembly. Cuban legislation also undercuts the right to a fair trial, by allowing the country's highest authorities to control the courts and prosecutors, granting broad authority for warrantless arrests and pretrial detentions, and restricting the right to a defense. Unfortunately, Cuban courts have failed to observe the few legal guarantees of due process available to defendants under the law.

In recent years, rather than modify its laws to conform with international human rights standards, Cuba has approved legislation further restricting fundamental rights. Only a restoration of religious freedoms stands out as a notable exception to this trend. But Cuba has consistently refused to reform the most objectionable elements of its laws. Cuba's concurrent refusal to amnesty political prisoners and its continued prosecutions of nonviolent activists highlight the critical role of Cuba's laws in its machinery of repression.[27]

Cuban Constitution

The Cuban constitution guarantees "the full freedom and dignity of men, [and] the enjoyment of their rights...."[28] However, multiple constitutional provisions undermine these guarantees. The constitution nullifies freedoms when they are contrary to "the goals of the socialist State," "socialist legality," or the "people's decision to build socialism and communism."[29] The breadth of these terms allows for arbitrary, politicized denials of fundamental rights. The constitution has been used to undermine international human rights treaties ratified by Cuba by providing that any treaty, pact, or concession that disregards or diminishes Cuba's "territorial sovereignty" is illegal and void.[30] In international fora for the protection of human rights, Cuba often invokes sovereignty as a justification for non-compliance and non-cooperation.

The constitution also grants citizens a right "to fight, using all means, including armed struggle... against anyone attempting to overthrow the political, social, and economic order established by the constitution."[31] René Gómez Manzano, a prominent Cuban dissident attorney who was sentenced to a four-year prison term in March 1999 for inciting sedition, has challenged this provision as an invitation to government sympathizers to intimidate nonviolent government opponents.[32]

---

[27] For further discussion of these concerns, see *Political Prosecutions, Treatment of Political Prisoners,* and *Routine Repression.*

[28] Constitution of the Republic of Cuba (1992), Article 9(a). Translation by Human Rights Watch.

[29] Ibid., Articles 10 and 62. Translation by Human Rights Watch.

[30] Ibid., Article 11. Translation by Human Rights Watch.

[31] Ibid., Article 3. Translation by Human Rights Watch.

[32] René Gómez Manzano, "Constitución y Cambio Democrático en Cuba," in *Cuba in Transition - Volume 7* (Washington: Association for the Study of the Cuban Economy, 1997), p. 407. Gómez Manzano is a member of the Internal Dissidents' Working Group. Cuban authorities arrested four of the group's leaders, including Gómez Manzano, on July 16, 1997. For further discussion of their case, see *Political Prosecutions.*

Beyond the conditionality of rights created by the provisions detailed above, several constitutional articles restrict the very rights they claim to ensure. The freedoms of speech and press, for example, exist "in keeping with the goals of the socialist society." In a strange twist, the constitution claims to ensure free speech and press by mandating that "press, radio, television, films, and other mass media are state or social property, and may in no instance be the object of private ownership."[33] Similarly, the constitution tempers the rights to assembly, demonstration, and association with a proviso that government-backed "mass and social organizations have all the facilities for carrying out [these rights], in which their members enjoy the most extensive freedom of speech and opinion."[34] The constitution detracts from Cuba's laudable efforts to provide universal education with restrictions on academic freedom. Cuba's educational and cultural policy must adhere to "the ideology of Marx and Martí"; promote communist training; and allow for "free artistic creation, provided that its content is not contrary to the Revolution."[35]

Constitutional provisions guaranteeing religious and economic rights offer more consistent statements of rights. Cuba's broad guarantees of religious rights, which were adopted in 1992 constitutional reforms and marked a shift away from an atheistic state, provide that:

> The State, which recognizes, respects, and guarantees freedom of conscience and religion, simultaneously recognizes, respects, and guarantees the freedom of every citizen to change religious creeds, or not to have any; and to profess the religious worship of their choice, based on respect for the law.[36]

Yet, the constitution does condition religious freedom, according to the potentially expansive requirement that professions of faith are "based on respect for the law." While Cuba's record of respect for religious rights has improved in recent years, the

---

[33] Cuban constitution, Article 53. Translation by Human Rights Watch.

[34] Ibid., Article 54. Translation by Human Rights Watch.

[35] Ibid., Article 39(a), (c), and (ch). Translation by Human Rights Watch.

[36] Ibid., Article 55. The constitution also provides for religious freedom under Article 8. Translation by Human Rights Watch.

government continues to impose some undue restrictions on religious freedom and tightly controls the freedom of conscience.[37]

In the economic realm, the constitution guarantees the rights to work, social security, medical care, and education, and aspires to provide comfortable dwellings for all citizens.[38] The government has had notable successes in guaranteeing these rights. Nevertheless, Cuba continues to discriminate politically in the provision of economic rights, most notably in the arena of labor rights, by banning all independent unions.[39]

The constitution explicitly grants women equal economic, political, cultural, social, and familial rights with men and bars discrimination based on "race, skin color, sex, national origin, religious creeds, and any other type [of discrimination] offending human dignity."[40] Yet Cuban nationals are routinely barred from enjoying amenities open to foreigners. In a phenomenon popularly known as "tourist apartheid," the best hotels, resorts, beaches, and restaurants are off limits to most Cubans, as are certain government health institutions.[41]

Regarding due process guarantees, the constitution bars any violence or coercion to force individuals to make statements, voids any coerced statements, and provides for the right to a defense.[42] While these provisions should serve as important deterrents to human rights abuses, in practice the Cuban legal system has failed to protect these rights.[43] Similarly, Cuba often disregards the constitutional right to freedom from arbitrary arrest and search, and the privacy of

---

[37] For discussions of religious rights in Cuba, see *Routine Repression* and the religious visits section of *General Prison Conditions.*

[38] Cuban constitution, Article 9(b). Translation by Human Rights Watch.

[39] For a discussion of Cuba's violations of economic rights, see *Labor Rights.*

[40] Cuban constitution, Articles 41 and 42. Translation by Human Rights Watch.

[41] Ironically, the constitution states that these are rights "won by the Revolution" for the enjoyment of all citizens, "without distinction based on race, skin color, sex, religious creeds, [or] national origin...." Ibid., Articles 43 and 44. Translation by Human Rights Watch. For further discussion of the tourist industry, see *Labor Rights.*

[42] Ibid., Article 59.

[43] Cuban legal procedures are discussed below, at *Due Process Denied.*

correspondence and telephone communications.[44] Cuba's utter lack of judicial and prosecutorial independence contributes to these abuses.

The constitutional provision stating that judges are "independent, and owe obedience solely to the law" is completely at odds with constitutional directives regarding the structure of Cuba's government.[45] The constitution provides that Cuba's National Assembly selects the Supreme Court, the attorney general and the deputy attorneys general. Cuba's judges and prosecutors must then report regularly to the National Assembly, which also retains the authority to remove them.[46] This structure clearly allows for the National Assembly to exercise political control over judges' and prosecutors' activities. Although Cuba allows voters to elect members of the National Assembly, only one candidate may sit for each seat.[47] The constitution further clarifies that the courts are "subordinate in the line of authority to the National Assembly... and the Council of State," as is the Office of the Attorney General.[48] The Council of State has authority to issue instructions to both the courts and the Office of the Attorney General.[49] The Council of State is an entity presided over by President Castro, selected by the Cuban National Assembly, and considered the "supreme representation of the Cuban State" under Cuban law.[50]

---

[44] Cuban constitution, Articles 56, 57, and 58.

[45] Ibid., Article 122. Translation by Human Rights Watch.

[46] Ibid., Articles 75(m) and (n), 126, 129, and 130. Translation by Human Rights Watch.

[47] Ibid., Article 71. Cuba expert Prof. Jorge Domínguez commented that Cuba's electoral law "appears to have been designed by politicians who were terrified that a dissident could be chosen for the National Assembly. The law establishes an awkward and complex mechanism that seeks to control the election more than the representativeness of its results." Translation by Human Rights Watch. Jorge Domínguez, "La Democracia en Cuba: ¿Cúal es el Modelo Deseable?" *La Democracia en Cuba y el Diferendo con los Estados Unidos* (Havana: Centro de Estudios sobre América, 1995), p. 120. Since the publication of this book, the Cuban government closed the Center for American Studies.

[48] Ibid., Articles 121 and 128. Translation by Human Rights Watch.

[49] Ibid., Article 90(h) and (I).

[50] Ibid., Article 89.

Cuba's constitution also provides for important guarantees that state officials who commit abuses will face consequences and victims will receive restitution, but in practice, Cuba has not enforced these rights.[51] The most vigorous provision on accountability provides that:

> Any person who suffers damage or injury wrongfully caused by State officials or agents, in connection with the discharge of the duties inherent in their positions, is entitled to demand and obtain the pertinent reparation or compensation in the manner stipulated by law.[52]

The constitution directs that state officials responsible for coercing statements "shall incur the penalties established by law."[53] Another provision grants every citizen the right "to address complaints and petitions to the authorities," and to receive a response "within a suitable period of time, according to law."[54]

The constitution recognizes the Communist Party as "the superior leading force of the society and the State."[55] This distinction endorses government-mandated political discrimination, necessarily relegating any other political party to an inferior status. Of course, given the concurrent limits on the freedoms of speech, association, and assembly, Cubans face serious impediments to the exercise of their political rights. As noted above, elections for the National Assembly are non-competitive. According to Cuba's justice minister, Roberto Díaz Sotolongo, the National Assembly also has the authority to accept or reject any prospective candidates for public office.[56] Given the heavy hand of the government in the electoral process, and the absence of any choice, the constitutional provision that the National Assembly "represents and expresses the sovereign will of the people" rings hollow.

---

[51] Cuba's failure to provide effective remedies for victims of human rights violations is discussed below, at *Impunity*.

[52] Cuban constitution, Article 26. Translation by Human Rights Watch.

[53] Ibid., Article 59. Translation by Human Rights Watch.

[54] Ibid., Article 63. Translation by Human Rights Watch.

[55] Ibid., Article 5. Translation by Human Rights Watch.

[56] Human Rights Watch interview with Justice Minister Roberto Díaz Sotolongo, New York, June 11, 1998.

Codifying Repression

The Cuban Criminal Code lies at the core of Cuba's repressive machinery, unabashedly criminalizing nonviolent dissent. With the Criminal Code in hand, Cuban officials have broad authority to repress peaceful government opponents. Cuba's criminal laws are designed to crush domestic dissent and keep the current government in power by tightly restricting the freedoms of speech, association, assembly, press, and movement.

Cuban authorities go through strained circumlocutions to deny the existence of political prisoners in Cuba. Despite admitting that Cuban law bars vocal opposition to Castro and other officials, Cuban Justice Minister Roberto Díaz Sotolongo claimed in an interview with Human Rights Watch that Cuba holds no political prisoners. He said that Cuban criminal laws only penalize conduct, not thought, and as an example, distinguished between the illegality of committing an overt act in the furtherance of a murder versus the legality of merely thinking about it.[57] Yet numerous Cuban criminal provisions explicitly penalize the exercise of fundamental freedoms while others, which are so vaguely defined as to offer Cuban officials broad discretion in their interpretation, are often invoked to silence government critics.

Cuban authorities regularly refer to peaceful government opponents as "counterrevolutionaries." But Cuba's invocation of state security interests to control nonviolent dissent—for acts as innocuous as handing out "Down with Fidel" flyers—represents a clear abuse of authority. Under the Universal Declaration of Human Rights restrictions of fundamental rights are only permissable:

> for the purpose of securing due recognition and respect for the rights and freedoms of others and of meeting the just requirements of morality, public order and the general welfare in a democratic society.[58]

Cuba's efforts to silence critics fall well outside these limits.

An international team of legal scholars, diplomats, and U.N. rights specialists, meeting at a 1995 conference in Johannesburg, South Africa, drafted a set of principles that provide further guidance regarding permissable justifications for restricting rights. In particular, the Johannesburg Principles on National Security,

---

[57] Human Rights Watch interview with Roberto Díaz Sotolongo, New York, June 11, 1998.

[58] Universal Declaration on Human Rights, Article 29(2).

Freedom of Expression and Access to Information distinguish between legitimate and illegitimate invocations of national security interests. Legitimate reasons to invoke national security interests are:

> protecting a country's existence or its territorial integrity against the use or threat of force, or its capacity to respond to the threat or use of force, whether from an external source, such as a military threat, or an internal source, such as incitement to violent overthrow of the government.

In contrast, illegitimate justifications for invoking national security interests include:

> protecting the government from embarrassment or exposure of wrongdoing, or to entrench a particular ideology, or to conceal information about the functioning of its public institutions, or to suppress industrial action.[59]

The Johannesburg Principles also specify that certain types of expression should always be protected, including criticizing or insulting the state and its symbols; advocating nonviolent change of government or government policies; and communicating human rights information.[60] Cuba's state security laws violate these principles, illegitimately restricting fundamental rights both in the phrasing of the laws themselves and in their application against nonviolent dissidents.

The human cost of Cuba's repressive Criminal Code is high. Thousands of Cubans have faced wrongful prosecutions and imprisonment since the Castro government came into power in 1959. Despite growing international criticism of the Criminal Code, the Cuban government has roundly refused to reform its most offensive provisions and has continued arrests and prosecutions of government opponents, detailed below at *Prosecutions Continue* and *Routine Repression.*

In the past two years, Cuban prosecutors have relied heavily on the provisions against enemy propaganda and contempt for authority (*desacato*) to silence dissent. Prosecutors also have tried dissidents for defamation, resisting authority,

---

[59] The full text of the Johannesburg Principles is available in *The New World Order and Human Rights in the Post-Cold War Era: National Security vs. Human Security*, papers from the International Conference on National Security Law in the Asia Pacific, November 1995 (Korea Human Rights Network, 1996).

[60] Ibid.

association to commit criminal acts (*asociación para delinquir*), dangerousness (*el estado peligroso*), and other acts against state security (*otros actos contra la seguridad del estado*) during this period. Cuba's prisons confine scores of citizens convicted for the exercise of their fundamental rights, or in some cases, convicted without ever having committed a criminal act, for dangerousness. Cuba also detains nonviolent political prisoners who were tried for crimes against state security, such as enemy propaganda, rebellion, sabotage, and revealing secrets concerning state security. Individuals convicted of state security crimes for having exercised their fundamental rights often are serving sentences of ten to twenty years. Prisoners also are wrongfully serving sentences for contempt for authority and illegal exit. The government's inhuman treatment of its detainees, which in some cases rises to the level of torture, is detailed below at *General Prison Conditions, Treatment of Political Prisoners,* and *Labor Rights: Prison Labor*.

Positive Provisions

Cuba's Criminal Code includes a number of positive provisions, such as those criminalizing genocide and apartheid.[61] The law also requires prosecution of public functionaries who abuse their authority, "with the purpose of taking advantage of someone (*perjudicar*) or gaining an illicit benefit."[62] Individuals found guilty of abusing their authority face prison terms of one to three years. Although this provision might allow for some penalties, particularly where abuses arose in the context of corruption, Cuba's record on punishing those who commit human rights abuses is extremely poor. Similarly, the crime of wrongful deprivation of liberty, which the law defines as the failure to free or turn over a detainee to the proper authorities within the legally-mandated period, offers the possibility that abusive officials could face punishment under the law.[63] Unfortunately, even though Cuba is bound to criminalize acts of torture due to its obligations under the Convention against Torture, which it ratified in May 1995, no crime of torture exists in Cuban law. The Criminal Code includes several provisions regarding the protection of

[61] Criminal Code, Law No. 62 (1988), Articles 116 and 120.

[62] Ibid., Article 133. Translation by Human Rights Watch. Accountability in Cuba is discussed below, at *Impunity*.

[63] Ibid., Article 280.

constitutional rights, such as the protection of equal rights without discrimination based on sex, race, or national origin.[64]

Crimes Against State Security Crush Nonviolent Dissent

Cuba prosecutes crimes against state security to repress nonviolent government opponents. While the crime of enemy propaganda explicitly violates the fundamental freedoms of expression and association, other state security crimes include objectionable references to preserving the socialist system and are defined in elastic terms that frequently have been used to punish the exercise of fundamental rights. Cuba's Criminal Procedure Code, which is discussed below at *Due Process Denied*, grants Cuban officials expansive authority to repress those accused of state security crimes. Under the law, Cuban authorities may conduct warrantless arrests of any person accused of a state security crime, must hold the accused in pretrial detention, and must try the person in a closed trial in a special state security tribunal. In order to increase the likelihood that officials will take action against the crimes of rebellion or sedition, which the Criminal Code defines to include nonviolent acts, officials failing to do so risk three-to eight-year prison terms for "violation of the duty to resist" (*infracción de los deberes de resistencia*).[65]

Enemy Propaganda

Under Cuban law, a person engaged in enemy propaganda "incites against the social order, international solidarity, or the socialist State, through oral or written propaganda, or in any other form" or "manufactures, distributes, or posseses [such] propaganda." Cuba punishes these actions with one-to eight-year sentences. The law further provides that, "the individual who spreads false news or malicious predictions tending to cause alarm or discontent among the population, or public disorder, incurs the sanction of deprivation of liberty for one to four years." Anyone using the mass media to engage in enemy propaganda faces a possible seven-to fifteen-year sentence.[66] The crime of enemy propaganda clearly infringes on the universally recognized rights to free speech, free exchange of information, and free association. The particularly heavy sanctions for the crime work as a powerful deterrent to the free expression of ideas. A prohibition on enemy

---

[64] Ibid., Article 295.

[65] Ibid., Article 101(1). Translation by Human Rights Watch.

[66] Ibid., Article 103. Translation by Human Rights Watch.

propaganda might be acceptable in times of war, if narrowly defined. Yet, the broadly-defined Cuban provision does not allow for such an exception, undercutting Cuban claims that restrictions on free speech are legitimate in the struggle against the United States.

Cuba perpetuates shocking injustices under the guise of prosecuting counter-revolutionaries who engage in enemy propaganda. Some cases are discussed below, at *Political Prosecutions*.

Rebellion

Cuba broadly defines rebellion as "any act leading, directly or indirectly, by means of violence or other illicit means," to any of the following objectives:

a) imped[ing] completely or in part, even temporarily, the superior organs of the state and the government from the execution of their functions;

b) chang[ing] the economic, political, and social regimen of the socialist state;

c) chang[ing], completely or partially, the constitution or the form of government established by it.

These extremely broad terms have been applied to bar peaceable efforts to criticize or change the government. Acts leading to rebellion are punishable by seven to fifteen years, and armed rebellion is punishable by ten to twenty years or a death sentence.[67]

Decisions under this provision issued by Cuban judges in military and civilian courts reveal a total disregard for freedom of expression and opinion.[68] A sentencing document obtained by Human Rights Watch justifies the October 17, 1994, conviction of five "counterrevolutionaries" to ten years each for rebellion. In the sentencing document, the Cuban judges characterized the actions of the opposition group members as nonviolent. However, the judges found that they had prepared and distributed "counterrevolutionary propaganda" consisting of flyers marked "Wake up, Cuban!" and "exhorted changes in the country's social, political, and economic systems, supported by three declarations from the Universal Charter [sic] of Human Rights that the [accused] said were being violated in Cuba." Other

---

[67] Ibid., Articles 98 and 99. Translation by Human Rights Watch.

[68] Cuba often denies political prisoners copies of their own sentences, leaving them uncertain as to what evidence the government has against them and how the government has justified its actions. Human Rights Watch obtained a number of sentencing documents from former Cuban political prisoners, tried in the early 1990s, who only received copies at the time Cuba released them from prison. This practice violates criminal defendants' rights to know the evidence against them, which is discussed below, at *Right to Know Charges and Review Evidence of Alleged Crime*.

prison at this writing. Alberto Manuel Boza Vázquez received a twelve-year sentence, while Juan Carlos González Vázquez received an eight-year sentence. The court also sentenced an Interior Ministry official, Augusto César San Martín Albistur, to seventeen years. Prison authorities released several other activists upon completion of their sentences.[73]

The government based its charge on Chaviano González's alleged effort to identify government infiltrators in his organization. The judges concluded that Chaviano participated in a document fraud scheme to entice representatives of the Interior Ministry (including a former ministry official, Boza Vázquez, and San Martín Albistur) to reveal the identity of State Security agents. Furthermore, the judges found that Chaviano and his fellow activists obtained several documents for use in their "counterrevolutionary activities." These documents included two pamphlets that were classified secret: "Economic Crime in the Commercial, Gastronomical, and Service Sector" and "Economic Crime in Activities relating to Energy" and one denouncing prison abuses.[74]

Sedition

The crime of sedition also penalizes nonviolent opposition to the government, and like many other provisions, protects the status quo of the "socialist order." Those who "perturb the socialist order or the celebration of elections or referendums, or impede the completion of any sentence, legal disposition or measure dictated by the government, or by a civil or military authority in the exercise of their respective functions, or refuse to obey them" can face from ten to twenty years in prison if they affect state security, even if they do so "without relying on arms or employing violence."[75]

Sabotage

Under another extremely expansive Cuban law, a person commits sabotage who, "with intent to impede or obstruct the normal use or function, or possessing knowledge that this result may be produced, destroys, alters, damages or harms in any way" one of the country's socioeconomic or military units. These include

[73] Abel del Valle Díaz served a three-year sentence in a work camp and Pedro Miguel Labrador Gilimas and Ernesto Aguilera Verde each served two-year sentences.

[74] Sentencing Document 420, Case 132 of 1995, Tribunal Militar, Ministerio del Interior, April 21, 1995. Translation by Human Rights Watch.

[75] Criminal Code, Article 100. Translation by Human Rights Watch.

energy sources, land transportation services, communications, teaching centers, public buildings, businesses, and sites of administrative, political, social or recreational organizations. If grave damage results, "no matter what means were used," the person will face ten to twenty years or the death penalty.[76] Cuban courts have prosecuted nonviolent dissent under this provision.

Additional Crimes Against State Security

Cuba also penalizes the distribution of "false information for the purpose of disturbing the international peace, or to endanger the prestige or credibility of the Cuban State or its good relations with another State." The penalty for spreading false news contrary to international peace is one to four years.[77] Cuba relies on the crime of "other crimes against state security" (*otros actos contra la seguridad del estado*) as the catch-all measure under the state security category. While the crime legitimately penalizes violent actions, it also permits prosecution on illegitimate grounds that violate freedom of expression and association. The provision bars one or more persons from coming together and resolving to commit any of the crimes against state security, such as enemy propaganda. The provision also penalizes anyone who fails to report any knowledge of a planned or executed state security crime to the authorities with six months to three years.[78]

Measures Against Persons Demonstrating Criminal Tendencies

Two Cuban criminal provisions permit the authorities to imprison or take other measures against individuals who have committed no criminal act. The dangerousness and official warning provisions violate the universally recognized principle of legality, by which criminal behavior must be explicitly defined by law before it can be penalized. The measures, particularly official warnings, are employed with alarming frequency against human rights activists, independent journalists, and government opponents, as detailed in *Routine Repression*. The laws also single out developmentally-disabled Cubans.

---

[76] Ibid., Articles 104 and 105. Translation by Human Rights Watch.

[77] Ibid., Article 115. Translation by Human Rights Watch.

[78] Ibid., Articles 124, 125, and 128. The cases of Juan Carlos Recio Martínez and several members of the Pro Human Rights Party of Cienfuegos are discussed below, at *Political Prosecutions.*

Dangerousness

Cuban law defines dangerousness (*el estado peligroso*) as "the special proclivity of a person to commit crimes, demonstrated by conduct that is observed to be in manifest contradiction with the norms of socialist morality." Signs of dangerousness include "anti-social conduct" or general behavior that "perturbs the order of the community." The law states that "mentally deranged [persons] and persons with retarded mental development" are guilty of dangerousness if they represent a threat to the "social order" or to the security of others.[79] The breadth of the dangerousness law permits Cuban authorities to employ it for politicized or discriminatory reasons.

If Cuba determines that someone is dangerous, the Criminal Code allows the state to impose "pre-criminal measures," including surveillance by the National Revolutionary Police and reeducation for periods of one to four years. The state may detain the person during this time. The law also provides for "therapeutic measures," including detention in a psychiatric hospital, that are continued "until the dangerousness disappears from the subject."[80] The open-ended nature of this punishment affords the state extraordinary authority to abuse the rights of political opponents and the developmentally disabled.

Official Warning

For those outside the ample reach of the dangerousness measure, the Criminal Code creates restrictive mechanisms to control an expansively defined group of those who have "links or relationships with persons who are potentially dangerous to the society and the social, economic, and political order of the socialist State." In order to prevent these persons—who now comprise the vast majority of Cuba's human rights activists, independent journalists, members of independent professional organizations and labor unions, and other nonviolent dissidents—from "committing socially dangerous or criminal activities," the law directs Cuban authorities to provide them with an official warning. Cuban authorities rely heavily on these warnings, which usually are accompanied by threats to cease opposition activities and a mention of the various crimes that activists could be prosecuted for and the maximum penalties for each.[81]

[79] Ibid., Articles 72, 73, and 74. Translation by Human Rights Watch.

[80] Ibid., Articles 78, 79, 80, 81, and 82. Translation by Human Rights Watch.

[81] The use of official warnings is detailed below, at *Routine Repression*.

Crimes Against Public Authorities and Institutions

Justice Minister Roberto Díaz Sotolongo acknowledged to Human Rights Watch Cuba's interest in protecting its "king" from insults. Cuba's criminalization of insults of public officials, public monuments, mass organizations, and the country's dead heroes represents an extraordinary government effort to deny freedom of speech.

Contempt for the Authority of a Public Official

Cuba's provision regarding contempt for authority (*desacato*) penalizes anyone who "threatens, libels or slanders, defames, affronts (*injuria*) or in any other way insults (*ultraje*) or offends, with the spoken word or in writing, the dignity or decorum of an authority, public functionary, or his agents or auxiliaries." Such actions are punishable by three months to one year in prison, plus a fine. If the person demonstrates contempt for "the President of the Council of the State, the President of the National Assembly of Popular Power, the members of the Council of the State or the Council of Ministers, or the Deputies of the National Assembly of the Popular Power, the sanction is deprivation of liberty for one to three years."[82]

While the crime of contempt for authority (*desacato*) existed in Cuba prior to the 1959 revolution, the Castro government expanded the definition to cover a broader possible range of speech and to apply explicitly to the government's highest authorities. More troubling still, the Castro government also eliminated a pre-revolutionary provision that allowed those charged with contempt to invoke the truthfulness of their statements as a defense.[83]

Cuba has prosecuted scores of Cubans for contempt, including several prisoners who were tried on the basis of having criticized prison conditions and abuses.[84] In January 1997, Cuban police arrested one of Cuba's prominent dissident leaders, Héctor Palacios Ruíz, the president of the Democratic Solidarity Party (Partido Solidaridad Democratica, PSD). In September 1997, a Havana court convicted him of contempt for the authority of Fidel Castro and sentenced him to eighteen months, which he served. Ironically, he had challenged the likelihood of President Castro complying with the Viña del Mar Declaration, a document

[82] Criminal Code, Article 144. Translation by Human Rights Watch.

[83] Ofelia Nardo Cruz, "El Delito de Desacato en Cuba," *Cuba Press*, June 25, 1998.

[84] For further discussion of retaliatory measures against political prisoners, see *Treatment of Political Prisoners*, below.

endorsing human rights and democracy that Cuba's leader had signed at the Sixth Ibero-American Summit in Chile in November 1996.[85]

Defamation of Institutions, Mass Organizations, Heroes, and Martyrs

The Criminal Code mandates a three-month to one-year sentence for anyone who "publicly defames, denigrates, or scorns the Republic's institutions, the political, mass, or social organizations of the country, or the heroes or martyrs of the nation."[86] This sweeping provision potentially outlaws mere expressions of dissatisfaction or disagreement with government policies or practices, clearly violating free expression. The protection from insult of lifeless entities, and state-controlled institutions and organizations in particular, appears designed solely to preserve the current government's power.

Insulting the Nation's Symbols

Cuba also punishes someone who "insults or with other acts shows disrespect to the Flag, the [National] Anthem, or the National Seal," (*escudo*) with three months to one year of imprisonment.[87] In past years, the government used this provision against Cuba's community of Jehovah's Witnesses, whose religion bars them from swearing allegiance to any flag.

Clandestine Printing

Like defamation of public institutions and symbols, clandestine printing appears as a crime against public order in the Criminal Code. Preserving public order does not sufficiently justify the law's extremely broad prohibition on free expression and a free press. Anyone who "produces, disseminates, or directs the circulation of publications without indicating the printer or the place where it was printed, or without following the established rules for the identification of the author or origin, or reproduces, stores, or transports" such publications, risks from three months to one year in prison.[88]

---

[85] "Video Constituirá Prueba Contra Héctor Palacios," *Infoburo*, January 22, 1997.

[86] Criminal Code, Article 204. Translation by Human Rights Watch.

[87] Ibid., Article 203. Translation by Human Rights Watch.

[88] Ibid., Article 210. Translation by Human Rights Watch.

Abuse of the Freedom of Religion

Under Cuban law, anyone who, "abusing the freedom of religion (*cultos*) guaranteed by the constitution, uses a religious basis to oppose educational objectives, the duty to work, the defense of the Homeland with arms, reverence for its Symbols, or any other established by the Constitution" risks three months to one year in prison.[89] This provision, which is defined as a crime against public order, allows the state to penalize a broad range of religious activities that would not endanger public order.

Disobedience and Resistance

While Cuba's criminalization of disobedience of and resistance to government authority may be legitimate, the government has employed these provisions specifically to repress peaceful dissidents. Someone who "disobeys the decisions of the authorities or public functionaries" may face a three-month to a one-year sentence.[90] An individual who "resists an authority, public functionary, or his agents or auxiliaries in the exercise of his functions," also risks three months to one year, but if the resistance occurs while the authority is carrying out arrests, the penalty can rise to five years.[91]

Crimes Restricting Freedom of Association

The Criminal Code highlights the conditionality of Cuba's constitutional guarantee of free association. Cuba uses alleged crimes against state security as its most aggressive weapon against nonviolent opposition organizations, but the Criminal Code offers the government additional legal grounds as well for repressing freedom of association.

Failure to Comply with the Associations Law

Cuba's Associations Law effectively bars any genuinely independent association from receiving government authorization, as discussed below. Those involved in associations not registered under the law risk one to three months of imprisonment, while directors risk three months to one year in prison.[92] If members

---

[89] Ibid., Article 206. Translation by Human Rights Watch.

[90] Ibid., Article 147. Translation by Human Rights Watch.

[91] Ibid., Article 143. Translation by Human Rights Watch.

[92] Ibid., Article 208.

or directors participate in meetings or demonstrations, they face, respectively, one to three months, or three months to a year, and fines.[93]

Criminal Association

Cuba's law against criminal association penalizes groups of three or more persons who form a band to commit crimes with a one-year to three-year prison term. While this provision may serve legitimate ends, its application against dissidents violates the right to free association. The second section of the law vaguely states that groups planning "to provoke disorders... or commit other antisocial acts" could be punished with three months to one year of imprisonment.[94] The overbroad nature of this provision, which does not require a criminal act, has facilitated its politically discriminatory application.

Crimes Restricting Freedom of Movement

Cuban law includes measures that restrict freedom of movement within the boundaries of one's country and the right to leave the country, in violation of the Universal Declaration of Human Rights, which states that: "Everyone has the right to leave any country, including his own, and to return to his country."[95] The 1997 law created to control migration to Havana is discussed below, at *Decree 217: Heightened Control of Internal Movement.*

Illegal Exit

The Criminal Code provision against illegal exit punishes individuals who, "without completing legal formalities, leave or take actions in preparation for leaving the national territory" with one to three years in prison. Someone who "organizes, promotes, or incites" an illegal exit can be punished with two to five years imprisonment, while someone who "provides material assistance, offers information, or in any way facilitates" an illegal exit, risks one to three years behind bars.[96] In May 1995, Cuba reached an accord on emigration with the United States in which it pledged not to apply the illegal exit law against repatriated Cubans. Cuba reportedly sentenced Abel Denis Ambroise to fourteen months for illegal exit

---

[93] Ibid., Article 209.

[94] Ibid., Article 207(2). Translation by Human Rights Watch.

[95] Universal Declaration of Human Rights, Article 13.

[96] Criminal Code, Articles 216 and 217. Translation by Human Rights Watch.

in October 1996, but Human Rights Watch does not know of further prosecutions since that time. Cuba's failure to revoke this law, however, seriously calls into question its willingness to legitimize the basic right of its citizens to leave their country.

Beyond the prison terms served by the scores of Cubans convicted of illegal exit, this law has contributed to numerous tragic efforts to flee Cuba surreptitiously. The government's apparent ire at those who attempted to circumvent the illegal exit law reached its peak with the government's March 1994 sinking of a tugboat, the *13 de Marzo*, that was loaded with fleeing Cubans.[97]

Illegal Entry

While Cuba has unquestionable authority to control its national borders, the broadly-defined crime of illegal entry would allow prosecutions of Cuban citizens attempting to return to their homeland. Someone who enters Cuba "without completing legal formalities or immigration requirements" risks one to three years of imprisonment.[98] Former political prisoners that Cuba forced into exile could risk prosecution for failing to comply with "legal formalities."

Restrictions on Residence

Cuba also employs the criminal penalty of banishment (*destierro*), defined as "the prohibition from living in a determined place or the obligation to remain in a determined place." Such residence restrictions may be used to penalize persons convicted of a crime in all cases where "the presence of the sanctioned person in the place is socially dangerous," and can last from one to ten years.[99]

Additional Crimes Subject to Abusive Application:

Failure to Comply with the Duty to Denounce

Cuba has discriminatorily applied the duty to report criminal acts against independent activists and government opponents. The law, which requires that

[97] The case is discussed below, at *Impunity: Impunity for the Sinking of the 13 de Marzo.*

[98] Criminal Code, Article 215. Translation by Human Rights Watch.

[99] Ibid., Article 42. Translation by Human Rights Watch. The cases of Nestor Rodríguez Lobaina and Radames García de la Vega are discussed below, at *Political Prosecutions.*

someone knowing of the commission or intent to commit a crime must report it to the authorities, creates an obligation for all Cubans to participate in the government's repression of nonviolent dissidents.[100]

Insult, Calumny, and Defamation

The elastic definitions of Cuba's crimes of insult, calumny, and defamation permit Cuban authorities to use them to silence government opponents. The most loosely-defined of these crimes, insult, applies to someone who, "by written or spoken word, through pictures, gestures or acts, offends the honor of another," and results in a three-month to one-year sanction.[101] Calumny applies to an "individual who knowingly divulges untruths that excessively discredit an individual," with six months to two years of imprisonment.[102] Defamation is said to occur when a person "before a third party, accuses someone of conduct, an act, or a characteristic that is dishonorable, and which could damage the person's social reputation, diminish the public's opinion of him/her, or expose him/her to the loss of the confidence necessary for him/her to carry out his/her job, profession, or social function." Defamation results in sanctions of three months to one year of imprisonment. Unlike contempt for authority, truth is a defense against charges of defamation, as are statements made in the defense of a "socially justifiable interest."[103]

Due Process Denied

Cuba frequently denies its citizens internationally recognized due process guarantees.[104] In law and in practice, Cuba impedes the right to a public hearing by an independent and impartial tribunal where the accused has sufficient guarantees for his or her defense.

The case of Francisco Pastor Chaviano González, a dissident leader who received a fifteen-year sentence for revealing state secrets, highlights several of the

---

[100] Ibid., Article 161.

[101] Ibid., Article 320. Translation by Human Rights Watch.

[102] Ibid., Article 319. Translation by Human Rights Watch.

[103] Ibid., Article 318. Translation by Human Rights Watch.

[104] The Universal Declaration on Human Rights includes due process guarantees, ensuring fair and public hearings by independent and impartial tribunals, as well as the presumption of innocence and necessary defense guarantees, at Articles 10 and 11.

obstacles facing criminal defendants in Cuba.[105] Chaviano González and some of his co-defendants remain in Cuban prisons. Cuban authorities arrested Chaviano González in March 1994 and held him in pretrial detention for over one year. The April 21, 1995, trial in a military court was closed to the public, press, and human rights activists, yet the courtroom was packed with dozens of State Security agents. Chaviano said that on the morning of the trial a government official gave him a sandwich that he believed contained a drug, since after eating it he found that he could not communicate and was slurring his speech. The government did not allow the defendants to review the evidence against them.[106] The principal evidence against Chaviano was a packet of documents delivered to his house the morning of his arrest by a stranger, who said he was acting in the name of other human rights activists.

Courts Lack Independence and Impartiality

Cuba's constitution grants the National Assembly the authority to name judges, to receive regular reports from them, and to remove them from office.[107] The constitution explicitly states that the courts are "subordinate in the line of authority to the National Assembly... and the Council of State," and that the Council of State may issue the courts instructions.[108] This structure seriously compromises the independence and impartiality of Cuban courts. The Council of State is an entity presided over by President Castro, selected by the Cuban National Assembly, and considered the "supreme representation of the Cuban State" under Cuban law.[109] Cuba also permits civilians to be tried in military courts, where the court's independence and impartiality also are in question. If any defendant in a criminal

---

[105] Sentencing Document 420, Case 132 of 1995, Tribunal Militar, Ministerio del Interior, April 21, 1995. This case is discussed above, at *Codifying Repression: Revealing Secrets Concerning State Security.*

[106] Human Rights Watch interview with a defendant in the case, Pedro Miguel Labrador Gilimas, Miami, April 15, 1997.

[107] Cuban constitution, Articles 75(m) and (n), 122, 126, 129, and 130.

[108] Ibid., Articles 90(h) and (i), 121, and 128. Translation by Human Rights Watch.

[109] Ibid., Article 89. Translation by Human Rights Watch.

trial is a member of the military, Cuban law requires that a military court try all of the suspects.[110]

Closed Trials

As in Chaviano González's case, Cuban judges occasionally choose to try nonviolent government opponents behind closed doors, violating the right to a public trial. The Criminal Procedure Code grants tribunals broad authority to close trials at any stage for reasons of state security, morality, or public order. While these could serve as legitimate justifications for barring the public from a trial, Cuba's closed trials appear designed to coverup its denial of due process to dissidents and to restrict opportunities for the public to hear their views. The law bars everyone related to the defendant except his lawyer from attending closed trials.[111] Brothers José Antonio Rodríguez Santana and José Manuel Rodríguez Santana received ten-year sentences for rebellion and enemy propaganda at a closed trial in August 1993. While José Antonio was forced into exile in Canada in early 1998, José Manuel Rodríguez Santana remains in prison in Cuba.[112]

Arrests and Pretrial Detentions

The Criminal Procedure Code allows the police and other non-specified "authorities" to carry out warrantless arrests of anyone accused of a crime against state security or of a crime that "has produced alarm or has been committed frequently in the municipal territory."[113] While the first provision, singling out suspects in state security crimes, leaves political dissidents at risk, the phrasing of the second provision is so vague as to allow the police legally to conduct warrantless arrests with minimal justification.

Cuba's Criminal Procedure Code allows the police and prosecutorial authorities to hold a suspect for a week before any court reviews the legality of the detention. This violates international norms requiring that a court review any detention

---

[110] Ibid., Article 5.

[111] Criminal Procedure Code, Law No. 5 (annotated edition issued in 1997), Article 305.

[112] Human Rights Watch interview with José Antonio Rodríguez Santana, Toronto, April 13, 1998.

[113] Criminal Procedure Code, Article 243. Translation by Human Rights Watch.

"without delay."[114] During the first week after an arrest, the police may detain the suspect for up to twenty-four hours.[115] The prosecutorial investigator (*instructor*) then may keep the suspect in custody for an additional seventy-two hours, while deciding whether to pass custody of the suspect to the prosecutor (*fiscal*) or release him or her.[116] The law grants the prosecutor an additional seventy-two hours to send the accused to jail, release him or her, or impose less-severe restrictions. Only if the prosecutor chooses to imprison the accused or impose other restrictions does a court review the legality of the detention.[117]

Equally troubling, authorities are not required to notify the accused of his or her right to an attorney until after the court decides on the legality of the detention, which may take up to seventy-two additional hours, passing through several layers of authorities. Failing to notify the accused of this right until up to ten days after an arrest deprives the detainee of legal assistance during a critical period and enables authorities to take advantage of the detainee through interrogations or intimidations.[118] However, in practice Cuban authorities have not even complied with the narrow provisions of its own legislation.

The Criminal Procedure Code grants judges broad latitude in determining whether to hold suspects in pretrial detention. Judges often abuse this authority with respect to government critics, such as the four members of the Internal Dissidents' Working Group who spent well over a year in pretrial detention without charge.[119] The law requires pretrial detentions when two vaguely defined circumstances occur simultaneously: the judge is aware of "actions showing the existence of a deed that has the characteristics of a crime," and "sufficient reasons to suppose criminal responsibility for the crime by the accused, independent of the

---

[114] American Declaration on the Rights and Duties of Man (May 2, 1948), Article 25.

[115] Criminal Procedure Code, Article 245.

[116] Ibid., Article 246.

[117] Ibid., Article 247.

[118] The discussion of pretrial detentions, at *Political Prisoners,* details several cases of police abuse following arrests.

[119] Their case is discussed below, at *Political Prosecutions.*

depth and quality of proof required."[120] This provision sets a very low standard of proof for holding a suspect in pretrial detention. The law also fails to justify the deprivation of liberty on the grounds of the severity of the crime or the likelihood a suspect would flee, foregoing less severe measures that also would ensure that a suspect appears at trial.

While bail and house arrest are alternatives to pretrial detention under Cuban law, a detainee lacking "good personal antecedents and conduct" cannot be considered for these measures.[121] In March 1985, the Council of State issued an accord, signed by President Castro and with the stated purpose of reducing the number of pretrial detainees, that defined good personal antecedents and conduct as "the qualities of a citizen who is respectful of socialist legality...who has not been subject to a detention (*medida de seguridad detentiva*), nor to three official warnings (*advertencias oficiales*)."[122] This definition likely excludes most of Cuba's dissidents. The accord also stated that even if a suspect demonstrated good conduct, no suspects in crimes against state security or the crimes of illegal exit or entry were eligible for conditional liberty with bail.[123]

Cuba permits habeas corpus petitions for "persons deprived of liberty...without the formalities and guarantees provided in the Constitution and the laws...."[124] In 1975 reforms eliminated habeas corpus from the Cuban constitution, but retained the protection under the criminal law.[125] Unfortunately, given the extraordinary authority granted police, prosecutors, and judges under Cuban law to carry out warrantless arrests and prolonged pretrial detentions with minimal evidence or for political reasons, this option offers Cuban detainees little hope. On July 30, 1998, the four members of the Internal Dissidents' Working Group filed a habeas corpus petition. A Havana tribunal dismissed it the next day as inadmissable. A Cuban

---

[120] Criminal Procedure Code, Article 252(1) and (2). Translation by Human Rights Watch.

[121] Ibid., Article 253. Translation by Human Rights Watch.

[122] Accord of the Council of State, March 8, 1985, First Section, para. (a). Translation by Human Rights Watch.

[123] Ibid., third section, para. (a).

[124] Criminal Procedure Code., Article 467.

[125] Gómez Manzano, "Constitución y Cambio Democrático en Cuba," (Washington: Association for the Study of the Cuban Economy) p. 402.

court rejected a second habeus corpus petition on October 16, apparently on the grounds that the order of preventive detention for the four leaders was well-founded.[126]

The Criminal Procedure Code states that the preparatory phase of the prosecutorial investigation should be completed in sixty days, unless special circumstances require the extension of this period to a maximum of six months.[127] A Cuban delegation reported to the U.N. that 96 percent of cases are tried before the close of the first sixty-day period and that only 8 percent of Cuba's inmates were pretrial detainees.[128] Since Cuba releases no detailed information on its prisons, and does not allow domestic or international monitors to enter them, it is unclear whether these figures are accurate. However, the routine extremely long pretrial detentions of political prisoners, which are detailed at *Treatment of Political Prisoners*, suggest that Cuba has regularly failed to observe these time limits, or has applied them discriminatorily. Cuban law requires authorities to hold pretrial detainees in different sites from convicted criminals.[129] Nevertheless, Cuba often sends dissident pretrial detainees to maximum-security prisons, where they are held with convicts and subjected to physical and psychological abuse.

Confessions and Witness Tampering

Cuba's constitution bars the use of violence or coercion to force individuals to make statements and requires judges to void any coerced statements.[130] In encouraging provisions, the Criminal Procedure Code states that judges cannot convict solely on the basis of a confession nor may an authority require a person to declare against his or her interest, nor employ coercion, deception, or false promises to induce a person to testify. Moreover, judges are required to notify defendants

---

[126] "Cuba Denies Habeas Corpus for Four Dissidents Group," *Agence France Presse*, August 11, 1998; and Jesús Zuñiga, "Familiares de Los Cuatro de la Patria Envían Carta a Parlamento Cubano," *Cooperativa de Periodistas Independientes*, January 14, 1999.

[127] Criminal Procedure Code, Article 107.

[128] Cuban report to the Committee Against Torture, CAT/C/SR.310/Add.1, Geneva, March 3, 1998, para. 31.

[129] Criminal Procedure Code, Article 247.

[130] Cuban constitution, Article 59.

of their right not to testify at trial.[131] Unfortunately, during long-term pretrial detentions, which in the case of political prisoners are often incomunicado, Cuban authorities have violated these provisions, brutalizing detainees while subjecting them to lengthy interrogations. Several of these cases are detailed below, at *Treatment of Political Prisoners.* Despite abuses committed during pretrial detentions, Cuban courts have not excluded coerced statements from trials of political prisoners, which almost unfailingly lead to convictions. Cuban authorities also have engaged in witness intimidation.

Timing of Trials

Under the Criminal Procedure Code, judges may convene extremely rapid trials (*juicios sumarísimos*) when "exceptional circumstances recommend it."[132] While a prompt trial is a laudable goal, summary trials convened on short notice impede the right to a defense. Cuba's use of this practice to try dissidents, such as Del Toro Argota, highlights the danger that the term "exceptional circumstances" could be applied for political purposes. Cuban detainees are far more likely, however, to languish in pre-trial detention, in several cases lasting well over a year, despite a Criminal Procedure Code provision that judicial tasks be addressed "without delay."[133]

Restrictions on the Right to a Lawyer

The Cuban constitution states that citizens have the right to a defense,[134] but Cuba's procedural laws, the banning of an independent bar association, and powerful, politicized judicial and prosecutorial authorities seriously debilitate this right. The fact that the Criminal Procedure Code permits detentions of up to ten days without requiring detainees to be notified of their right to an attorney, much less appointed an attorney, represents a clear failure to secure a genuine right to a defense.

The close ties of the government with judges, prosecutors and state-appointed or approved attorneys leave many defendants with little belief that their attorneys can or will do anything but request a slightly shorter sentence. Raúl Ayarde Herrera

---

[131] Criminal Procedure Code, Articles 161, 166, 183, and 312.

[132] Criminal Procedure Code, Article 479. Translation by Human Rights Watch.

[133] Ibid., Article 31. Translation by Human Rights Watch.

[134] Cuban constitution, Article 59.

remembered his state-appointed attorney advising him, "Everything is proven. Admit your error and see if they'll lower your sentence."[135] René Portelles, who received a seven-year sentence for enemy propaganda in 1994, stated that the court did not allow him to hire a private attorney. His state-appointed attorney was an avowed communist who first met with him three days before the trial for about ten minutes. He recalled asking her, "How can you defend me since I'm a member of the opposition?" At trial, she merely asked that he not receive the maximum sanction.[136] Former political prisoner Adriano González Marichal said that:

> Lawyering in Cuba is a fantasy. Lawyers have no means to defend the accused. They defend, but it's as if they were never there. I did not want a lawyer. I was assigned a government lawyer, and she said to me "Mr. Marichal, this trial is already over. The only thing you can ask for is seven years rather than ten."

At trial, the prosecutors recommended twelve years and the court sentenced him to ten.[137] Similarly, Alberto Joaquím Aguilera Guevara said that even though he had a private lawyer at his 1992 trial, it was the same thing as having a state-appointed attorney. "There are no private lawyers. They have to represent the interests of the state. Lawyering is a mechanism that does not function."[138]

Collective Law Firms

In 1973 Cuba eliminated private law firms and required all attorneys who did not work directly for the state to join "collective law firms" (*bufetes colectivos*).[139] A reorganization of the collective law firms in 1984 required all members to reapply, demonstrating that they "possess[ed] moral qualities in accord with the

---

[135] Ayarde received a ten-year sentence for espionage. Human Rights Watch telephone interview with Raúl Ayarde Herrerra, Toronto, April 21, 1998.

[136] Human Rights Watch telephone interview with René Portelles, Toronto, April 21, 1998.

[137] A Havana court tried González Marichal in November 1993. Human Rights Watch interview with Adriano González Marichal, Toronto, April 12, 1998.

[138] Human Rights Watch interview with Alberto Joaquím Aguilera Guevara, Toronto, April 12, 1998.

[139] Organization of the Judicial System, Law. No. 1250 (1973).

principles of our society."[140] The Justice Ministry denied readmission to several lawyers known for defending human rights cases and criticizing the government.[141] In February 1995, the National Organization of Collective Law Firms (Organización Nacional de Bufetes Colectivos) expelled and effectively disbarred Leonel Morejón Almagro, a member of the Agramontist Current (Corriente Agromontista). The Agramontist Current is an independent group named for Ignacio Agramonte, a nineteenth century Cuban lawyer. Morejón Almagro and other members of his organization had defended several dissidents in prominent political trials. In February 1997, Cuba justified Morejón Almagro's expulsion to the United Nations on the grounds of "serious failures to carry out his professional duties."[142] But the purported deficiencies were so insignificant that Morejón Almagro's supervisor reportedly had recommended a simple warning. On February 23, 1996, a Havana court sentenced Morejón Almagro, who had continued to speak out against government abuses as a leader of a coalition of nongovernmental organizations known as the Cuban Council (Concilio Cubano), to fifteen months for contempt of authority and resisting authority. Other lawyers, including René Gómez Manzano, the imprisoned member of the Internal Dissidents' Working Group, have suffered serious consequences for their defense of dissidents and opposition to human rights violations in Cuba.

René Gómez Manzano first requested legalization of the Agromontist Current under the Associations Law (discussed above at *Associations Law*) in August 1990. He filed a revised application in 1991 but as of late 1995 received no response from the government, despite six additional communications. In February 1997, the Cuban government told the U.N. that it had rejected Gómez Mánzano's application to register his group "because it would have similar objectives to those of the existing National Union of Jurists of Cuba," a state-controlled organization.[143]

---

[140] The Practice of Law and the National Organization of Collective Law Firms, Decree-Law 81 (1984), Article 16(a). Translation by Human Rights Watch.

[141] The Association of the Bar of the City of New York, "Human Rights in Cuba: Report of a Delegation of the Association of the Bar of the City of New York, " July 1988, pp. 11-19.

[142] Cuban Communication, United Nations Report of the Special Rapporteur on the Independence of Judges and Lawyers, Mr. Param Cumaraswamy, E/CN.4/1998/39, February 12, 1998, para. 3.

[143] Cuban Communication, United Nations Report of the Special Rapporteur on the Independence of Judges and Lawyers, para. 5.

In March 1999 the director of the National Organization of Collective Law Firms, Dr. Raúl Mantilla Ramírez, announced that the group would conduct a national review of its 2,000 members to assess their "professionalism." Mantilla Ramírez's concurrent endorsement of Cuba's recently passed Law for the Protection of Cuban National Independence and Economy (a repressive measure that is discussed below) on behalf of all of the organization's members cast further doubt on the likelihood that dissident lawyers could belong to the group.[144]

Right to Know Charges and Review Evidence of Alleged Crime

In practice, Cuban authorities do not always inform detainees of the charges against them, nor allow them to review the purported evidence of their crimes. Besides demonstrating the arbitrary nature of the detentions, this practice undoubtedly impedes defendants in the preparation of their defense. Cuban authorities only notified the four detained leaders of the Internal Dissidents' Working Group of the charges against them in September 1998, more than a year after their July 1997 arrest. From Guillermo Ismael Sambra Ferrándiz's arrest in January 1993 until a few days before his July 1993 trial, he and his fellow defendants did not know what crime they allegedly had committed. When they learned the prosecutors had charged them with rebellion, they still did not know of the evidence against them or precisely what they allegedly had done. After the trial, a State Security captain told Sambra Ferrándiz that the trial was necessary to give the local community an example of why they should not dissent from the government. While Cuba forced Sambra Ferrándiz (who received an eight-year sentence) into exile in Canada, his co-defendants Víctor Bressler and Emilio Bressler remain in Cuban prisons.[145] Cuba often denies political prisoners copies of their own sentences, leaving them uncertain of the evidence the government has against them and how the government has justified its actions, impeding an appeal.

Appeals

Not surprisingly, dissidents and former political prisoners place little confidence in appeals. Luis Alberto Ferrándiz Alfaro, who was tried with Sambra Ferrándiz and sentenced to twelve years, said that the attorney representing him for his appeal told him he was "indefensible" because he had spoken out against the

[144] Iraida Calzadilla Rodríguez, "En Bufetes Colectivos, Próximo Sistema de Parámetros de Calidad," *Granma Diario*, March 3, 1999.

[145] Human Rights Watch telephone interview with Guillermo Ismael Sambra Ferrándiz, Toronto, May 8, 1998.

government at the original trial. He noted with pride that he had declared at trial that Cuba should have free elections, free speech, and an end to dictatorship. His appeal confirmed his sentence. He concluded that,

> Appeals are worthless. If you are sanctioned for political crimes, the sentence you get is the one you'll keep. Sometimes they will lower a sentence if the person repents or if they did not testify at trial. But if you maintain your position, you'll get the full sentence.[146]

Associations Law

Although Cuba's Associations Law claims to guarantee the "right of association,"[147] the law effectively bars the legalization of any genuinely independent association.[148] Cuba reported to the United Nations that some 2,000 groups—among them "non-profit scientific and technical, cultural and artistic, public-interest and sports associations and friendship and solidarity groups"—have been granted legal status to operate under the Associations Law.[149] But these putative nongovernmental organizations (NGOs) include Cuba's Communist Party-supported and government-controlled mass organizations, as well as groups formed by government ministries. Cuba's most prominent women's organization, the Federation of Cuban Women (Federación de Mujeres Cubanas, FMC), called into question the legitimacy of its NGO status by participating as both an NGO and as Cuba's official government representative at the Fourth World Conference on Women, which was held in Beijing in 1995.[150]

---

[146] Human Rights Watch interview with Luis Alberto Ferrándiz Alfaro, Toronto, April 13, 1998. Translation by Human Rights Watch.

[147] The Associations Law refers to Article 53 of the February 1976 constitution. The text of that article appears unchanged as Article 54 of the 1992 constitution. Translation by Human Rights Watch.

[148] Associations Law, Law No. 54 (1985) and Regulations for the Associations Law (1986).

[149] Cuban Report to the Committee on the Elimination of Racial Discrimination, August 13, 1998 (CERD/C/SR.1291), issued August 18, 1998, para. 12.

[150] Approximately one-fifth of the recognized groups are sports leagues. Homero Campa, "El Gobierno les Ve con Recelo y las Somete a Estrictos Controles," *Proceso*, Mexico, May 18, 1997.

The government consistently has refused to recognize organizations critical of its policies and practices. Cuba has not legalized any political party under the law, since recognized groups cannot violate the constitution (which endorses the Communist Party) or engage in state functions. Cuba has rejected human rights groups by alleging that, in fact, they are political parties.[151] Cuba expert Gillian Gunn-Clissold, Ph.D., explained that:

> The Cuban state is uneasy about NGOs. They are deemed useful because they capture resources that otherwise would not enter Cuba and relieve social tensions by resolving problems the state is unable to address. NGOs are also viewed with suspicion, however, because they represent an independent resource base for citizens whose desires do not always coincide with those of the state. Before Soviet subsidies disappeared, the state would have simply taken over those NGOs deemed inconvenient. To do so now would be self-defeating, for if Cuban NGOs are perceived as state front organizations, foreign donations will dry up. Therefore, the state seeks to indirectly control NGOs without overtly dominating them.[152]

While many independent organizations have requested legalization under the Associations Law, Human Rights Watch is not aware of any group that is openly critical of the government's human rights or labor rights practices that has received government authorization to operate. Typically, the government fails to respond at all or harasses petitioners.[153]

Cuba's Justice Ministry can only grant legal status to associations willing to accept broad state interference in their activities and arbitrary state authority to shut them down. Under the Associations Law, members of human rights groups, professional organizations of doctors, economists, and teachers, independent labor unions, women's rights groups, and other independent organizations risk prosecution simply for belonging to their group or for carrying out any activities

---

[151] Gillian Gunn, Ph.D., "Cuba's NGOs: Government Puppets or Seeds of Civil Society?" *Cuba Briefing Paper Series: Number 7*, Georgetown University Caribbean Caribbean Project, February 1995.

[152] Ibid.

[153] The difficulties that independent groups face are detailed below, at *Routine Repression*, *Labor Rights,* and *Limits on Religious Freedom.*

without authorization.[154] As discussed above at *Codifying Repression*, persons involved in unauthorized associations risk criminal sanctions ranging from three months to a year, plus fines.[155] Several other criminal code provisions also restrict the freedom of association.[156]

Application Review Process

The first level review of a potential association is carried out by highly-politicized government bodies. If aspiring groups seek to function at the municipal or provincial level, then the local Executive Committee of the Assembly of Popular Power reviews their application. If a group plans work on the national level, then it must present its application to the "state organ, organism, or dependency that is related to the objectives and activities that the association will carry out."[157] The first review must be completed in ninety days, after which the Justice Ministry has sixty days to accept or reject the prospective application.

Government reviewers have ample authority to reject aspiring associations for arbitrary or politicized reasons. The Associations Law bars groups "whose activities could prove damaging to social interests"or "whose applications demonstrate the impossibility of attaining their proposed objectives and activities," and rejects organizations when there is another group with similar interests already inscribed, as it did with an independent lawyers group.[158]

---

[154] The Associations Law does not govern the functioning of mass organizations, religious organizations, agricultural cooperatives, credit and service organizations, and other groups "authorized by law." Associations Law, Article 2. Cuba treats agricultural cooperatives as labor entities. Cuban constitution, Articles 19 and 20 and Law No. 49, Article 7(ch).

[155] Criminal Code, Articles 208 and 209.

[156] These provisions are discussed above, at *Crimes Against State Security Crush Nonviolent Dissent* and *Crimes Restricting Freedom of Association.*

[157] Ibid., Article 6. Translation by Human Rights Watch.

[158] Ibid., Article 8(c), (ch), and (d). Translation by Human Rights Watch. Cuba's refusal to recognize the lawyers' group is discussed above, at *Restrictions on the Right to a Lawyer*.

Coordination and Collaboration with State Entities

The law provides that an unrecognized organization must create internal regulations that detail how the organization will "coordinate" and "collaborate" with the counterpart state entity.[159] This coordination and collaboration effectively require the association to subjugate itself to the government organization. To comply, the association must allow a representative of the state entity to attend and speak at any planned or unplanned meetings; notify the government entity in advance of any publications; coordinate with the government entity regarding participation in any national or international event, conference or activity; allow the government entity to carry out periodic inspections; regularly report to the government entity on its activities; and provide prior notice of the date and hour of any planned or unplanned meetings, events, or other activities.[160] The law further provides that the relationship between the association and the state entity is immutable, unless the state entity approves changes in the nature of the relationship.[161]

Inspections

The Justice Ministry maintains a registry of national associations, while municipal offices keep local registries. The Associations Law and regulations grant the ministry's designated registrars or the local government entities reporting to them broad authority to inspect associations.[162] Municipal registrars have authority to assist in the supervision, control, and inspection of national associations in their region.[163] The law provides for no government notification prior to an inspection. The law demands that all association directors and members must "offer every assistance in the carrying out of the inspection." Thus, association members must allow government representatives to enter the premises and "in particular, examine their books and other documents."[164]

---

[159] Regulations for the Associations Law, Article 12(f). Translation by Human Rights Watch.

[160] Ibid., Article 28 (b), (c), (ch), (d), (e), and (f) and Article 29.

[161] Ibid., Article 28.

[162] Ibid., Articles 35, 36, and 73.

[163] Ibid., Article 36(g).

[164] Ibid., Article 75. Translation by Human Rights Watch.

A government official told Cuba expert Gunn-Clissold that the inspection provisions of the Associations Law were not being fully enforced. But when asked whether the inspections requirement should thus be lifted, the official emphasized that any revised law would still need to prohibit the registration of groups using human rights as a "cover for efforts to overthrow the government."[165]

Dissolution

The inspector must report any violations of the Associations Law or other laws to the Justice Ministry's Associations Department within fifteen days of an inspection. Based on the findings in the inspector's report, the chief of the department can apply any appropriate sanction, including the dissolution of the association. Grounds for dissolving an association include the failure to comply with its internal rules, failure to observe the Associations Law, and the broad category of "activities destructive to the social welfare."[166] Recognized Cuban associations attempting to express dissent from the government, or trying to carry out activities without tight government supervision, risk prompt disbanding. While the regulations provide thirty days for associations to appeal a dissolution decision, the Justice Ministry can nonetheless order the association dissolved in the interim if it is in the "public interest" to do so or if not doing so would cause "irreparable harm."[167]

New Legal Measures Expand Government Control

Far from relinquishing control over freedom of expression, association, press, and movement, in recent years the Cuban government has created new mechanisms to strengthen its repressive authority.

Law for the Protection of Cuban National Independence and the Economy

The Law for the Protection of Cuban National Independence and the Economy (*Ley de Protección de la Independencia Nacional y la Economía de Cuba*, hereafter protection law), which took effect in March 1999, created harsh penalties

---

[165] Gillian Gunn Ph.D., "Cuba's NGOs: Government Puppets or Seeds of Civil Society?" *Cuba Briefing Paper Series: Number 7*, February 1995.

[166] Regulations for the Associations Law, Article 79. Translation by Human Rights Watch.

[167] Ibid., Articles 87 and 88. Translation by Human Rights Watch.

for actions that could be interpreted as support of the Helms-Burton law. Helms-Burton, which became U.S. law in March 1996, tightened the U.S. economic embargo on Cuba.[168] In publicly expressing his support for the protection law, President Fidel Castro referred to the law as a weapon in Cuba's struggle against the United States. He said that "it is vital to defend ourselves with clean weapons, legal [ones], without violations of the law...."[169] Castro's language echoes the text of the preamble to the protection law, which provides that it will not infringe upon the rights and guarantees afforded by the Cuban constitution. While Cuba's claims to respect legality ring true in an insular, domestic context, this law, like Cuba's constitution, undermines internationally protected rights. In early March, Cuban police reportedly warned a prominent independent journalist and an opposition leader that they might be the first to face twenty-year sentences under the protection law's provisions.[170] The new law prohibits,

> those actions designed to support, facilitate, or collaborate with the objectives of the "Helms-Burton" Law, the blockade, and the economic war against our people, leading toward the destruction of internal order, the destabilization of the country and the liquidation of the socialist state and the independence of Cuba.[171]

While the protection law describes potentially cataclysmic consequences for the prohibited actions, most of the specific actions detailed in the law are nonviolent expressions of opinion or exchanges of information—activities that should be protected rather than penalized. The law's over broad definitions of prohibited activities further the risk that Cubans could be penalized for exercising their fundamental rights.

For example, the law criminalizes the accumulation, reproduction or diffusion of "material with a subversive character" for the purposes described above with

---

[168] The Helms-Burton law is discussed in detail below, at *International Policy.*

[169] "Esta Trinchera Tenemos que Defenderla," *Granma Diario*, February 17, 1999. Translation by Human Rights Watch.

[170] Pablo Alfonso, "Raúl Rivero and Oswaldo Paya Seriously Threatenend," *El Nuevo Herald*, March 5, 1999.

[171] Law for the Protection of Cuban National Independence and the Economy, Law 88 (1999), Article 1. Translation by Human Rights Watch.

three to eight years of imprisonment.[172] Cubans risk two to five years in prison for "collaborating in any way with radio or television stations... or other foreign media" toward the objectives detailed above.[173] The law's heaviest penalties are directed toward those who "provide information to the United States government, its agencies, dependencies, representatives or officials, to facilitate the objectives..." Persons convicted of this crime face seven to twenty years of imprisonment.[174] The law also creates seven-to twenty-year penalties for persons who commit "any act designed to impede or prejudice the economic relations of the Cuban state or the economic relations of any industrial, commercial, or financial institution or any other type of institution." Those whose actions lead the U.S. government to take measures against foreign investors in Cuba face the longest sanctions under this provision.[175]

Ironically, while the protection law penalizes extraterritorial actions by the U.S. government, Cuba's Justice Minister Roberto Díaz Sotolongo said that persons violating the law while outside Cuban territory could also be subject to punishment under its provisions.[176]

The protection law serves as the implementing legislation for a law passed in late December 1996, the Law Reaffirming Cuban Dignity and Sovereignty (*Ley de Reafirmación de la Dignidad y Soberanía Cubanas*), which Cuba described as "a response to the Helms-Burton Law."[177] According to the Cuban government, the U.S. law "has as its end the colonial reabsorption" of Cuba. In response, Cuba created broad restrictions on free expression, criminalizing even the appearance of support for U.S. policies. These provisions earned the December 1996 law a new

---

[172] Ibid, Article 6.1. Translation by Human Rights Watch.

[173] Ibid., Article 7.1. Translation by Human Rights Watch.

[174] Ibid., Article 4.1 and 4.2. Translation by Human Rights Watch.

[175] Ibid., Article 9.1 and 9.2. Translation by Human Rights Watch. The Helms-Burton provisions against companies investing in Cuba are discussed below, at *International Policy*.

[176] "Esta Trinchera Tenemos que Defenderla," *Granma Diario*, February 17, 1999.

[177] Law Reaffirming Cuban Dignity and Sovereignty, Law 80 (1996), Article 8. Translation by Cuban government.

name, in common parlance the "gag law" or "antidote law" (*ley mordaza* or *ley antídoto*).

Throughout the first months of 1997, Cuba undertook a nationwide campaign to demonstrate support for the gag law. The government circulated a petition celebrating the law, the Declaration of the Mambises of the Twentieth Century (Declaración de los Mambises del Siglo XX, in honor of those who fought for Cuba's independence), to mass organizations, schools, universities, and workplaces. In each office or institution, workers or students were expected to demonstrate publicly their support for the initiative. The government is said to have verbally harassed a few who refused to sign. On March 19, 1997, in the Vedado area of Havana, a handful of students at the Adalberto Gómez Núñez Primary School refused to sign the declaration. School officials reportedly took down their names, called their parents, and warned them that the children's failure to sign could have negative consequences.[178] On the afternoon of April 7, 1997, Cuban authorities reportedly detained the father of one of the children, Fidel Emilio Abel Tamayo, who is a member of the Cuban Social Democratic Party (Partido Social Demócrata Cubano).[179] Meanwhile, the Cuban press provided ample coverage of the delivery of signed petitions to the government. On March 15, 1997, President Castro culminated the campaign with a ceremony marking the presentation of the signed declaration, which he declared to be "of the people and loved by the people."[180]

Regulations for International Press

The Cuban government permits a small number of international press agencies to operate permanent news bureaus in Cuba, including the *British Broadcasting Corporation* (BBC), *Reuters*, the Mexican news agency *Notimex*, the Spanish wire service *EFE* and daily *El País*. In March 1998, Cuba granted the U.S.-based *Cable*

---

178 "Lista parcial de las amenazas, agresiones y demás occurridas en Cuba en las últimas semanas," *Cuba S.O.S.*, April 2, 1997.

179 "Detenido Padre de Niño que no Firmó Apoyo a Ley 80," *Cuba S.O.S.*, April 2, 1997.

180 "Discurso Pronunciado por el Comandante en Jefe Fidel Castro Ruz, Primer Secretario del Comité Central del Partido Comunista de Cuba y Presidente de los Consejos de Estado y de Ministros, en el 'Acto de Entrega de la Declaración de los Mambises del Siglo XX,' Efectuado Ante el Monumento a Jose Martí, en la Plaza de la Revolución, el Día 15 de Marzo de 1997, Año del 30 Aniversario de la Caída en Combate del Guerrillero Heróico y sus Compañeros," *Granma Internet*, Año 2, Número 12, April 2, 1997. Translation by Human Rights Watch.

News Network (CNN) permission to establish an office and in November 1998 it allowed the *Associated Press* (AP) to do so. While the U.S. government approved licenses for eight additional media to open Cuban bureaus, the Cuban government has not granted these companies permission to do so.[181] Beyond the restrictions on establishing offices in Cuba, in February 1997, Foreign Minister Roberto Robaina signed a ministerial resolution regulating foreign media reporting from Cuba. The new regulations require that foreign correspondents demonstrate "objectivity, adhering strictly to the facts and in consonance with the professional ethics that govern journalism," or face reprimand or the withdrawal of credentials. Reporters also may not work for any media outlet other than the one for which they are accredited.[182] Human Rights Watch is not aware of any cases where Cuba has applied this law against foreign news outlets. Nonetheless, such regulations produce a chilling effect on international news coverage of Cuba.[183]

Decree 217: Heightened Control of Internal Movement

In a public address on April 4, 1997, President Castro urged the populace to fight against the "indiscipline" favored by the "enemy" and demonstrated by "illegal immigration" to Havana and announced that the state was planning to halt such movement.[184] He justified such actions by explaining that free movement to the capital would endanger Cuba's security due to the state's insufficient control and knowledge of the identities of Havana's residents and guests. International human rights law assures the right to liberty of movement within a country's borders and

---

[181] These U.S. media are: ABC, CBS, Dow Jones News Service, the *Chicago Tribune*, the *St. Petersburg Sun-Sentinel*, the *Miami Herald*, and *Cuba Info*. Patricia Zengerle, "Cuban Exiles Say CNN is the 'Castro News Network,'" *Reuters News Service*, March 18, 1997.

[182] Frances Kerry, "Cuba Introduces New Regulations for Foreign Media," *Reuters News Service*, June 4, 1997.

[183] Other government pressures on international reporters are detailed below, at *Routine Repression: International Journalists Covering Cuba*.

[184] "Discurso Pronunciado por el Comandante en Jefe Fidel Castro Ruz," *Granma Internet,* April 2, 1997. Translation by Human Rights Watch.

the right to enter and leave one's country of origin.[185] President Castro called upon the Committees for the Defense of the Revolution (Comités para la Defensa de la Revolución, CDRs), pro-government groups that have taken part in intimidations of government opponents, to work with the police to gather information on Havana residents. The president also mentioned problems with overcrowding, overbuilding, and crime that had resulted from increased population pressures in Havana. On April 22, 1997, President Castro signed Decree 217, creating internal migratory regulations for Havana.

Decree 217 explains restrictions on internal movement as being due to public health, welfare, and public order concerns. While these issues in some circumstances justify narrowly-tailored restrictions on movement, President Castro's prior statements highlighting the government's interest in minimizing "indiscipline" and maintaining tight control over citizens' movement for security reasons call into question the government's motivation in creating Decree 217. By late April 1997, the Cuban press announced that more than 1,600 "illegal residents" of Havana had been returned to their home provinces "using persuasive methods."[186] By mid-May, many more Havana residents had received government notices that they had forty-eight hours to regularize their status in the city or face fines and the "obligation to return immediately to their place of origin."[187] The government's provision of an extremely brief period for Havana residents to demonstrate the legitimacy of their presence in the capital raised additional concerns about whether the Cuban authorities were ensuring sufficient due process guarantees. By June 1998, the Cuban government reported that some 27,717 people had left Havana since the law took effect, although not necessarily due to its application, while 22,560 others had moved to Havana, resulting in a net population

[185] Universal Declaration of Human Rights, Article 13. The International Covenant on Civil and Political Rights (ICCPR), Article 12, which Cuba has not ratified, also protects this right. International norms do permit some restrictions on the freedom of movement and residence, but only where the state must do so to protect "national security, public order, public health or morals, or the rights and freedoms of others, and [is] consistent with other rights...." ICCPR, Article 12, Section 3. As discussed above, at *Codifying Repression*, Cuba retains a prohibition on illegal exit, in violation of international norms.

[186] "Havana Mayor Reports 1,600 Illegals Returned to Provinces," *Prensa Latina*, April 27, 1997.

[187] Decree 217, Article 8. Translation by Human Rights Watch.

decrease of over 5,000 residents.[188] While diplomats noted that the law had not resulted in massive round-ups and deportations, Cuban migrants to Havana expressed frustration that they could not choose where to live and that police demands for their personal papers and proof of "legal" residency had increased.[189]

---

[188] "Havana's Population Strain Eases After Decree," *Reuters News Service*, June 17, 1998.

[189] Larry Rohter, "Cuba's Unwanted Refugees: Squatters in Havana's Teeming Shantytowns," The *New York Times*, October 20, 1997.

IV. POLITICAL PROSECUTIONS

Cuban authorities continue to treat as criminal offenses nonviolent activities such as meeting to discuss the economy or elections, writing letters to the government, reporting on political or economic developments, speaking to international reporters, or advocating the release of political prisoners. While the number of political prosecutions has diminished in the past few years, Cuban courts continue to imprison human rights activists, independent journalists, economists, doctors, and others—all of whom are subjected to the Cuban prison system's inhuman conditions.[190] Even as Cuba released some political prisoners early in 1998—most of whom had completed the majority of their sentences—subsequent trials replenished the ranks of the incarcerated. Prison terms remained a plausible threat to any Cubans considering nonviolent opposition. Yet, in the cases of four prominent dissident leaders arrested by Cuban authorities in July 1997, charged only in September 1998, and tried in March of 1999, the arbitrariness of Cuban repression reached new heights. The prosecutions detailed below occurred in 1997, 1998, and 1999.

Manuel Antonio González Castellanos, Leonardo Varona González, and Roberto Rodríguez Rodríguez

On May 6, 1999, a court in Holguín found two journalists and one of their companions guilty of "contempt for authority" (*desacato*). Manuel Antonio González Castellanos, of the Cuba Press agency, reportedly was tried because he had criticized Fidel Castro and the local authorities in the course of a difficult conversation with local police in late 1998. The police apparently had verbally harassed González Castellanos earlier in the day. The court sentenced him to two years and seven months.

The day after González Castellanos's October 1, 1998 arrest, Leonardo Varona González, of Santiago Press, reportedly protested his detention by putting up anti-government signs at Varona González's residence. The same day, a local Committee for the Defense of the Revolution subjected the home to a violent attack. Roberto Rodríguez Rodríguez, a friend who previously had been tried for enemy propaganda, was present when the repudiation meeting was carried out.

---

[190] Throughout this report, Human Rights Watch is using the term "political prosecution" to mean the wrongful prosecution of individuals based on the exercise of fundamental civil and political rights. Similarly, we use the term "political prisoners" to refer to persons incarcerated as a result of these prosecutions.

National Revolutionary Police arrested both men and Joannys Caridad Varona González on October 2, 1998. Leonardo Varona González received sixteen months, while Rodríguez Rodríguez was sentenced to seventeen months in prison. The court reportedly postponed Joannys Caridad Varona González's trial.[191]

Martha Beatriz Roque Cabello, René Gómez Manzano, Félix Bonne Carcassés, and Vladimiro Roca Antúnez

On March 1, 1999, a Havana court tried the four leaders of the Internal Dissidents' Working Group (Grupo de Trabajo de la Disidencia Interna, GTDI) for "other acts against the security of the state" based on their allegedly inciting sedition. The trial occurred after the four, economists Martha Beatriz Roque Cabello and Vladimiro Roca Antúnez, engineering professor Félix Antonio Bonne Carcasses, and attorney René Gómez Manzano, had spent over nineteen months in pretrial detention.[192] The trial was closed to the public, the press, and international observers. Only nine of the dissidents' family members were allowed to attend. The court forbade Gómez Manzano, the leader of a group of independent attorneys whom the government had previously disbarred, from defending himself.[193] On March 15, the court found the four guilty, sentencing Roca Antúnez to five years, Bonne Carcassés and Gómez Manzano to four years each, and Roque Cabello to three and one-half years.

---

[191] Human Rights Watch telephone interviews with Efrén Martínez Pulgarón, journalist with Cuba Press, Havana, January 13, 1999, and Gerardo Sánchez Santacruz, Cuban Commission for Human Rights and National Reconciliation, May 11, 1999. Ricardo González Alfonso, "Sancionados Periodistas Independientes," *Cuba Press*, May 7, 1999. Letter from Ann K. Cooper, executive director of the Committee to Protect Journalists, to Fidel Castro Ruz, president of Cuba, October 16, 1998. CDR's are discussed further below, at *Routine Repression.*

[192] Each of the dissidents also leads an independent Cuban organization: Roca Antúnez heads the Social Democrat Party (Partido Socialdemócrata); Roque Cabello heads the Cuban Institute of Independent Economists (Instituto Cubano de Economistas Independientes); Gómez Manzano heads the Agromontist Current (Corriente Agromontista); and Bonne Carcassés heads the Cuban Civic Current (Corriente Cívica Cubana).

[193] Alberto Pérez Giménez, "España: La Fiscalía Insistió en sus Penas y Acusó al 'Grupo de los Cuatro' de 'Saboteadores,'" *ABC*, March 3, 1999. Cuba's restrictions on independent lawyering are discussed above, at *Impediments to Human Rights in Cuban Law: Collective Law Firms.*

The government based the detention and trial of the four leaders on their activities with the GTDI. On May 5, 1997, the GTDI held a press conference in Havana encouraging a boycott of elections planned for late 1997. Representatives of more than fifteen foreign press agencies attended the event, at which the GTDI declared that one-party elections do not offer the electorate genuine choices.[194] The lack of government interference at the press conference marked a rare departure from usual government practices. The four dissident leaders followed the press conference with the June release of a paper titled "The Homeland Belongs to All" (*La Patria es de Todos*), which offered an analysis of Cuba's economy and discouraged foreign investment, proposed reforms to the Cuban Constitution, discussed human rights, and challenged Cuba's exclusive recognition of one political party.

On July 16, 1997, Cuban police arrested the four leaders of the GTDI, categorizing their peaceful protests as "counterrevolutionary crimes." The government sent each of the leaders to separate prisons, where they were held with convicted violent criminals and subjected to the extremely poor conditions prevailing in Cuba's prisons.[195] During their pretrial detention, government authorities repeatedly encouraged the dissidents to go into exile. In September 1997, Cuban Foreign Ministry official Carlos Fernández de Cossio explained that the Cuban government intended to prosecute the dissidents because, "They tried to harm the Cuban economy, and they were performing under the instructions of a foreign government."[196] On June 25, 1998, a Havana-based State Security police official, Col. Nelson de Armas, reportedly visited Roca Antúnez in the Ariza Prison in Cienfuegos Province. De Armas asked Roca Antúnez about his dissident activities and about "The Homeland Belongs to All."[197] Marking the one-year anniversary of his detention, Roca Antúnez reportedly wrote in a July 1998 letter, "It is not my intention to challenge the authorities or to seek a confrontation

---

[194] Pascal Fletcher, "Cuban Dissidents will Oppose One-Party Elections," *Reuters News Service*, May 5, 1997, and Juan O. Tamayo, "Disidentes Cubanos Piden en La Habana Boicotear Elecciones," *El Nuevo Heraldo*, May 6, 1997.

[195] These conditions are described below, at *General Prison Conditions* and *Treatment of Political Prisoners.*

[196] Howard LaFranchi, "Cuba Backslides on Reform, Arrests Dissidents," The *Christian Science Monitor*, September 9, 1997.

[197] Human Rights Watch telephone interview with Magalys de Armas Chaviano (Roca Antúnez's wife), Havana, July 2, 1998.

because my position continues to be one of reconciliation, tolerance, forgiveness, reunification of all Cubans and nonviolence."[198] Cuba only charged the four leaders with a crime in September 1998, after they had spent more than a year in prison.[199]

Following their trial, on March 1, 1999, Cuba undertook a media campaign to discredit the GTDI leaders and justify the government's actions.[200] The state-controlled Communist Party daily, *Granma Diario*, reported that the four leaders' "counterrevolutionary" actions had resulted in the "unavoidable necessity to arrest [them] and put [them] at the disposition of the courts...." *Granma* labeled "The Homeland Belongs to All" as "the most indignant insult to the history of our Homeland" and further stated that

> The history of a country is its fundamental weapon.... To destroy this history is to destroy its identity, its independence, its life. Those who so repugnantly have acted at the service of powers who harm our country...are truly traitors to the nation....[201]

Granma also termed the international response to the arrests and trial, which included requests from the pope and the Canadian Prime Minister Jean Chrétien for the dissidents' release, as "an intense campaign of defamation." After the verdicts were announced, the president of Cuba's National Assembly, Ricardo Alarcón, said that the sentences were "not too severe." Alarcón stated that the convictions did not represent punishments for the dissidents' having expressed their opinions, but were based on their ties to a foreign government. He stressed that the court had "judged

---

[198] Herald Wire Services, "Jailed Cuban Dissident Seeks Public Trial," The *Miami Herald*, July 16, 1998.

[199] Sedition and other crimes against state security are discussed above, at *Impediments to Human Rights in Cuban Law: Crimes Against State Security Crush Nonviolent Dissent.*

[200] "Quienes son los Disidentes y los Presos de Conciencia en Cuba," *Granma Diario*, March 4, 1999; "Nota de Televisión Cubana," *Granma Diario*, March 5, 1999; and, Andrew Cawthorne, "Cuba: Cuba Attacks 'Traitor' and 'Mercenary' Dissidents," *Reuters News Service*, March 4, 1999.

[201] "Quienes son los Disidentes," *Granma Diario*, March 4, 1999.

these people in accordance with Cuban law."[202] Alarcón's point highlighted the repressive nature of Cuba's legal system, which had provided a legal framework for the government's actions.

Jesús Joel Díaz Hernández

On January 18, 1999, Cuban police detained Jesús Joel Díaz Hernández, the director of the Cooperative of Independent Journalists of Ciego de Avila (Cooperativa Avileña de Periodistas Independientes), in Morón, Ciego de Avila province. The next day, the Municipal Tribunal of Morón found him guilty of dangerousness (*el estado peligroso*) and sentenced him to four years. The extremely brief period between Díaz Hernández's arrest and conviction made it difficult for him to prepare an adequate defense.[203] The court reportedly based its verdict on Díaz Hernández's having met with delinquents and disturbed the public order. On January 22, the Ciego de Avila Provincial Tribunal confirmed Díaz Hernández's sentence. Shortly after his trial, Cuban prison officials confined him in a punishment cell in the Canaletas Prison.[204]

Lázaro Constantín Durán

Cuban police arrested Lázaro Constantín Durán, the leader of the Friends Club of the College of Independent Teachers (Club de Amigos del Colegio de Pedagogos Independientes), on December 10, 1998, when he was participating in a celebration of the fiftieth anniversary of the Universal Declaration of Human

---

[202] Cawthorne, "Cuba Attacks 'Traitor' and 'Mercenary' Dissidents," *Reuters News Service*, March 4, 1999. Cuba's reliance on legal measures to restrict human rights is discussed above, at *Impediments to Human Rights in Cuban Law.*

[203] Several barriers to full due process protections, including extremely rapid trials *(juicios sumarisimos)*, are discussed below, at *Impediments to Humans Right in Cuban Law: Due Process Denied.*

[204] Ramón Alberto Cruz Lima, "Condenan a Disidente Cubano Tras Arbitrario Juicio," *Nueva Prensa Cubana*, January 20, 1999; "Cuba: Journalist Given Four-Year Jail Term for 'Dangerous Social Conduct,'" *ABC* published by the *BBC Monitoring Summary of World Broadcasts*; Letter from Ann K. Cooper, executive director of the Committee to Protect Journalists, to Fidel Castro Ruz, president of Cuba, February 3, 1999; and Human Rights Watch telephone interview with Ricardo González Alfonso, Cuba Press, Havana, February 1, 1999.

Rights in the Butari Park in Havana. On December 16, 1998, a Havana tribunal sentenced Constantín Durán to a four-year prison term for dangerousness.[205]

On January 7, 1999, the Cuban government daily newspaper, *Granma*, published a remarkable article justifying the government's imprisoning of Constantín Durán and calling into question his legitimacy as a "dissident." The article refers to Constantín Durán's alleged participation in a robbery in Cuba, prior to his 1980 departure from the country as part of the Mariel exodus. Upon his return to Cuba from the United States in 1990, he served out a sentence for this alleged crime. The government also repeatedly notes that Constantín Durán allegedly committed an assault and served time for it in the United States. In addition to these ten-and almost twenty-year-old allegations, for which the Cuban government admits that Constantín Durán already served prison time, the *Granma* article accuses him of "having been warned on several occasions for maintaining relations with unsavory persons, as well as habitually consuming alcoholic beverages and moving around the area near the Central Park of Havana, where among other things, he tried to become an illegal guide for foreign tourists." The Cuban tribunal "t[ook] into account these antecedents in Cuba and in the United States," when sending him to prison for four years of "reeducation."[206]

The government article also criticizes Constantín Durán and human rights defenders and independent journalists as "Made in USA dissident[s]" ("*disidente Made in USA*"). While admitting that some Cubans do not sympathize with the revolution and asserting that "they have the right to think in this way," Cuba's government paper dismisses these activists as fabrications of the U.S. government's Central Intelligence Agency.[207] Yet, while calling Constantín Durán a "vulgar wrongdoer," the government article points to no recent criminal act as the basis of

---

[205] Human Rights Watch telephone interview with Odilia Collazo, president of the Pro Human Rights Party (Partido Pro Derechos Humanos), Havana, January 11, 1999. In the course of gathering information on this case, several of our telephone calls to Cuba were abruptly terminated.

Dangerousness is a criminal provision that allows the Cuban government to take measures against persons demonstrating an alleged tendency to commit a crime. Dangerousness is discussed above, at *Impediments to Human Rights in Cuban Law: Measures Against Persons Demonstrating Criminal Tendencies.*

[206] Nicanor Leon Cotayo, "El Disidente," *Granma Diario*, January 7, 1999.

[207] Ibid. Cuba's harassment of human rights activists, independent journalists, and members of other independent organizations is discussed below, at *Routine Repression* and *Labor Rights.*

his prison term. On January 8, 1999, a Havana court reaffirmed Constantín Durán's sentence.

Reynaldo Alfaro García

The Cuban government arrested Reynaldo Alfaro García, the vice-president of the Association for the Struggle Against National Injustice (Asociación para la Lucha Frente a la Injusticia Nacional, ALFIN) and also a member of the Democratic Solidarity Party (Partido de Solidaridad Democrática, PSD), on May 8, 1997, and detained him without trial for more than a year, much of that time in the Valle Grande Prison in Havana province. The Cuban government did not accede to the pope's request for Alfaro García's release.[208] On August 28, 1998, a Havana court sentenced Alfaro García to three years for spreading false information against international peace, a state security crime in Cuba's Criminal Code.[209] Cuban police jailed Alfaro García shortly after he joined an organization of mothers of political prisoners in preparing a letter asking the government to free their sons and daughters. On May 7, 1997, Alfaro read the letter for a *Radio Martí* transmission. Cuban authorities detained him the next day and charged him with enemy propaganda. At trial, the government apparently based its charge of spreading false news on Alfaro García's having denounced beatings of prisoners and calling upon the National Assembly to free prisoners held for crimes against state security.[210]

After the conviction, a Cuban government-controlled radio announcer criticized Alfaro García over the airwaves as a liar undeserving of being called "prisoner of conscience." Rather, the *Radio Havana* Cuba journalist alleged that,

---

[208] "Juzgarán a un Activista Pese a Petición Papal," *Agencia EFE*, August 25, 1998.

[209] Radio Havana Cuba, "Radio Denounces Western Media Handling of 'Prisoners of Conscience,'" broadcast on September 1, 1998, *BBC Monitoring Summary of World Broadcasts*, September 3, 1998. This and other state security crimes are discussed above, at *Impediments to Human Rights in Cuban Law: Crimes Against State Security Crush Nonviolent Dissent.*

[210] "Cuban Dissident Sentenced to Three Years Amid Rare Street Protest," *Agence France Presse*, August 28, 1998, and Luis López Prendes, "Pide Fiscalía 12 Años de Prisión a Reynaldo Alfaro García," *Buró de Prensa Independiente de Cuba: CubaNet*, February 14, 1998.

> It is possible that Reynaldo Alfaro García has collected dollars for his news dispatches based on lies. Whether this is true or not, the fact is that there are mass media organizations that act as vehicles for anti-Cuban campaigns, and this applies not only to the ill-called *Radio* and *Television Martí*. At the trial held in Havana, it has just been demonstrated that Reynaldo Alfaro García and those who once again have transmitted anti-Cuban slander, have lied.[211]

On August 28, 1998, some twenty protesters gathered outside the court where Alfaro García's trial was taking place to demonstrate on his behalf and for the release of political prisoners. Shortly after they assembled, another group of protesters reportedly arrived chanting pro-government slogans.[212] In September, Cuban police arrested a number of those who had protested against his trial.[213]

After completing over twenty-two months of the three-year sentence, Cuban authorities granted Alfaro García conditional freedom in March 1999.[214]

Julio César Coizeau Rizo

On April 24, 1998, a court in Santiago de Cuba found Julio César Coizeau Rizo, a member of the Gerardo González Ex-Political Prisoners Club (Club de Ex-Presos Políticos "Gerardo González"), guilty of contempt of authority. The government reportedly based its prosecution on Coizeau Rizo's activities with the ex-prisoners' group and his alleged posting of some twenty anti-government flyers.

---

[211] Radio Havana Cuba, "Radio Denounces Western Media," *BBC Monitoring Summary of World Broadcasts*, September 3, 1998. Alfaro García's trial highlights the heavy-handed measures the government uses to respond to criticisms of prison abuses, which are discussed below, at *Treatment of Political Prisoners: Criminal Charges for Denouncing Prison Abuses*. Pressures on Cuban human rights activists who are not imprisoned are detailed below, at *Routine Repression: Cuba's Human Rights Activists.*

[212] "Cuban Dissident Sentenced," *Agence France Presse*, August 28, 1998.

[213] These detentions are detailed below, at *Routine Repression.*

[214] Human Rights Watch interview with Elizardo Sánchez Santacruz, leader of the Cuban Commission for Human Rights and National Reconciliation (Comisión Cubana para los Derechos Humanos y la Reconciliación Nacional), Washington, March 26, 1999.

The court sentenced him to three years and incarcerated him in the Aguadores Prison in Santiago Province.[215]

Cecilio Monteagudo Sánchez and Juan Carlos Recio Martínez

Cuban police arrested Cecilio Monteagudo Sánchez, a vice-delegate of the Democratic Solidarity Party (Partido Solidaridad Democrática, PSD), on September 15, 1997, in Villa Clara. On February 13, 1998, a Santa Clara tribunal sentenced Monteagudo Sánchez to four years in prison for enemy propaganda. He was tried on the basis of having drafted a document calling for abstention from local elections, a paper he never published. At this writing, the Cuban authorities had imprisoned Monteagudo Sánchez in the Guamajal prison, Villa Clara Province, known as the "White Shark."[216]

Cuban authorities also tried Juan Carlos Recio Martínez, a local journalist whom Monteagudo Sánchez had asked to type his handwritten draft. On February 13, 1998, the Santa Clara tribunal convicted Recio Martínez for other acts against state security (*otras actas contra la seguridad del estado*), for having failed to denounce Monteagudo Sánchez.[217] Recio Martínez, of the Cuba Press agency, received a one-year sentence in a labor camp without internment *(correcional sin internamiento*); he must report for work every day but may sleep at his home. In June 1998, he began serving his sentence at the Abel Santamaría Cooperative, near Camajuaní in Villa Clara province.[218]

---

[215] Human Rights Watch telephone interview with Mirna Riverón Guerrero, deputy director of the Eastern Free Press Agency (Agencia de Prensa Libre Oriental, APLO) and member of the Cuban Party of Orthodox Renovation (Partido Cubano de Renovación Ortodoxa), Santiago, July 3, 1998. Ana Luisa Lòpez Baeza, "Juzgado Hermano del Joven Desaparecido," *Cuba Press*, April 29, 1998.

[216] Human Rights Watch telephone interview with Héctor Trujillo Pis, Villa Clara correspondent for Cuba Press, July 3, 1998.

[217] This provision and other state security crimes are discussed above, at *Impediments to Human Rights in Cuban Law: Crimes Against State Security Crush Nonviolent Dissent.*

[218] Ibid. The government's prosecution of individuals based on their political opinions and the sentencing of those individuals to labor camps violates Cuba's obligations under the International Labor Organization's (ILO) Abolition of Forced Labor Convention, which Cuba ratified in 1958. Article 1(a) and Article 2, Convention 105: Abolition of Forced Labor, ILO (1957). Cuba's prison labor programs are discussed below, at *Labor Rights: Prison Labor.*

Israel García Hidalgo, Benito Fojaco Iser, Angel Nicolas Gonzalo, José Ramón López Filgueira, and Reynaldo Sardiñas Delgado

In October 1997, Cuban authorities arrested five members of the Pro Human Rights Party of Cuba (Partido Pro Derechos Humanos de Cuba, PPDH) in Cienfuegos. The men's activities with the group included denunciations of local human rights abuses. At trial on March 12, 1998, the court found all five guilty of "other acts committed against state security." This crime covers all persons forming groups to commit state security crimes, such as enemy propaganda. Cuban authorities could employ it to punish the nonviolent exercise of fundamental rights. The tribunal sentenced García Hidalgo and Fojaco Iser to two years in prison, while López Filgueira received a one-year sentence. Authorities incarcerated the three men in Ariza prison in Cienfuegos Province. Sixty-nine-year-old Gonzalo's and sixty-six year-old Sardiñas Delgado both received one-year sentences to labor camps without internment. Given Gonzalo and Sardiñas Delgado's advanced ages, Cuba's sentencing them to forced labor was particularly egregious.

Bernardo Arévalo Padrón

A Cienfuegos court sentenced Bernardo Arévalo Padrón, a journalist with the Linea Sur Agency, to six years in prison for contempt for the authority of Fidel Castro and Carlos Lage, a member of the Cuban Council of State, in November 1997. The court reportedly based the charge on accusations by the journalist that the two leaders had lied, due to the Cuban government's failure to uphold the Viña del Mar Declaration, a document signed by Castro at the Sixth Ibero-American Summit, which was held in Viña del Mar Chile in November 1996. Arévalo Padrón, a former official of the Ministry of the Interior, made his comments to a Miami radio station.[219] Cuban authorities previously had tried Héctor Palacios Ruíz, the president of the Democratic Solidarity Party, when he challenged Castro's willingness to comply with the Viña del Mar agreement. Following his January 1997 arrest and September 1997 trial, Palacios Ruíz served most of an eighteen-month sentence for contempt for authority until his release in early 1998, after the pope appealed for his freedom.[220]

---

[219] Reporters Sans Frontieres, "RSF Protests Conditions of Two Journalists," *IFEX-News from the International Freedom of Expression Community*, September 1, 1998.

[220] "Video Constituirá Prueba Contra Héctor Palacios," *Infoburo*, January 22, 1997.

Since his incarceration, prison guards reportedly have beaten Arévalo Padrón, held him in an isolation cell, and refused to provide him with medicine brought by his family members.[221]

Eleven Members of the Pro Human Rights Party of Villa Clara

On August 7, 1997, Cuban police detained Daula Carpio Mata, the leader of the Villa Clara branch of the Pro Human Rights Party, charging her with assault, apparently based on her having spoken out at an earlier trial of a PPDH colleague, Israel Feliciano García. The police released Carpio Mata but arrested her again on October 9, 1997. At trial on October 29, the Santa Clara court sentenced Carpio Mata to sixteen months internment in a work camp. Carpio Mata protested the sentence, refused to report to the work camp, and commenced a hunger strike. In December, Cuban police arrested her and imprisoned her in the women's section of the Guamajal Prison.[222]

Following Carpio Mata's initial arrest, several other members of the Villa Clara branch of the PPDH initiated a hunger strike to protest her detention. On October 23, 1997, a Santa Clara court convicted ten members of the PPDH of "association to commit criminal acts" *(asociación para delinquir)* and "disobedience," with sentences ranging from one year of house arrest for María Felicia Mata Machada to one and one-half years in prison or at a prison work camp for José Antonio Alvarado Almeida, Ileana Peñalver Duque, Roxana Alina Carpio Mata, Lilian Meneses Martínez, Arélis Fleites Méndez, Iván Lema Romero, Danilo Santos Méndez, Vicente García Ramos, and José Manuel Yera Benítez. The judge reportedly allowed the defense attorney less than ten minutes to present its case, including the testimonies from all of the defendants.[223]

In early 1998, Cuban authorities took stronger measures against the group, apparently to retaliate for the activists having undertaken prolonged hunger strikes and garnering the attention of the international press covering Pope John Paul II's Cuba pilgrimage. Local authorities imprisoned several of the activists who previously had received lighter sentences. Cuban authorities incarcerated Santos

---

[221] His treatment in prison is detailed below, at *Treatment of Political Prisoners: Beatings*.

[222] Human Rights Watch telephone interviews with Ricardo González and Héctor Trujillo Pis, journalists with Cuba Press, Havana, July 3, 1998, and Odilia Collazo, Pro Human Rights Party, Havana, August 6, 1998.

[223] Ibid.

Méndez and García Ramos at the "Nieves de Morejón" Prison in Sancti Espiritu; Yera Benítez at the Manacas Prison in Villa Clara; Lema Romero in the Villa Clara Provincial Prison, known as "El Pre"; Peñalver Duque and Fleites Méndez in El Pre's women's section; Meneses Martínez in the women's section of the Guamajal Prison in Santa Clara (where Daula Carpio Mata remained); and Alvarado Almeida in the Guamajal Prison's men's section. Cuban authorities granted Roxana Alina Carpio Mata temporary permission to leave prison (*licencia extrapenal*) due to her pregnancy.[224]

Beyond facing harsh prison conditions, several of the PPDH members who had stayed on extended hunger-strike were suffering physical deterioration from the experience. Ivan Lema's 120-day hunger strike, during which he took only broth and water, left him hospitalized after he lost 47 pounds. In mid-1998, Cuban authorities reportedly denied Lema's request for temporary permission to leave prison due to his serious medical problems.[225] Daula Carpio Mata reportedly had persistent abdominal pain and problems with her hearing, while José Manuel Yera Meneses suffered memory loss. Nonetheless, as of July 1998, Alvarado Almeida undertook yet another hunger strike to protest his detention with violent common prisoners who were aggressively threatening him.[226]

Dr. Dessy Mendoza Rivero

In June 1997, Dr. Dessy Mendoza Rivero, the founder and president of the Independent Medical College of Santiago de Cuba (Colegio Médico Independiente de Santiago de Cuba), alerted the international press of a dengue fever epidemic in Santiago.[227] Even though large numbers of people had fallen ill from the disease,

---

[224] Ibid.

[225] Héctor Trujillo Pis, "Niegan la Libertad a Prisionero," *Disidente Universal de Puerto Rico*, September 1998.

[226] Human Rights Watch telephone interviews with González and Trujillo Pis, Cuba Press, July 3, 1998, and Collazo, PPDH, August 6, 1998.

[227] Dengue fever and dengue hemorrhagic fever are mosquito-borne diseases that can lead to death. The World Health Organization (WHO) considers dengue a serious and growing health threat worldwide. World Health Organization, "Dengue and DHF Prevention and Control: Burden and Trends," WHO Division of Control of Tropical Diseases website, February 25, 1998. Dr. Mendoza informed the international press that between twenty and forty people had died from dengue fever between January 1997 and mid-June 1997, and that approximately 3,000 people had fallen ill of dengue during the

Dr. Mendoza had been dismayed that the state-controlled Cuban press had not reported on the severity of the crisis. Between June 15 and June 18, 1997, Dr. Mendoza granted interviews to several international news outlets, including *Radio Martí* (the U.S.-government sponsored station broadcasting to Cuba), the Spanish news service *ABC*, *Radio Netherlands*, and the Mexican newspaper *La Reforma*.[228]

Cuban state security agents arrested Dr. Mendoza on June 25, 1997. Prosecutors unsuccessfully urged him to sign an admission that he had "propagated an epidemic" (*propagación de epidemia*). Prosecutors then charged him with illicit association, based on his activities with the doctors' group and with the Pacifist Pro Human Rights Movement of Santiago, (Movimiento Pacifista pro Derechos Humanos de Santiago de Cuba), and with enemy propaganda based on his public discussion of the dengue outbreak. On November 18, 1997, a Santiago tribunal tried him and found him guilty of enemy propaganda. Yet, the court document justifying his sentence also cited government evidence of a dengue epidemic in the region. The same document referred to Dr. Mendoza as a "counterrevolutionary" for his activities with his medical colleagues and with human rights activists, but did not judge him guilty of illicit association. The tribunal sentenced him to eight years, of which he served over one and one-half years in the maximum-security Boniato prison in Santiago.[229] In November 1998, Cuba released Dr. Mendoza on the condition that he abandon Cuba for Spain.[230]

Orestes Rodríguez Horruitiner

On November 11, 1997, a Santiago tribunal found Orestes Rodríguez Horruitiner guilty of enemy propaganda and sentenced him to four years in prison. He was a member of the Cuban Party of Orthodox Renovation and a vice-president of the Ex-Political Prisoners Club (Club de Ex-Presos Políticos).[231] Cuban police

---

same period. Human Rights Watch telephone interview with Dr. Caridad del Carmen Piñon Rodríguez (Dr. Mendoza Rivero's wife), Santiago de Cuba, June 25, 1998.

[228] Ibid.

[229] Ibid.

[230] "Prisioneros Políticos Liberados Tramitan Viaje a España," *EFE*, December 1, 1998.

[231] Adalberto Yero, "Sentencian al Activista de Derechos Humanos Orestes Rodríguez Horruitiner," *Corresponsalia Turquino/Agencia de Prensa Independiente de Cuba: CubaNet*, November 21, 1997.

arrested him in July 1997 after searching his home and seizing several books from it, apparently including books by José Martí, Máximo Gómez, and Antonio Maceo, and books printed outside Cuba. At trial, these books reportedly served as the foundation for the prosecution's enemy propaganda charge. Prosecutors argued that any book edited outside of Cuba contained ideological diversions. The prosecutors also expressed dissatisfaction with Rodríguez Horruitiner's activities with nongovernmental organizations.

Cuban authorities detained Rodríguez Horruitiner in the La Caoba Prison in Santiago Province. While imprisoned, his high blood pressure worsened, leading to his prolonged hospitalization at the Boniato Prison hospital. Prison authorities only allowed him visits with two members of his immediate family once every two months for two hours. The Standard Minimum Rules for the treatment of prisoners urge prison authorities to assist prisoners in maintaining and improving their relationships with their family, and in providing for regular contact with family and friends.[232]

Maritza Lugo Fernández and Raúl Ayarde Herrera

In June 1997, in an apparent effort to stifle criticism of the government, a Havana tribunal found Maritza Lugo Fernández and Raúl Ayarde Herrera guilty of bribery. At the time of the trial, Ayarde Herrera was serving a ten-year sentence for espionage. The Cuban prosecutors who tried him in 1991 following his unsuccessful effort to leave Cuba presented no evidence of espionage. Prosecutors at the 1997 trial alleged that Ayarde Herrera and Lugo Fernández, a member of the Frank País 30th of November Party (Partido 30 de Noviembre Frank País), had conspired to bribe a guard at the Unit 1580 Prison in Havana Province (also known as "El Pitirre") to bring a tape recorder into the prison.[233] Cuban authorities, who often were frustrated by prisoners' outspoken criticism of prison conditions and abuses, apparently targeted Ayarde Herrera and Lugo Fernández in order to prevent the dissemination of information about Cuban prisons. The court sentenced Lugo Fernández to two years and Ayarde Herrera to three years. In April 1998, the Cuban government released Ayarde Herrera from prison on the condition that he

---

[232] Standard Minimum Rules for the Treatment of Prisoners, Articles 37 and 61.

[233] Cuban courts also had prosecuted Lugo Fernández's husband Rafael Ibarra Roque, the president of the 30th of November Party, after arresting him in June 1994. At this writing, he was serving a twenty-year sentence for sabotage in the maximum security Kilo 8 Prison in Camagüey Province. Mercedes Moreno, "Irá a Juicio Joven Opositora," *Agencia Nacional de Prensa ANP: CubaNet,* September 2, 1997.

go into exile in Canada. At this writing, Lugo Fernández was serving her sentence under house arrest in Havana.[234]

Cecilio Ruíz Rivero

Cuban police arrested Cecilio Ruíz Rivero, a member of the Association Struggling Against Injustice (ALFIN), on July 14, 1997. In September 1997, a Havana tribunal reportedly found him guilty of contempt for authority, resisting arrest, and assault on authority (*desacato, resistencia al arresto, y atentado a la autoridad*) and sentenced him to nine years in prison. He previously had served a three-year sentence for enemy propaganda. Cuban authorities sent him to the Quivican prison in Havana Province.[235] As described above, on August 28, 1998, a Havana court sentenced Ruíz Rivero's colleague, Reynaldo Alfaro García, ALFIN's vice-president, to three years for spreading false news.

Lorenzo Paez Núñez and Dagoberto Vega Jaime

On July 10, 1997, Cuban authorities detained Lorenzo Paez Núñez, a journalist with the Independent Press Bureau of Cuba (Buró de Prensa Independiente de Cuba, BPIC) and the president of the José de la Luz y Caballero Nongovernmental Human Rights Center (Centro No Gubernamental para los Derechos Humanos "José de la Luz y Caballero"), and Dagoberto Vega Jaime.[236] On July 11, the Municipal Tribunal in Artemisa found both guilty of defaming the police and contempt for authority. The court sentenced Paez Núñez to eighteen months and Vega Jaime to one year in prison. The extremely short period between their arrest and trial compromised their ability to prepare for the trial, particularly since the government did not permit either defendant to name a defense attorney. The court found both defendants guilty of defaming a former Interior Ministry official by alleging that he beat several youths. In rendering this decision, the court ignored testimony the youths reportedly provided confirming the defendants' allegations. The contempt of authority charge reportedly arose after Paez Núñez described an

---

[234] Human Rights Watch telephone interview with Raúl Ayarde Herrera, Toronto, Canada, April 21, 1998. Julio Martínez, "Condenada a Dos Años de Privación de Libertad la Opositora Maritza Lugo Fernández," *Habana Press: CubaNet*, September 7, 1997.

[235] Human Rights Watch telephone interview with Odilia Collazo, PPDH, Havana, August 6, 1998. Ariel Hidalgo and Tete Machado, "Disidente Será Condenado," *Infoburo*, November 24, 1997.

[236] Amnesty International, "Cuba: Prisoners of Conscience Lorenzo Paez Núñez and Dagoberto Vega Jaime," *An Amnesty International Report*, August 7, 1997.

ongoing police search to a contact in Miami who later broadcast his interview on a radio station accessible to Cubans. Vega Jaime appeared to have no role in this incident, but nonetheless was found guilty of contempt. A Havana tribunal ratified the sentence on July 24.[237] Cuba released both men upon the completion of their sentences.

Nestor Rodríguez Lobaina and Radamés García de la Vega

Cuban authorities tried and convicted Nestor Rodríguez Lobaina, the president of the Movement of Young Cubans for Democracy (Movimiento de Cubanos Jóvenes por la Democracia), of contempt for authority and resisting authority in early April 1997. He reportedly had criticized government plans for a youth festival that allowed no participation of independent groups. He was released in October 1997 after serving his full eighteen-month sentence. Following his detention, Cuban authorities reportedly also subjected his family members and colleagues to harassment and threats of prosecution for political crimes.[238] Cuban police also detained Rodríguez Lobaina's colleague, Radamés García de la Vega, the vice-president of the Movement of Young Cubans for Democracy, later that month. In June 1997, a Santiago tribunal sentenced García de la Vega to eighteen months for contempt of authority. In July the court confirmed the sentence on appeal. After completing his sentence, García de la Vega left Cuba for exile in the United States. The government repeatedly had detained both Rodríguez and García on previous occasions and in June 1996, had sentenced both to residence restrictions, insisting that they leave Havana and return to their hometowns in eastern Cuba.[239]

---

[237] Reporters Without Borders, "Two Journalists Still Detained," *IFEX - News from the International Freedom of Expression Community*, February 9, 1998.

[238] Human Rights Watch telephone interview with a representative of the Cuban Commission for Human Rights and National Reconciliation (Comisión Cubana para los Derechos Humanos y la Reconciliación Nacional), Havana, May 15, 1997; "Lider Juvenil Disidente en Pésimas Condiciones," *Infoburo*, May 27, 1997, "Hostigan a Familiares y Amigos de Joven Prisionero," *Infoburo*, May 30, 1997; and Omar Rodríguez Saludes, "Celebrado Juicio a Joven Disidente," *Agencia Nueva Prensa: CubaNet*, July 23, 1997.

[239] Cuba's controls over the freedom of movement, including the sanction of internal exile, are discussed above, at *Impediments to Human Rights in Cuban Law: Crimes Restricting the Freedom of Movement.*

Ana María Agramonte Crespo

In mid-May 1997 Cuban authorities convicted Ana María Agramonte Crespo, a member of the Nationalist Action Movement (Movimiento de Acción Nacionalista, MAN), to eighteen months for contempt of authority and resistence to authority. Cuban authorities detained her in the Manto Negro Prison in Havana. Her warrantless arrest on May 1, 1997, followed shortly after she protested the government's directive that dissidents should refrain from any activities on May Day. Cuban authorities arrested and searched the homes of five other dissidents that day, holding them in Villa Marista (the state security detention center in Havana) for several days. The five dissidents held were Alberto Perrera Martínez, the president of Peace, Progress, and Liberty (Paz, Progreso y Libertad); Jesús Pérez Gómez and Lorenzo Pescoso, the vice-president and secretary, respectively, of the same organization; Aquileo Cancio Chong, the president of the Nationalist Action Party (Partido de Acción Nacionalista, PAN); and Gabriel Leyva.[240]

Enrique García Morejón

In February 1997, a Cuban court found Enrique García Morejón, a member of the Christian Liberation Movement (Movimiento Cristiano de Liberación, MCL), guilty of enemy propaganda and sentenced him to four years in prison, which he began serving in the Cerámica Roja prison in Camagüey. Reportedly, the charge arose from his having worked in late 1996 to collect signatures for the MCL's legalization. The MCL, a Catholic nongovernmental organization, repeatedly has solicited government legalization without success. Initially charged with "illegal association," the government later based his prosecution for enemy propaganda on an accusation of distributing flyers saying "Down with Fidel."[241]

---

[240] "Cuban Dissident Jailed for 18 Months," *Reuters News Service*, May 20, 1997. Human Rights Watch telephone interview with representative of the Cuban Commission for Human Rights and National Reconciliation, Havana, May 23, 1997.

[241] Human Rights Watch telephone interview with Odilia Collazo, PPDH President, Havana, August 6, 1998. Cuba's pressures on the MCL and other religious organizations are detailed below, at *Limits on Religious Freedom*.

V. GENERAL PRISON CONDITIONS

> *Imprisonment and other measures which result in cutting off an offender from the outside world are afflictive by... depriving [the person] of his liberty. Therefore the prison system shall not, except as incidental to... the maintenance of discipline, aggravate the suffering inherent in such a situation.*
>
> *Article 57, United Nations Standard Minimum Rules for the Treatment of Prisoners*

Cuba confines its sizable prison population in substandard and unhealthy conditions, where prisoners face physical and sexual abuse. Cuban prison practices fail in numerous respects to comply with the Standard Minimum Rules for the Treatment of Prisoners, which provide authoritative guidance on the treatment of prisoners under international law and treaties.[242] Despite grave problems in its prisons, Cuba has asserted its full compliance with the Standard Minimum Rules.[243] Cuba told the U.N. that in May 1997 its Interior Ministry promulgated new prison regulations that "took into account" the Standard Minimum Rules, as well as Cuba's constitution and other legislation.[244]

Cuba's refusal to allow domestic or international human rights monitors to conduct regular visits to its prisons casts a veil of secrecy over its extensive prison system, reportedly one of the largest per capita in Latin America and the Caribbean. Cuba refuses to disseminate even the most basic prison statistics, such as prison population figures. Cuba's Penitentiary Establishment Directorate, however, reportedly maintains a centralized, computerized system that would readily make

---

[242] Standard Minimum Rules for the Treatment of Prisoners, approved by the U.N. Economic and Social Council by resolutions 663 C, July 31, 1957, and 2076, May 13, 1977.

[243] "Informe de la Fiscalía General de la República de Cuba," presented by Blanca Gutiérrez, Cuba's Attorney General for the Control of Legality in Penitentiary Establishments at the Instituto Latinoamericano de las Naciones Unidas para la Prevención del Delito y el Tratamiento del Delincuente conference, San José, Costa Rica, February 1997, p. 5.

[244] Cuban report to the Committee Against Torture, November 17, 1997 (CAT/C/SR.310/Add.1), March 25, 1998, para. 17.

available detailed information about all detainees in Cuba's prisons.[245] Cuba has promised to do so with respect to the racial makeup of its prison population, in response to questions as to whether persons of African descent are over-represented.[246] In late 1996 Cuba reportedly operated some forty maximum security prisons, thirty minimum security prisons, and over 200 work camps.[247] Prisoners reportedly completed the construction of Cuba's newest prison in early 1998. The facility, which has space for 300 inmates and is next to the maximum-security Valle Grande prison in Havana, apparently is being used to hold the increasing numbers of women accused of prostitution. However, in late 1997 the Cuban government told the U.N. that "there were only nineteen closed prisons in Cuba, together with a number of open prisons." The government did not detail the distinction between closed and open prisons. Cuba also said that, "whatever the case, the number of places of detention in Cuba, including police stations, was less than 250."[248] Our research suggests that the government's figures are artificially low.

In preparation for this report, Human Rights Watch interviewed dozens of former Cuban prisoners and family members of current and former prisoners

---

[245] The government also has stated that it maintains files at each prison that are regularly updated to reflect the prisoner's legal and medical status. Prison officials and government prosecutors reportedly examine each of these files when they conduct prison inspections. Ibid., p. 6. Several former prisoners interviewed by Human Rights Watch stated that prison officials told them that they could not be released until the officials had received computer authorization from Havana to do so.

[246] In August 1998, Cuba told the U.N. Committee on the Elimination of Racial Discrimination that it would begin to compile statistics on the racial makeup of its prison population in order to submit these to treaty bodies in the future. Cuba unconvincingly argued that its not having compiled racial breakdowns previously demonstrated that the government did not discriminate. Consideration of the Report Submitted by Cuba to the Committee on the Elimination of Racial Discrimination, August 13, 1998 (CERD/C/SR.1291), issued August 18, 1998, para. 7. One scholar noted that in the late 1980s "blacks and mulattoes [were] over-represented in the prison population." Alejandro de la Fuente, "Recreating Racism: Race and Discrimination in Cuba's Special Period," *Cuba Briefing Paper Series*, July 1998, p. 5.

[247] "Lista Parcial de Prisiones y Centros Correccionales," *Comisión Cubana de Derechos Humanos y Reconciliación Nacional* (Cuban Commission of Human Rights and National Reconciliation, hereinafter, the Cuban Commission), Havana, December 31, 1996.

[248] Cuban Report to the Committee Against Torture, para. 27.

(gathering information on twenty-four of Cuba's maximum security prisons and numerous other detention centers, such as police stations and state security offices), as well as human rights activists within Cuba, many of whom are former political prisoners. Our interviews reveal that male and female Cuban prisoners, including political prisoners whose treatment is discussed in greater detail below, at *Treatment of Political Prisoners*, endure severe hardships in Cuba's prisons. Most prisoners suffer malnourishment from an insufficient prison diet and languish in overcrowded cells without appropriate medical attention. Some endure physical and sexual abuse or long periods in isolation cells. Prison authorities insist that all detainees participate in politically oriented "reeducation" sessions or face punitive measures. In many prisons, authorities fail to separate all of the pretrial detainees from the convicts and minors from adults. Cuba has stated that only 8 percent of its detainees have not been tried, but qualified this assertion with an unusual description of a "trial" as, typically, "a six-to-nine month" period before any sentence is handed down.[249] This explanation suggests that Cuba has a far larger percentage of pretrial detainees, who are imprisoned without being convicted of any crime, for periods of six to nine months or longer. Minors risk indefinite detention in juvenile facilities, without benefit of due process guarantees or a fixed sentence.

The Cuban Interior Ministry runs the prison system, with soldiers often serving as prison guards and labor camp overseers. Each prison's staff includes a reeducator, usually a military official, assigned to direct the prison population's pro-government political indoctrination. In facilities holding political prisoners, special units of the state security police reportedly take responsibility for overseeing the detainees' sentences. Prison guards in men's facilities name prisoners to powerful positions as members of "prisoners' councils" or "disciplinary councils," (*consejos de reclusos* or *consejos de disciplina*) and rely on these prisoners to maintain internal discipline. Prison authorities apparently select members of the prisoners' councils because they have records of violence or "thuggery" (*matonismo*) and sometimes allow them to carry sticks.[250] One prisoner held in the Agüica maximum security prison in Matanzas from late 1996 to February 1998 said that three or four members of the prisoners' councils took charge of discipline and food distribution for each company of approximately 150 prisoners.[251] The council members commit

---

[249] Ibid., para. 31.

[250] Human Rights Watch interview with Víctor Reynaldo Infante Estrada, Toronto, April 14, 1998.

[251] Ibid.

some of Cuba's worst prison abuses, including beating fellow prisoners as a disciplinary measure and sexually abusing prisoners, under direct orders from or with the acquiescence of prison officials.[252]

Bar on Domestic and International Monitoring of Prison Conditions

The Cuban government bars regular access to its prisons by domestic and international human rights and humanitarian monitors. While the government allowed a representative from Human Rights Watch to visit Cuba and interview twenty-four political prisoners in 1995, as part of a human rights mission with France-Libertés, the Federation Internationale des Droits de l'Homme, and Medicins du Monde, the government strictly controlled the access to the prisoners and did not allow us beyond the administrative sections of any prison visited.[253] We later learned that Cuban authorities surreptitiously audiotaped our interviews with the prisoners and based decisions to release or continue to imprison them on the content of their conversations with us (specifically, their positions for or against the U.S. embargo on Cuba).[254] The Cuban government has not allowed Human Rights Watch to return officially to Cuba since 1995. While the Cuban government allowed two groups restricted access to a juvenile detention center in the past year, we know of no Cuban or international organization granted open access to Cuba's prisons and prisoners. Cuba never allowed U.N. Special Rapporteur on Human Rights in Cuba Ambassador Carl Johan-Groth to enter the country, much less its prisons.

The International Committee for the Red Cross (ICRC), which visits prisoners in custody for political and security offenses all over the world, last conducted prison visits in Cuba in 1988 and 1989. ICRC delegates carry out strictly humanitarian work: they interview prisoners to determine their material and

---

[252] The Standard Minimum Rules prohibit prison authorities from granting prisoners any disciplinary authority over other prisoners. Article 28(1). As Human Rights Watch concluded in our global prison report: "No inmate should ever be placed in a position to exercise significant authority over other prisoners." Human Rights Watch, *Global Report on Prisons* (Human Rights Watch: New York, 1993), p. 46.

[253] Frances-Libertés, Federation Internationale des Ligues des Droits de l'Homme, Medecins du Monde, and Human Rights Watch/Americas, *Cuba: Situation des Prisonniers Politiques: Mission du 28 Avril au 5 Mai 1995: Rapport de Mission*, December 1995. See also, Human Rights Watch/Americas, *Improvements without Reform*, October 1995.

[254] Human Rights Watch interviews with former political prisoners; names withheld for security.

psychological needs and, if necessary, provide them with supplies, such as medicine, toiletries, and clothing. They also observe the treatment afforded detainees and ask the authorities to take needed steps to improve that treatment.[255] In 1989, the agreement between the Cuban government and the ICRC was suspended, and the visits foreseen for 1990 could not take place. Cuba's refusal to allow human rights and humanitarian groups access to its prisons represents a failure to demonstrate minimal transparency. Moreover, the government's barring of the ICRC, which works behind the scenes to protect the rights of political prisoners and does not publicize its findings, shows a profound lack of concern for those prisoners' welfare.[256]

Food

Cuban prisoners measure their prison rations by the spoonful, rather than by the bowl or plate. Most prisoners suffer malnutrition on the prison diet—typically losing significant amounts of weight while serving their sentences.[257] A former prisoner at the Provincial Prison of Holguín recalled that during his four-year incarceration in the prison (from March 1994 until February 1998), his daily food ration would fit into one small cup.[258] When asked what she received for her evening meal, one former prisoner simply said "no," explaining that she never had received more than two servings of food per day. One former prisoner said that in his six years in Cuban prisons, his food rations included a total of six eggs and "never a single piece of chicken." He recalled that for breakfast, he typically received a cup of water with some sugar and for lunch, four or five spoonfuls of

---

[255] International Committee of the Red Cross, *ICRC Annual Report: 1996* (Geneva: ICRC, 1996), p. 8.

[256] During the January 1998 papal visit to Cuba, authorities reportedly used an ambulance marked with a red cross to remove an anti-government demonstrator from the pope's January 23 open air mass in Havana. Juan Tamayo, "Cruz Roja Investiga Uso Indebido de Ambulancia," *El Nuevo Herald*, March 6, 1998. This incident called into question Cuba's respect for internationally recognized human rights and humanitarian standards, and specifically, the protective emblem of the International Red Cross and Red Crescent Movement.

[257] The Standard Minimum Rules call for "food of nutritional value adequate for health and strength, of wholesome quality and well prepared and served." Article 20(1).

[258] Human Rights Watch interview with Edelberto Del Toro Argota, Toronto, April 12, 1998.

rice and a small bowl of unidentifiable soup (*caldo loco*). He said that he would not have survived but for his family's persistent deliveries of food.[259] Several former prisoners said prison authorities served them foul and poorly cleaned food that was both revolting and potentially harmful to eat. Prisoners recalled meals composed of rice or beans that were infested with pests, rotting fish innards, excrement, and putrified cow's and pig's blood. Several prisoners told Human Rights Watch that receiving food in this condition was one of the most degrading experiences of their prison terms.

The Cuban government claimed in late 1997 that "...despite the [U.S.] economic blockade, the penitentiary population was sufficiently nourished. The prisoners can raise poultry and other animals appropriate for their nourishment. They are guaranteed three meals per day...."[260] Another government report stated that all prisoners receive 2,160 calories a day, served in three meals, and that any prisoners who are underweight receive additional food and vitamin supplements.[261] The government's assertions are contradicted by consistent reports from Cuban prisons that detainees receive inadequate nutrition. Moreover, the prison officials' practice of granting control over food to the prisoners' councils aggravates the nutritional crisis in Cuba's prisons.[262] Prisoners' councils routinely abuse this authority, hoarding food for themselves, using it to discipline prisoners or to bribe hungry prisoners for sexual favors. And while Cuban prisoners often work on prison farms, guards typically forbid them from eating the produce or livestock they raise. Moreover, prisoners interviewed by Human Rights Watch had gleaned information from prison overseers that the food raised on Cuban prison grounds was destined for Cuba's military forces or tourist restaurants.[263] Prisoners' family members often encounter difficulties when attempting to leave food for their

---

[259] Human Rights Watch interview with Víctor Reynaldo Infante Estrada, Toronto, April 14, 1998.

[260] Excerpted from Cuba's December 1997 report to the United Nations Committee Against Torture, by Pablo Alfonso, "Comida en Prisiones es Balanceada, Dice Gobierno," *El Nuevo Herald*, February 12, 1998.

[261] "Informe de la Fiscalía General," p. 8.

[262] As mentioned above, this practice violates the Standard Minimum Rules prohibition on granting prisoners authority over one another. Article 28(1).

[263] Prison labor conditions are discussed below, at *Labor Rights: Prison Labor*.

imprisoned relatives. Prisoners and their family members recalled cases of prison guards refusing to accept food or taking it but failing to give it to prisoners. Cuban prison authorities needlessly aggravate prisoners' suffering with these practices.

Health Concerns

Cuban prisoners also endure overcrowded, squalid conditions that one former prisoner called "primitive and anti-hygienic." Prisoners rarely have regular access to clean drinking water, and bathing water often is filthy or insufficient.[264] Toilets are usually filthy holes in the floor. One former prisoner recalled that the toilet near his cell drained into the corridor and onto his cell floor.[265] Overcrowding in some facilities requires prisoners to sleep on the floor until other prisoners leave. Mattresses and sheets are rare. Prisoners with mattresses described them as rough sacks stuffed with leaves that were infested with biting insects. Prison authorities rarely permit visitors to bring bedding, clothes, or writing materials. Nevertheless, Cuba has stated that "despite the limitations arising from the economic blockade...all of the areas used by prisoners, including the dormitories, are maintained in a perfectly hygienic sanitary state...."[266]

Malnutrition leaves Cuban prisoners at risk of numerous diseases.[267] Overcrowding and poor hygiene contribute to widespread disease in Cuban prisons. Mosquito-infested, filthy cells are breeding grounds for skin diseases, tuberculosis, conjunctivitis, and scabies. Many prisoners suffer from uncomfortable fungal infections under their arms and between their legs, which could be prevented by improved hygiene and exposure to sunlight. A physician who served over six years as a political prisoner said he had seen prisoners suffering from malnutrition, beriberi, anemia, polineuropatitis, hepatitis, girardia, lectoperosis (transmitted by rat bites), amoebiasis, vomit and diarrhea, and meningitis. Prisoners also had a high

---

[264] The Standard Minimum Rules call for prisoners to have access to drinking water whenever they need it. Article 20(2).

[265] Human Rights Watch telephone interview with José Miranda Acosta, Toronto, May 7, 1998.

[266] "Informe de la Fiscalía General," p. 8.

[267] Glenn R. Randall and Ellen L. Lutz, *Serving Survivors of Torture: A Practice Manual for Health Professionals and Other Service Providers*, (Washington: American Association for the Advancement of Science, 1991), p. 20.

incidence of psychological disorders, including neuroses, anxiety, and depression.[268]

Despite the serious medical problems affecting Cuban prisoners, prison authorities routinely deny them access to medical care and even refuse to provide prisoners with medicines brought by family members. The Standard Minimum Rules call for prison doctors to visit sick inmates daily and for prisons to provide dental care.[269] While many Cuban prisons have medical staff on the prison grounds, prisoners still do not receive prompt attention and appropriate medicines. On occasion, prison authorities treat prisoners suffering from acute conditions in hospitals off prison grounds. But prisoners complain that most ailments go untreated, even extremely painful conditions such as broken bones or multiple cavities. In some cases, prisoners died due to prison doctors' failure to treat them swiftly and sufficiently.[270] Prison authorities deny political prisoners medical care as a punishment for anti-government views, as discussed below at *Treatment of Political Prisoners.*

Restrictions of Visits

Cuban prison authorities impose severe limits on visits from family members and friends. Given the poor prison conditions, the reduction of family visits denies prisoners mental and physical support, including the provision of food and medicine. The Standard Minimum Rules urge prison authorities to assist prisoners in maintaining and improving relationships with their families, and in providing for regular contact with family and friends.[271] Prison guards place detainees on specific regimens, which link the frequency of visits to the prisoners' behavior. The most severe regimens only allow two-hour family visits, with a maximum of two immediate family members, every two or three months. Guards arbitrarily reduce these visits even further, by barring visits for several months or by cancelling family

---

[268] Ibid., pp. 35-36. Human Rights Watch interview with Dr. Omar del Pozo Marrero, Toronto, April 14, 1998.

[269] Articles 25(1) and 22(3), Standard Minimum Rules.

[270] The cases of Aurelio Ricart Hernández, who died on February 19, 1997, in the Micro 4 Prison in Havana, and Pedro Armenteros Laza and Sebastian Arcos Bergnes—two political prisoners who Cuban prison doctors failed to treat for serious conditions and who died as a result of those illnesses after their releases—are discussed below, at *Treatment of Political Prisoners: Denial of Medical Treatment.*

[271] Articles 61 and 37.

visits at the last minute, often after family members have traveled long distances under difficult conditions. Guards arbitrarily confiscate or refuse to accept food, medicines, and other belongings intended for the personal use of prisoners. Guards also penalize prisoners who refuse to participate in political reeducation sessions by reducing their family visits.

On a positive note, Cuban prison authorities grant some male and female prisoners conjugal visits. The Cuban government states that it allows female prisoners to keep their infants with them until they are one year old, after which they are sent to family or a government-run child-care center *(círculo infantil).*[272] One female prisoner held in a Havana prison for a lengthy term said that in practice, mothers must cede their infants to the government centers when they are six months old.[273]

Former prisoners and their family members told Human Rights Watch that guards routinely strip-search prisoners and visitors, including the elderly and, on occasion, children. The wife of one prisoner described how guards forced her to disrobe and perform deep knee bends before allowing her to take part in a conjugal visit. She said that the humiliation of the vaginal search made her feel like a prisoner herself.[274] The strip-searches were performed by same-sex guards.

Human Rights Watch is cognizant of prison security requirements and the difficulty of reconciling such constraints with humane visiting policies. Yet, family members, particularly children and the elderly, should not be subjected to degrading searches as the cost of a visit. Human Rights Watch agrees with a 1996 decision of the Inter-American Commission on Human Rights concluding that vaginal searches are only acceptable if, in each instance: 1) they are absolutely necessary for achieving a legitimate objective, 2) there is no alternative means of achieving the objective, 3) they are authorized by a judicial order, and 4) they are conducted by a health professional.[275]

---

[272] "Informe de la Fiscalía General," p. 11.

[273] Human Rights Watch interview with Rosalina González Lafita, Toronto, April 13, 1998.

[274] Strip-searches of several political prisoners' relatives are detailed below, at *Treatment of Political Prisoners: Hardships for Political Prisoners' Family Members.*

[275] *María Arena v. Argentina*, Case No. 10,506 (October 30, 1996). The commission ruled that such searches constitute degrading treatment, an arbitrary interference with personal privacy, and violate the right to protection of the family. For further discussion of this practice, see Human Rights Watch/Americas, *Punishment Before*

Restrictions of Religious Visits

The Standard Minimum Rules call for prison authorities to respect religious beliefs, to allow prisoners to meet with religious advisors in private, and to allow prisoners to participate in religious instruction.[276] In 1989, the Cuban Interior Ministry re-authorized the right of religious groups to provide for the spiritual needs of Cuban prisoners, which was banned in 1964. Nonetheless, prisoners face multiple barriers to receiving religious guidance in Cuba's prisons. Prison authorities apparently require prisoners to make written requests to prison directors noting their interest in religious attention, yet directors rarely inform prisoners of this requirement.[277] In late 1997 prison guards reportedly harassed and threatened to prosecute Augusto César San Martín Albistur, who was sentenced to seventeen years in 1994 for revealing secrets concerning the security of the state, reportedly because he had solicited religious attention.[278] Some prison guards subject prisoners to interrogations about their religious beliefs when they ask for pastoral care. The guards apparently explain that the prisoners must first "properly" answer questions such as: "why do you hold this faith?"; "why do you want religious assistance?"; or, "why do you prefer this religion over others?"[279] Nonetheless, the Cuban government allows some Catholic clergy to make limited prison visits while arbitrarily denying the requests of others. In April 1998, the Archdiocese of Havana expressed frustration at the government's refusal to allow detainees to meet with Catholic clergy.[280] But even when the authorities permit visits, prison guards often accompany the representatives.

Trial: Prison Conditions in Venezuela (Human Rights Watch: New York, 1997), pp. 82-86.

[276] Standard Minimum Rules, Articles 6(2), 41(2), 41(3), and 77(1).

[277] María de los Angeles González Amaro, "La Iglesia Católica y Pastoral Carcelaria," Agencia de Prensa Independiente de Cuba (APIC), June 18, 1996.

[278] Marvin Hernández Monzón, "Sufriendo por la Fé, " *Cuba Press*, February 23, 1998.

[279] Human Rights Watch interview with Dr. Omar del Pozo Marrero, Toronto, April 14, 1998.

[280] Agence France Presse, "Revista Dice Impiden Actos Religiosos a los Presos," *El Nuevo Herald*, April 19, 1998.

Political Indoctrination

Cuba requires prisoners to undergo political indoctrination. The prison authorities' emphasis on political "reeducation," rather than broader educational opportunities, exercise, and recreational and cultural activities, runs counter to the Standard Minimum Rules' provisions to protect convicts' mental and physical health.[281] Cuba's insistence that all prisoners, whether held for political or common crimes, engage in pro-government activities also violates those prisoners' freedom of opinion.[282] Prison officials routinely punish prisoners who fail to participate in the political reeducation activities.

Obligatory prison reeducation programs, directed by the prison's reeducator who usually is a military official, require prisoners to shout pro-government slogans, including "Long Live Fidel," "Commander-in-Chief, Give Us Your Orders," "Socialism or Death," and "The Homeland or Death - We Will Win!" Prisoners also must participate in "cycles" (*ciclos*), where they study and take quizzes based on pro-government reading materials. Prisoners also noted that reeducators sometimes turn over the responsibility for carrying out reeducation sessions to the abusive prisoners' councils. Prison authorities force compliance with political reeducation programs by subjecting non-participating prisoners to beatings (often carried out by the prisoners' councils), denying food rations, transferring inmates to prisons with worse conditions, or suspending the right to conditional liberty, visits, access to sunlight, or other benefits.

Prisoners consider reeducators among the most abusive prison authorities. Former political prisoner Raúl Ayarde Herrera recalled that the reeducator at the Pinar del Río Provincial Prison, known as Osiris, told him "you have to reeducate yourself. Then you'll get more food." On November 9, 1997, nine days after Ayarde Herrera commenced a hunger strike to protest prison conditions and his detention in an isolation cell, Osiris and the prison official in charge of political prisoners, state security Lt. Mario Medina, beat him and cut his face with a piece of a broken mirror.[283]

Cuban prisons provide limited educational and recreational opportunities. The Standard Minimum Rules recommend that all prisons have libraries stocked with

---

[281] Articles 21(1) and (2), 77(1), and 78.

[282] The Universal Declaration of Human Rights provides that everyone has the right to hold opinions without interference and the right to manifest his or her beliefs in public. UDHR, Articles 19 and 18.

[283] Human Rights Watch telephone interview with Raúl Ayarde Herrera, Toronto, April 21, 1998.

recreational and instructional books that are accessible to all inmates.[284] But Cuban prison authorities typically provide limited access to reading materials and ban any books that might contain anti-government content. Prisoners complain that they are rarely permitted outside for exercise or simply to be in the sun (many suffer ailments related to sunlight deprivation).

Prison Labor

Cuba provides prisoners with opportunities to work, which in some cases provide helpful job-training, but these programs do not always satisfy the Standard Minimum Rules' regulations governing prison labor programs. The Standard Minimum Rules require prisons to have physically fit convicts to take part in vocational training and to engage in meaningful, rehabilitative work for equitable remuneration.[285] Cuba's insistence that some political prisoners participate in work programs and its inappropriate pressuring of inmates to work without pay in inhuman conditions violate international labor and prison rights standards. Prison labor conditions are discussed in detail below, at *Labor Rights: Prison Labor.*

Isolation

The Cuban government has stated that "it does not practice, nor allow, corporal punishment, nor are there any darkened cells, nor degrading or cruel punishments, nor punishments that humiliate or minimize the dignity of a detainee."[286] Unfortunately, this assessment bears little relation to the reality of Cuban prisons, where guards frequently mete out long punishment periods in darkened isolation cells. The use of this extremely destructive and unnecessary practice is detailed below, at *Treatment of Political Prisoners: Abusive Pretrial Detentions* and *Post-Conviction Isolation.*

Beatings by Police, Guards and Prisoners' Councils

Cuban prison guards and prisoners' councils reportedly use beatings as a disciplinary measure, to punish political opinions, to intimidate prisoners for sex,

---

[284] Standard Minimum Rules, Article 40.

[285] Ibid., Articles 71, 72, and 76(1).

[286] "Informe de la Fiscalía General," p. 11.

or for other reasons.[287] Several former prisoners believed that prison guards grant disciplinary authority to prisoners' councils, in direct violation of the Standard Minimum Rules, in order to avoid becoming directly involved in physically abusing prisoners themselves. Prison authorities reportedly are quite sensitive to criticism of their human rights practices and typically punish prisoners who criticize prison abuses or attempt to publicize them.[288] Prisoners in pretrial detention, particularly political prisoners, also face beatings. Some prisoners interviewed by Human Rights Watch recalled minor actions taken by Cuban authorities against prison guards implicated in abuses, in one case a transfer to another post. We have learned of one 1998 case where two guards beat a political prisoner in which the government reportedly intended to prosecute the wrongdoers. We know of no incident when prison authorities disciplined a member of a prisoners' council who was implicated in beating a fellow prisoner.

In a report to the U.N. Committee Against Torture, Cuba provided some information about internal efforts to establish accountability for a broad range of rights and specifically mentioned receiving complaints of abuse in its prisons. Since Cuba permits no independent prison monitoring, and has not even released the number of prisoners currently detained in its prisons, it is impossible to confirm the veracity of this information. Without providing specific details of any cases, the government stated that in 1997 it had received thirty-seven complaints of ill-treatment in prison or in custody; had taken "administrative or disciplinary measures" in ten of those cases; and had sent ten cases to the courts, one of which resulted in an eight-year sentence.[289] If true, Cuba's actions would constitute encouraging steps toward establishing accountability for prisoners' rights abuses. A February 1999 Criminal Code reform provided that prisoners "cannot be the objects of corporal punishment, nor is it permitted to employ any means against them to humiliate them or to lessen their dignity."[290] The failure to create any penalties for committing such acts or to define them explicitly as crimes diminishes the potential impact of this reform. Furthermore, Cuba's retaliations against

---

[287] Several cases of guards beating prisoners due to their political opinion are discussed below, at *Treatment of Political Prisoners: Beatings.*

[288] This practice is discussed further below, at *Treatment of Political Prisoners: Criminal Charges for Denouncing Abuses.*

[289] Cuban report to the Committee Against Torture, March 3, 1998, para. 25.

[290] Law Number 87 (1999), Article 1, modifying Law Number 62 (1988), Article 30.

prisoners who denounce prison abuses and conditions and its ban on prison monitoring suggest a determination to cover up—rather than expose and punish—prison abuses.

Cuba detains untried individuals in a variety of institutions, ranging from police stations to state security headquarters and maximum security prisons (where they are improperly detained with convicted violent offenders). Heavy reliance on incommunicado pretrial detention heightens the risk that police or prison guards will brutalize detainees. On June 30, 1998, Cuban police arrested Reinery Marrero Toledo, alleging that he had ties with some neighbors who had been charged with slaughtering livestock (*sacrificio ilegal de ganado*).[291] On July 9, 1998, agents of the Technical Department of Investigations in Havana (Departamento Técnico de Investigaciones, DTI) told his family that he had committed suicide by hanging himself with a sheet. However, a family member who viewed his corpse noted that it was heavily bruised and recalled that the police had cancelled his scheduled family visit the day before his death.[292]

On July 18, 1998, prisoners at the Nieves Morejón prison in Sancti Spiritus beat Adiannes Jordán Contreras, who was serving a ten-year sentence for piracy. Reportedly, the victim and her sister, Mayda Bárbara Jordán Contreras, who was serving a fifteen-year term for piracy, had decided not to wear prison uniforms or comply with other prison rules. The sisters believed that the prison's reeducator, Yeni Sánchez López, and two guards had ordered the beating as a reprisal.[293]

One former political prisoner who served in the Las Tunas Provincial Prison from August 1997 to February 1998 recalled several instances when guards used iron bars about the size of baseball bats, lightly-covered with cloth, to beat common prisoners. Some of these beatings occurred after prisoners insisted on a lightening of the prison regimen. He said that during his term at the Micro 4 Prison in Havana, in 1996 and 1997, guards got drunk on weekends and on several occasions took prisoners out of their cells to practice martial arts techniques on them.[294]

---

[291] Criminal Code, Article 240.

[292] Orlando Bordón Gálvez, "Sospecho 'Suicidio' de Recluso," *Cuba Press*, July 9, 1998.

[293] Public letter from Amado J. Rodríguez, Coordinator, Human Rights in Cuba, Miami, August 13, 1998.

[294] Human Rights Watch interview with Marcos Antonio Hernández García, Toronto, April 13, 1998.

Sexual Abuse

Members of prisoners' councils apparently commit widespread sexual abuse with the acquiescence of prison authorities. To a lesser extent, prison guards also commit sexual abuse and engage in sexual misconduct with prisoners under the guise of "consensual" sexual relationships. The prison systems' youngest inmates are most vulnerable to sexual abuse. While the former prisoners interviewed by Human Rights Watch did not know the exact ages of young prisoners who had suffered sexual abuse, they believed that many of these prisoners were under the age of eighteen. Cuba's full compliance with the Standard Minimum Rules' bar on detaining minors in adult facilities would help protect youths from this type of abuse.

Given the near absolute authority that guards have over prisoners' lives, even so-called "consensual" sex between guards and inmates constitutes a serious form of misconduct.[295] Because prisoners are dependent on guards for the most basic necessities, guards' offer of, or the threat to eliminate, privileges or goods carries tremendous weight. Former detainees in women's prisons said that sexual relations between male guards and female prisoners were not uncommon. One prisoner recalled that when ranking prison authorities became aware of several of these relationships, they punished the prisoners, rather than the guards.[296] One prisoner interviewed by Human Rights Watch said that a male prison guard at Las Tunas had received oral sex from a male prisoner in 1997. It was not clear if the sexual contact was "voluntary." The guard later was moved from his post, but he was not fired.[297]

The prisoners' councils, which are active in men's facilities, apparently rape younger detainees, intimidate them with beatings, or lure them into sexual relationships with offers of food (since prison authorities grant them control of food distribution), drugs, or other hard-to-obtain goods. Prison guards apparently permit these abuses in order to ensure the loyalty of the prisoners' councils, who they have improperly imbued with internal prison disciplinary authority. Human Rights Watch learned from a credible source that members of a prisoner council had

---

[295] For a detailed discussion of this issue, see Human Rights Watch, *All Too Familiar: Sexual Abuse of Women in U.S. State Prisons* (Human Rights Watch: New York, 1996), pp. 4-5, 217.

[296] Human Rights Watch interview with Rosalina González Lafita, Toronto, April 13, 1998.

[297] Human Rights Watch interview with Marcos Antonio Hernández García, Toronto, April 13, 1998.

subjected one male detainee to repeated rapes, which left the victim emotionally devastated.[298] One former prisoner said that while the prisoners' council's sexual abuse was "constant," he knew of no case when a guard intervened.[299] Another former prisoner said that guards permit the council members to practice sodomy and that there are "many cases of rape."[300]

Juvenile Justice

Cuban courts do not prosecute minors under the age of sixteen. Rather, "child welfare councils" under the direction of the Minister of the Interior can order children detained for indefinite periods in "reeducation centers."[301] A multidisciplinary team examines the child and decides his or her fate. The child is represented by a lawyer from the Ministry of the Iinterior, but it is not clear whether the attorney represents the child's interests or the government's, nor if the attorney provides adequate representation.[302] The indefinite term of detention also is cause for concern, since international children's rights standards ratified by Cuba require that any restrictions on children's liberty are kept to a minimum.[303]

The Cuban system provides that juveniles from age sixteen to eighteen who receive prison sentences may serve those sentences in facilities holding detainees from the ages of sixteen to twenty, but they still risk being placed in prisons with

---

[298] Human Rights Watch interview; name withheld for security.

[299] Human Rights Watch telephone interview with Raúl Ayarde Herrera, Toronto, April 21, 1998.

[300] Human Rights Watch telephone interview with René Portelles, Toronto, April 21, 1998.

[301] United Nations Committee on the Rights of the Child, "Consideration of Reports Submitted by States Parties under Article 44 of the Convention," (CRC/C/8/Add.30.), issued February 15, 1996.

[302] Ibid. The U.N. Convention on the Rights of the Child, G.A. Res. 44/25, November 1989, entered into force September 2, 1990, Article 37(d). Cuba ratified the Convention on August 21, 1991.

[303] U.N. Convention on the Rights of the Child, Article 37(b); and U.N. Standard Minimum Rules for the Administration of Juvenile Justice (Beijing Rules), G.A. Res 40/33, November 29, 1985, Article 17.1(b).

adults.[304] Several former Cuban prisoners told Human Rights Watch that they encountered youngsters whom they believed were under eighteen in adult prisons. Mixing minors and adults in detention facilities violates strict international rules against such practices, principally because the youths are at risk of abuse by the older, more powerful adult prisoners.[305] Human Rights Watch also received reports that young Cuban prisoners were subjected to serious physical and sexual abuse in adult prisons.

[304] The February 1999 Criminal Code reform stated that minors younger than twenty should be held in separate establishments from older detainees or in separate areas of the same detention facilities. Law Number 87, Article 1. It is too early to tell whether this provision will result in the segregation of minor and adult detainees.

[305] Beijing Rules, Article 26.3.

VI. TREATMENT OF POLITICAL PRISONERS

Cuba's repressive machinery is used effectively against people who exercise their fundamental rights of free association, free expression, free opinion, or the freedom of movement. Scores of Cuban activists who suffer short-term detentions and who receive official warnings that they will face prosecutions for political crimes take seriously the risk of prosecution and imprisonment in Cuba's jails. And while the existence of hundreds of political prisoners is a deterrent to some potential opponents at home, Cuba also uses occasional prisoner releases to maximize political capital abroad. Cuba's deprivation of these individuals' liberty represents a shocking disregard for their fundamental rights. The government's failure to provide the prisoners with humane conditions and the punitive measures taken against them in prison represent additional layers of punishment for their "crimes" that, in several instances, rise to the level of torture.

High-ranking Cuban officials insist that Cuba has no political prisoners, relying on specious arguments and word-games to deny a glaring problem. In June 1998, Cuba's justice minister, Roberto Díaz Sotolongo, argued that Cuba had no political prisoners because its criminal code only penalizes conduct and not thought.[306] In July 1998, the Foreign Ministry spokesman, Alejandro González, invoked national sovereignty in his attempt to dodge reporters' questions about the lengthy pretrial detention of four members of the Internal Dissidents' Working Group and the confinement of hundreds of other political prisoners, saying that Cuba preferred the term "counterrevolutionary prisoners."[307]

The Cuban government's refusal to reveal the size of its prison population and its bar on domestic and international human rights monitoring impedes the collection of precise information on the numbers and condition of Cuban political prisoners. On several occasions, Human Rights Watch conducted telephone interviews to Cuba regarding political prisoners which were disrupted by persistent background noise that made conversation impossible or were terminated when lines went dead. Human Rights Watch interviews with former political prisoners, dissident groups, and prisoners' family members lead us to believe that Cuban prisons still hold several hundred political prisoners, and potentially hundreds more

---

[306] Human Rights Watch interview with Minister of Justice Roberto Díaz Sotolongo, New York, June 11, 1998.

[307] Pascal Fletcher, "Cuba Ducks Questions about Political Prisoners," *Reuters News Service*, July 9, 1998.

prosecuted for common crimes in retaliation for their real or perceived government opposition. Others have been imprisoned for dangerousness and illegal exit, in violation of fundamental human rights. In mid-1998, one of Cuba's nongovernmental human rights groups prepared a list of almost 400 political prisoners.[308] Other Cuban human rights organizations believe that the number of political prisoners is even higher, and point to continued arrests and prosecutions in 1998 and 1999.

While the numbers of Cuban political prisoners have dropped over recent years, this apparently has resulted from a trend toward shorter prison sentences (often eighteen months to four years versus past sentences of ten to twenty years), resulting in quicker turn-over. Most political prisoners serve out their entire sentences and virtually all are detained for more than one-third of their term, when Cuban convicts become eligible for parole. Nevertheless, Cuban prisons still detain scores of dissidents for extremely long terms—of ten to twenty years—and prosecutors have not uniformly reduced sentences.

Punitive Measures Against Political Prisoners

Like Cuba's general prison population, political prisoners frequently suffer dramatic weight loss due to meager food rations, serious and sometimes life-threatening health problems due to insufficient medical attention, and abuses at the hands of guards or other inmates. But political prisoners also encounter problems unique to their status as non-violent activists, for holding anti-government views or for criticizing human rights violations in the prisons. Every political prisoner we spoke to stressed that Cuba's confinement of non-violent prisoners with prisoners convicted for violent crimes, often in maximum-security facilities with Cuba's most hardened criminals, is degrading and dangerous. Prison authorities refuse to acknowledge political prisoners' distinct status and punish them for refusing to participate in political reeducation, not wearing prison uniforms, or denouncing human rights abuses in the prisons. Guards restrict political prisoners' visits with family members and subject relatives to harassment. Prisoners' relatives also face government intimidations outside the prison walls. Before trial, many Cuban

---

[308] Comisión Cubana de Derechos Humanos y Reconciliación Nacional, "Lista Parcial de Sancionados o Procesados por Motivos Políticos o Político Sociales," July 1998. The Commission's president, Elizardo Sánchez Santacruz, estimated that the government held between 1,000 and 4,000 additional prisoners convicted of common crimes in a political context. For example, the prevalence of black market activity in Cuba's economy provides police with an opportunity to selectively enforce laws prohibiting such activities against the government's political opponents. Human Rights Watch interview with Elizardo Sánchez Santacruz, Washington, March 24, 1997.

political prisoners routinely spend several months to more than a year in pretrial detention, often in isolation cells. Following conviction, they face additional punitive periods in solitary confinement. The government also crushes free expression inside the prison walls with criminal charges and prosecutions of previously-convicted prisoners who speak out about inhumane prison conditions and treatment.

Cuban police or prison guards often heighten the punitive nature of solitary confinement with additional sensory deprivation, such as completely blocking all light from entering a cell, blocking ventilation, removing beds or mattresses, seizing prisoners' clothes and belongings, forbidding prisoners from communicating with one another, or restricting food and water beyond the already meager prison rations. Prison and police officials also disorient prisoners by leaving lights on in cells for twenty-four hours a day, incorrectly setting the time on clocks, or incessantly playing loud music. Many prisoners said that their discomfort was aggravated by extreme heat and swarms of mosquitos biting them in the tightly closed cells. Experts in treating torture survivors recognize these as methods of physical and psychological torture.[309]

Abusive Pretrial Detentions

Prior to trial, government officials often disregard basic due process guarantees by confining suspected political opponents in incommunicado detentions for extended periods—often in maximum security prisons. The practice, which can include interrogations, threats, physical hardship, and psychological trauma, serves as a heavy punitive sanction prior to trial. While Cuban law limits pretrial detention to sixty days except in exceptional circumstances, political prisoners—particularly prominent ones—often spend far longer. The four leaders of the Internal Dissidents' Working Group spent over nineteen months in pretrial detention before their March 1, 1999 trial. A Havana court sentenced Reinaldo Alfaro García to three years in prison for spreading false news on August 28, 1998, but he already had spent over one year in detention—since May 1997, which the Cuban government typically counts as time served.

In the cases detailed below, Cuban authorities used pretrial isolation as a tool of intimidation and as punishment for nongovernmental activism. During these isolation periods, police or prison authorities barred or strictly limited contact with

---

[309] American Association for the Advancement of Science, *The Breaking of Bodies and Minds: Torture, Psychiatric Abuse, and the Health Professions*, edited by Eric Stover and Elena O. Nightingale (New York: W.H. Freeman and Company, 1985), pp. 62-69.

other prisoners, attorneys, family members, and friends, subjected the detainees to interrogations without lawyers present, and physically and mentally debilitated them. The former political prisoners interviewed by Human Rights Watch, who uniformly believed that the government had preordained the outcome of their trials, considered pretrial detentions the first stage of the government's punishment.[310]

Cuba only charged the four leaders of the Internal Dissidents' Working Group with a crime in September 1998, after they had spent fifteen months in detention.[311] During their nineteen-month pretrial detention, Cuba held Vladimiro Roca Antúnez, Martha Beatriz Roque Cabello, Félix Bonne Carcassés, and René Gómez Manzano in maximum-security prisons. Roque Cabello spent some periods in the prison ward of a Havana hospital. Vladimiro Roca's wife, Magalys de Armas Chaviano, visited her husband at the Ariza Prison in Cienfuegos on June 26, 1998.[312] She said that since his arrest, Roca had spent several months in an isolation cell where he had no contact with other prisoners and no access to sunlight. His punishment cell had one bare light bulb that guards kept illuminated day and night. Although prison authorities provided him with a medical check-up on June 12, he depended on his wife to supply him with medicine for his high blood pressure. Prison guards restricted his visits to one two-hour visit every three weeks, which only two family members could attend. De Armas Chaviano said that prison guards forbade her from bringing him books with any political themes.[313] Cuban authorities were holding Bonne Carcassés in similar conditions at the Guanajay Prison in Havana province. From the time of his incarceration, Bonne Carcassés, who suffers from diabetes, was not provided with an appropriate diet and received insufficient

---

[310] The right to a fair trial in Cuban courts is discussed above, at *Due Process Denied.*

[311] Their case is detailed above, at *Political Prosecutions.*

[312] Using public transportation, the approximate travel time between Havana, where Roca's family resides, and the prison where he was held, is eight hours each way. Cuban authorities often assign prisoners to prisons that are extremely remote from their families, diminishing the families' opportunities to visit them and to provide them with home-cooked meals.

[313] Human Rights Watch telephone interview with Magalys de Armas Chaviano, Havana, July 2, 1998.

medicine. The twenty-four-hour illumination in his cell reportedly contributed to vision loss.[314]

Most of the prisoners who were released in early 1998 on the condition that they leave Cuban territory told of harsh, lengthy pretrial detentions.[315] In some cases, the former prisoners who were forced into exile left behind co-defendants (*compañeros de causa*) in Cuban prisons, serving out sentences exacerbated by interrogations carried out under intimidating circumstances and poor treatment during pretrial confinement.

On October 11, 1992, state security agents in Bayamo in Granma Province arrested brothers José Antonio and José Manuel Rodríguez Santana, detaining them at Bayamo's state security headquarters. The officials confined the brothers, who both suffer from asthma, for four months in sealed cells, where they could see no sign of night or day and had minimal ventilation. Although family members tried to bring the brothers asthma medication, the officials did not always deliver it and in the sweltering, airless conditions, they suffered several severe asthma attacks. During this period, the state security agents interrogated the brothers several times.

After four months, Cuban authorities transferred José Antonio and José Manuel to the maximum security Las Mangas Prison in Granma, where each was assigned to a cell with ten or eleven common prisoners held for violent crimes. The common prisoners harassed and beat them and provided state security agents with false information about them that later led to difficult interrogations. When the brothers protested their treatment and human rights conditions in the prison, they were harassed further. At a closed trial in August 1993, both brothers received ten-year sentences for rebellion and enemy propaganda. While Cuba released José Antonio on the condition he go into exile in Canada in April 1998, José Manuel Rodríguez Santana remains in the Las Mangas Prison at this writing.[316]

In July 1993, a court in Santiago convicted eight local residents of enemy propaganda and rebellion. Human Rights Watch interviewed three of these

---

[314] Human Rights Watch telephone interview with Odilia Collazo, president of the Pro Human Rights Party, Havana, January 11, 1999.

[315] Unfortunately, those prisoners who did not spend long periods in pretrial detention were tried in such an expedited fashion that their ability to prepare and present an adequate defense was compromised. The rapidity of their trials, of course, was only one of many obstacles to their receiving full due process guarantees. These impediments are detailed above, at *Due Process Denied.*

[316] Human Rights Watch interview with José Antonio Rodríguez Santana, Toronto, April 13, 1998.

individuals, Guillermo Ismael Sambra Ferrándiz, Luis Alberto Ferrándiz Alfaro, and Xiomara Aliat Collado, who were exiled to Canada in early 1998. One of their co-defendants, Víctor Bressler Villazán, remains in the Cuatro Caminos Work Camp in Santiago serving a twelve-year sentence for rebellion, while Emilio Bressler Cisneros, a relative who tried to defend them, is serving an eight-year sentence for enemy propaganda in the maximum security Boniato Prison in Santiago. Cuban state security agents arrested all of the co-defendants in January 1993 and first detained them in the Santiago state security headquarters, known as Versalles. Sambra Ferrándiz remembered challenging the police searching his house on January 13, 1993, to present him with a warrant. Rather than produce one, they arrested him and took him to an isolation cell at Versalles, where he was detained for three months. The cell reminded him of a tomb. It was two meters by two meters and completely closed except for a very narrow, deep space, "like a canal," that allowed some air in. A hole in the floor served as his toilet. An incandescent 100 watt bulb remained lit twenty-four hours a day, heating the stuffy cell like an oven. When night fell, swarms of mosquitos emerged, which to Sambra Ferrándiz seemed like a nightmare and kept him awake through the night. He remembered one of the state security investigators, a Captain Seriocha, telling him that "the mosquitos are our principal allies." Sambra Ferrándiz spent fifteen days in incommunicado detention before seeing his family. He said that they wept when they first saw him because he was so swollen from mosquito bites.

State security agents began interrogating him on January 14, usually in very heavily air-conditioned offices, after he had emerged from the stifling heat of his closed cell. When he or his co-defendants arrived for questioning, the agents would shut him in the cold office for between thirty minutes and one hour before the interrogation began, leaving him shivering from the cold. He recalled an investigator, who had an overcoat in his arms, asking him several times if he was cold, yet refusing to give it to him. While going to and from the interrogations, guards required him always to face the wall, with his hands at his back, and not to look at his surroundings. From Versalles, state security agents moved Sambra Ferrándiz to the maximum security Mar Verde Prison in Santiago. A Santiago court convicted him of enemy propaganda and rebellion and sentenced him to twelve years in prison in July 1993.[317]

State security agents also detained Luis Alberto Ferrándiz Alfaro and his wife, Xiomara Aliat Collado, in Versalles. Aliat Collado said that during her forty-five-day detention in Versailles, state security agents tormented her psychologically,

---

[317] Human Rights Watch telephone interview with Guillermo Ismael Sambra Ferrándiz, Toronto, May 8, 1998.

telling her that her then five-year-old son—who suffers from asthma and had been left alone with his fourteen-year-old sister following their parents' arrest—was sick and that he would not receive medical treatment and might die if she did not talk.[318] Aliat Collado received a seven-year sentence. Cuban officials transferred Ferrándiz Alfaro to the maximum security Boniato Prison in May 1993, where guards detained him for three months with another prisoner in a closed cell, measuring six feet by six feet, with no light and minimal ventilation, that was full of insects. He said, "they did not explain why I was being held in that cell. I'd never been in prison before." During this period, a Santiago court sentenced him to twelve years for enemy propaganda and rebellion.[319]

On August 3, 1992, a Cuban military tribunal found Víctor Reynaldo Infante Estrada and Dr. Omar del Pozo Marrero guilty of revealing state security secrets and sentenced them, respectively, to thirteen and fifteen years. The court also sentenced Second Lt. Julio César Alvárez López to nineteen years for the same crime and for insubordination, and Carmen Julia Arias Iglesias to nine years as an accomplice to revealing state secrets. The Cuban government released Infante Estrada and Del Pozo Marrero into exile in Canada in 1998 and Arias Iglesias into exile in the United States in 1997, while Alvarez López remains in prison at this writing. Cuban prosecutors alleged that Alvarez López had provided the three others, who were human rights and political rights activists, with the names of government infiltrators in their organizations.

Their trial also followed harsh pretrial detentions. In April 1992, state security agents arrested Infante Estrada and Del Pozo Marrero and confined them in sealed cells (*celdas tapiadas*) in their Havana headquarters, known as Villa Marista. During the seventy-five days that state security agents held Infante Estrada in solitary confinement in Villa Marista, they repeatedly interrogated him about his human rights and opposition activities. He recalled that he could not tell day from night in his cell and he tried to mark the passage of time by listening for birds singing outside. Del Pozo Marrero spent eighty days in a cell that was

---

[318] Human Rights Watch interview with Xiomara Aliat Collado, Toronto, April 13, 1998.

[319] Human Rights Watch interview with Luis Alberto Ferrándiz Alfaro, Toronto, April 13, 1998.

approximately three-by-seven feet. He said that the guards never used his name, but only referred to him by a number.[320]

Adriano González Marichal spent almost two years in prison before his December 1993 trial. Police had arrested him in January 1992 for putting up anti-government posters, denouncing human rights violations, and participating in a September 1991 rally in front of the Villa Marista state security headquarters calling for the release of political prisoners. In March 1992, he was sent to the maximum security Quivicán Prison in Havana, where several guards and common prisoners beat him and sent him to a punishment cell for two months. The cell was approximately four feet by nine feet, with no lights. In July of the next year, still in pretrial detention, prison authorities moved him to the maximum security Combinado del Este Prison in Havana. Guards delivered him to the punishment section of the prison, a group of cells known as "forty-seven" and the "rectangle of death,"(*rectángulo de la muerte*) a unit with about ninety cells in three hallways. At the entrance, he remembered a large sign listing the rules, which include no speaking and no lying in bed from 5:00 a.m. until 10:00 p.m. The prison officials took his clothes, dressed him in a black uniform, took all his belongings, and handcuffed him for several hours. Each time prisoners entered or left the unit, guards forced them to face the wall with their hands behind their heads and their legs spread, or the guards would push their legs apart. Guards often beat prisoners who fell down. He spent twenty-one days in the isolation cells in that unit.

Post-Conviction Isolation

Following conviction, prison authorities frequently punish political prisoners with periods in isolations cells, either due to their status as dissidents or their speech or activities while in prison.

The case of René Portelles demonstrates how Cuba employs brutal measures to repress political prisoners. From his arrest in September 1993 until his release into exile in Canada in April 1998, prison authorities repeatedly used isolation, as well as beatings and prison transfers (which isolated him from family and friends and forced him to adapt to new, difficult prison environments), to punish him for his opposition to the government and criticisms of prison conditions. Prior to his trial, state security agents confined Portelles in an isolation cell in the Pedernal State Security Offices (Unidad de Seguridad del Estado) in Holguín for several months. In 1994, an Holguín court sentenced him to seven years for enemy

---

[320] Human Rights Watch interviews with Víctor Reynaldo Infante Estrada, Toronto, April 14, 1998, and Omar del Pozo Marrero, Toronto, April 14, 1998.

propaganda, apparently because he had served as the local president of the Social Democratic Party.

After his conviction, prison guards held Portelles in isolation cells in the Holguín Provincial Prison and the Holguín State Security Headquarters because he had organized hunger strikes to protest prison conditions. The agents also beat Portelles several times, in one case breaking a rib, to punish him for his criticisms. Portelles spent thirteen months in an isolation cell in 1995 and 1996 at the Canaleta Prison in Ciego de Avila. In early 1996, he undertook a hunger strike at the Ariza Prison in Cienfuegos. On February 29, guards attempting to end the strike beat several prisoners, including Portelles. The authorities sent Portelles to a punishment cell for one additional month in retaliation. In March 1996, guards transferred Portelles to the Valle Grande Prison in Havana, where they sent him to isolation cells on five separate occasions due to his defense of other prisoners' rights. In April 1997, prison authorities transferred him to the "punishment company" (*compañía de castigo,* the section of the prison where officials punish prisoners with isolation and other deprivations) of the Boniato Prison in Santiago de Cuba. After only a month, prison authorities transferred Portelles again, to the Combinado de Guantánamo Prison, where he spent three separate periods ranging from twenty days to three months in punishment cells in late 1997. Prison authorities imposed the three-month isolation period after granting Portelles a several day temporary release in August 1997 with orders that he solicit a visa to the United States. While at the United States Interests Section in Havana, Portelles denounced human rights violations at the Guantánamo prison.

Back in prison, guards beat him for his denunciations and for shouting "Down with Communist Slogans!" and "Down with the Communist Dictatorship!" In November 1997, prison authorities transferred Portelles to an isolation cell in the "rectangle of death," the punishment section of the Combinado del Este Prison in Havana. In late 1997, prison authorities transferred him across the country, detaining him in a tightly-sealed cell of the state security headquarters at the Combinado de Guantánamo Prison. To protest, he started a hunger strike. On January 14, 1998, state security agents beat him after he had shouted "Long live Pope John Paul II!" and "Long live the Social Democratic Party!" Shortly afterwards, Cuban authorities transferred Portelles again, to Villa Marista, prior to forcing him into exile in Canada in May 1998. Twice, state security agents in Villa Marista tied him up and left him on the floor of his isolation cell for a few hours.

Portelles said that state security agents at Villa Marista deceived him on five occasions, telling him to get ready for his "imminent" departure.[321]

In December 1997, authorities at the Las Mangas Prison in Granma transferred José Antonio Rodríguez Santana, who was serving ten years for enemy propaganda and rebellion, to a punishment cell at the state security headquarters in Bayamo, Granma. The transfer followed Rodríguez Santana's denunciation of serious physical abuse in the prison. Capt. Leonardo Miranda, the commander of the state security post, ordered Rodríguez Santana confined to the completely closed cell for seventeen days. The confinement in the airless cell, which Rodríguez Santana believed was an effort to intimidate him, provoked several asthma attacks.[322]

Cuban authorities kept Raúl Ayarde Herrera, who was serving a ten-year sentence for espionage, in a completely dark isolation cell in the maximum security Guantánamo Provincial Prison for one year and ten months, from March 1995 until December 1996. The cell measured three feet by seven feet. Prison guards took all of his belongings, leaving him only with some clothes. On several occasions when he asked for medical assistance, the guards punished him by leaving him naked for twenty-one-day periods. In December 1996, prison authorities transferred him to the maximum security Pitirre Prison in Havana, known as 1580, where they held him in a sealed punishment cell for two months. From April 1997 until February 1998, guards at the Kilo 5 ½ Provincial Prison in Pinar del Río confined him in an isolation cell. The Cuban government forced Ayarde Herrera into exile in Canada in April 1998.[323]

Cuba imprisoned Armando Alonso Romero, nicknamed Chino, who was serving a twelve-year sentence for "other acts against the security of the state," in the Las Tunas Provincial Prison from August 1997 until February 1998. Throughout this period, prison guards confined him in a punishment cell that measured approximately four feet by six feet. The cell was almost completely sealed, allowing little daylight to enter. He said that the prison had approximately

---

[321] Human Rights Watch telephone interview with René Portelles, Toronto, April 21, 1998.

[322] Human Rights Watch interview with José Antonio Rodríguez Santana, Toronto, April 13, 1998.

[323] Human Rights Watch telephone interview with Raúl Ayarde Herrera, Toronto, April 21, 1998.

forty-five isolation cells. From the time of his arrest in September 1993 until his April 1998 release, Alonso Romero spent over four years in isolation cells.[324]

Marcos Antonio Hernández García, who was arrested in April 1990, convicted of enemy propaganda, espionage, and sabotage in 1991, and sentenced to twenty years, also was confined in the Las Tunas Prison from August 1997 until February 1998. Guards confined him in an isolation cell during the entire period. The guards also placed him on a regimen they called the "harassment plan," (*plan de hostigamiento*) under which they pulled him out of his cell at ten to fifteen minute intervals from 10:00 p.m. until 6:00 a.m. every night.[325]

From December 1996 until March 1998, guards at the Cerámica Roja Prison in Camagüey held José Miranda Acosta, who was serving a twelve-year term for terrorism, in an isolation cell. Miranda Acosta, a member of the Christian Liberation Movement (Movimiento Cristiano de Liberación, MCL), was arrested in 1993 and charged with being the intended recipient of a box containing a grenade. He never received such a box, nor affirmed that it had ever existed. When he first arrived at the prison in September 1996, guards beat him several times.[326]

Víctor Reynaldo Infante Estrada spent the majority of his almost six years in prison in solitary confinement. Prison authorities placed him in punishment cells at the Toledo Prison in Havana, the Agüica Prison in Matanzas (in an area with sixteen isolation cells known as "La Polaca"), and the Combinado del Sur Prison in Matanzas (from early 1994 until December 1996). In La Polaca, where prison guards detained him in 1993 and again from December 1996 until April 1997, Infante Estrada's cell was completely dark at all hours of the day and night and for various periods guards seized his mattress and all his belongings. The guards did not permit him access to a nearby closed patio, where he said the sun entered directly only in July and August. At the Combinado del Sur Prison in Matanzas, where Infante Estrada spent almost two years in solitary confinement, the chief of internal order, Lt. Juan Araño, warned him to cease his denunciations of human

---

[324] Human Rights Watch interview with Armando Alonso Romero, Toronto, April 12, 1998.

[325] Human Rights Watch interview with Marcos Antonio Hernández García, Toronto, April 13, 1998.

[326] Human Rights Watch telephone interview with José Miranda Acosta, Toronto, May 7, 1998. The prosecution of another MCL member, Enrique García Morejón, is discussed above, at *Political Prosecutions*, while the challenges facing the MCL and other religious groups are discussed below, at *Limits on Religious Freedom.*

rights abuses in the prison. Infante Estrada recalled Araño telling him, "if you are a lion, then you have to be caged" (*si eres leon, tienes que estar enjaulado*).[327]

In September 1995, Guillermo Ismael Sambra Ferrándiz commenced a seven-month period of incommunicado detention in a four foot by six foot cell in the Bahia Larga Prison in Santiago. Prison authorities ordered his punishment there because he had refused to stand at attention for the visit of a general to the prison and had refused to cut his hair and shave.[328] Also in 1995, Omar del Pozo Marrero spent eight months in a punishment cell at the Guanajay Prison in Havana. While the guards called this step a "security measure" (*medida de seguridad*), they provided no evidence to justify this claim. During the same period, prison authorities also psychologically pressured him with threats to end his visits, beat him, and cause his family members to lose their jobs.[329]

Beatings

Prison guards or groups of common prisoners known as prisoners' councils, which act under the orders or with the acquiescence of prison authorities, punish outspoken Cuban political prisoners with beatings, according to the prisoners, human rights activists, prisoners, family members, and journalists interviewed by Human Rights Watch. In the first half of 1998, Guantánamo Provincial Prison authorities reportedly ordered beatings of political prisoners who denounced prison conditions, including Néstor Rodríguez Lobaina, Jorge Luis García Pérez, also known as Antúnez, Francisco Herodes Díaz Echemendía, and Orosman Betancourt Dexidor.[330] Since Antúnez commenced his seventeen-year sentence for enemy propaganda, sabotage, and "evasion" in 1990, prison guards reportedly have beaten him severely on numerous occasions and responded to his hunger strikes, in protest of prison conditions, by denying him family visits and medicine. In October 1998,

---

[327] Human Rights Watch interview with Víctor Reynaldo Infante Estrada, Toronto, April 14, 1998.

[328] Human Rights Watch telephone interview with Guillermo Ismael Sambra Ferrándiz, Toronto, May 8, 1998.

[329] Human Rights Watch interview with Omar del Pozo Marrero, Toronto, April 14, 1998.

[330] Luis López Prendes, "Maltratan a Presos en Guantánamo," *El Nuevo Herald*, June 29, 1998.

prison authorities reportedly transferred Antúnez to another prison, without notifying his family.[331]

In September 1997, Guantánamo prison guards beat Antúnez, Francisco Díaz Echemendia, and Nestor Rodríguez Lobaina.[332] Prison guards at the Kilo 8 Prison in Camagüey repeatedly beat Jesús Chamber Ramírez, who was sentenced to ten years for enemy propaganda in 1992. He suffered deteriorating health due to the beatings, periods spent in punishment cells, insufficient medical attention, poor nutrition, and denial of access to sunlight for months at a time.[333] In November 1998, Cuba announced that it would release Chamber Ramírez on the condition that he go into exile in Spain.[334] Upon his arrival there in December, he stated, "I've been through everything: I had my head cracked open, my legs smashed up and they put me in a corridor for six months to try to drive me mad."[335]

On April 11, 1998, two state security agents, Capt. Hermes Hernández and Lt. René Orlando, reportedly beat Bernardo Arévalo Padrón, a journalist serving a six-year sentence for contempt of authority at the Ariza prison in Cienfuegos. The officers, who apparently were angered after finding anti-government materials inside the prison, reportedly beat him with a wooden baton on the head, neck, and abdomen, while shouting at him and calling him a "worm" or traitor. In a positive step, Cuban military prosecutors are said to have accused both officers of wrongdoing in early May.[336] Arevalo Padrón remained in an isolation cell, where

---

[331] Olance Nogueras, "En Paradero Desconocido un Veterano Disidente," *El Nuevo Herald*, October 4, 1998.

[332] United Nations Commission on Human Rights, Report on the Situation of Human Rights in Cuba Submitted by the Special Rapporteur, Mr. Carl-Johan Groth, in Accordance with Commission Resolution 1997/62 (E/CN.4/1998/69), January 30, 1998, para. 60.

[333] Ibid., para. 59(c).

[334] His release is detailed below, at *Political Prisoner Releases*.

[335] "Spain: Released Cuban Political Prisoner Arrives in Spain," *EFE* distributed by the *BBC Monitoring Newsfile*, December 2, 1998.

[336] Olance Nogueras, "SIP Protesta por Golpiza a Periodista en Prisión," *El Nuevo Herald*, April 29, 1998, "Juzgarán a Oficiales que Golpearon a Preso," *El Nuevo Herald*, May 7, 1998, and "Journalist Assaulted in Prison," *IFEX-News from the International Freedom of Expression Community*, April 29, 1998.

prison guards confined him shortly after the beating, until September. His family members alleged that Lieutenant Orlando had refused to allow them to leave medicine for him, despite his complaints of severe stomach problems.[337] Other prisoners also reportedly stated that they had suffered beatings by Ariza guards.[338]

On April 5, 1998, common prisoners at the Canaleta Prison in Matanzas reportedly beat Jorge Luis Cruz Arencibia. Prison authorities reportedly refused to provide Cruz Arencibia with medical care for his injuries.[339]

On November 9, 1997, the reeducator at the Kilo 5 ½ Prison in Pinar del Río, known as Osiri, and a state security official at the prison, Lt. Mario Medina, reportedly beat Raúl Ayarde Herrera because he had commenced a hunger strike to protest prison conditions. During his transfer to the Pinar del Río Prison from the Pitirre Prison in Havana, on April 30, 1997, two state security officials, Col. Wilfredo Velásquez and one with the last name of Vargas, beat Ayarde Herrera throughout the trip. They also are said to have thrown all of his belongings and clothes out of the car window. Three days after his arrival, a common prisoner known as Veltoldo also reportedly beat him. Ayarde Herrera said that Veltoldo later approached him and said, "Damn, political prisoner. Forgive me. I had to do it." Veltoldo explained that Lt. Mario Medina had ordered him to beat Ayarde or risk losing his right to be transferred from the maximum security prison to a work camp (*correcional*).[340]

On several occasions, prison guards beat Víctor Reynaldo Infante Estrada, an outspoken human rights advocate who faced numerous other punitive measures while imprisoned. In June 1997, several prison guards entered Infante Estrada's isolation cell to cut his hair and beard, as they had done several times in the prior months. He had let his hair grow to protest his prolonged detentions in punishment cells and other human rights violations. Led by the prison's chief of internal order, Sec. Lt. Emilio Villacruz, several guards pinned down Infante Estrada, forcibly removed his clothes, buzz-cut his hair, and shaved his beard. When Infante Estrada

---

[337] Marvín Hernández Monzón, "Enfrenta Problemas Periodista Independiente," *Cuba Press*, September 29, 1998.

[338] Marvin Hernández Monzón, "Seguridad para los Presos Políticos," *Cuba Press*, October 3, 1998.

[339] Ariel Hidalgo and Tete Machado, "Presos Políticos Hostigados," *Infoburo*, May 20, 1998.

[340] Human Rights Watch telephone interview with Raúl Ayarde Herrera, Toronto, April 21, 1998.

tried to stop them, the guards beat his back with their batons. On July 13, 1997, Maj. Pedro López, a member of the state security political unit at the Agüica Prison, waved his pistol at Infante Estrada and, referring to a string of recent hotel bombings, said, "If anything else like this happens inside Cuba, I will come here to your cell and kill you myself." Before leaving, he accused Infante Estrada of being responsible for the bombings, called him a counterrevolutionary, and smacked him.[341]

In April 1997, the chief of internal order at the prison, Major Abreu, ordered Omar del Pozo Marrero out of his cell so that guards could search it for knives and drugs. Del Pozo Marrero refused, explaining that he was a political prisoner. Guards pulled him out of his cell and dragged him for about fifty meters while beating him.[342] In May 1997, Lieutenant Carrales at the Combinado del Este Prison in Havana handcuffed del Pozo Marrero and threw him on the ground because he did not want the official to search his prison cell.

Criminal Charges for Denouncing Prison Abuses

Cuba's prosecutorial efforts to stifle criticism reach inside prison walls as well, where prisoners protesting inhumane treatment face criminal charges, trial, and additional years added to their prison terms.

In September 1997 a Havana tribunal found Maritza Lugo Fernández and Raúl Ayarde Herrera guilty of bribery for allegedly paying a guard at the Pitirre Prison in Havana to bring a tape recorder into the prison.[343] The court sentenced Lugo Fernández to two years and Ayarde Herrera to three years on top of the sentences they were already serving. In April 1998 the Cuban government forced Ayarde Herrera into exile in Canada. Lugo Fernández served several weeks of her sentence

---

[341] Human Rights Watch interview with Víctor Reynaldo Infante Estrada, Toronto, April 14, 1998.

[342] Human Rights Watch interview with Omar del Pozo Marrero, Toronto, April 14, 1998.

[343] This case is discussed above, at *Political Prosecutions.* Cuban courts also had prosecuted Fernández's husband, Rafael Ibarra López, the president of the 30th of November Party. At this writing, he was serving a twenty-year sentence for sabotage in the maximum security Kilo 8 Prison in Camagüey Province. Mercedes Moreno, "Irá a Juicio Joven Opositora," *Agencia Nacional de Prensa ANP,* September 2, 1997.

in the Havana Province Women's Prison, known as Manto Negro, and then was ordered confined under house arrest.[344]

In September 1996 a Camagüey tribunal convicted Jesús Chamber Ramírez, who already was serving ten years for enemy propaganda at the Kilo 8 Prison, of contempt for the authority of the commander-in-chief and sentenced him to four more years. Chamber Ramírez, whom prison guards had repeatedly beaten, had shouted "Down with Fidel" and denounced human rights abuses in the prison.

During his six years in Cuban prisons, prison authorities routinely punished Víctor Reynaldo Infante Estrada for being an outspoken advocate for the rights of political and common prisoners. As detailed above, he spent most of his sentence in isolation cells. To further discourage his criticisms, Cuba turned to the Criminal Code. On December 10, 1996, a Matanzas court sentenced Infante Estrada to an additional year in prison for contempt for the authority of a prison guard. The trial arose from Infante Estrada's November 1996 denunciation of a Combinado del Sur prison official, Lt. Juan Araña, for beating a common prisoner who later was found hanging dead in his cell. Infante Estrada recalled having told Araña, "I don't respect assassins, and I don't respect your authority." After the trial, Infante Estrada closed himself in his cell and commenced a hunger strike. Araña threatened him, saying "you could wake up hanging, too."

In April 1997 Infante Estrada protested the prison's failure to treat his high blood pressure by writing anti-government slogans on many sheets of paper (including "Down with Fidel" and "Down with the Dictatorship"), attaching them to the end of a broomstick and waving it out of his isolation cell so that the sheets flew onto the prison grounds. Shortly afterwards, a state security official at the prison, Lt. Fidel Relovu, threatened to beat him and notified him that he had enemy propaganda charges pending against him. He recalled that Relovu said "against the Commander [Fidel], you cannot do this." Guards ordered Infante Estrada held twenty-one additional days in his punishment cell, removed the mattress, and seized all of his belongings.

In June 1997 several Agüica Prison authorities beat Infante Estrada. His effort to defend himself from the guards' rough handling resulted in Infante Estrada's being charged with "resistance."[345] When Cuba forced Infante Estrada into exile in

---

[344] Human Rights Watch telephone interview with Raúl Ayarde Herrera, Toronto, April 21, 1998. Julio Martínez, "Condenada a Dos Años de Privación de Libertad la Opositora Maritza Lugo Fernández," *Habana Press,* September 7, 1997.

[345] Human Rights Watch interview with Víctor Reynaldo Infante Estrada, Toronto, April 14, 1998.

Canada in early 1998, telling him it was his only option if he hoped to get out of prison, these charges were pending against him.

Denial of Medical Treatment

While the medical treatment afforded all Cuban prisoners is poor, prison authorities discriminatorily deny medical care to political prisoners. The refusal to treat sick prisoners is particularly egregious when guards or prisoners' councils are responsible for inflicting injuries. Due to the extremely difficult conditions in Cuba's prisons, the denial of medical care leaves prisoners with serious and sometimes life-threatening conditions. Cuban failures to provide medical care for political prisoners led to a number of prisoners' deaths while imprisoned and left scores of former prisoners suffering severe health problems.

On February 19, 1997, Aurelio Ricart Hernández died in the Micro 4 Prison in Havana. He was serving a fifteen-year sentence for enemy propaganda and espionage. Marcos Antonio Hernández García, who was imprisoned with him, recalled that he had been sick with a liver ailment for a long time and that his skin had turned yellow. He was hospitalized on February 15, when he began vomiting blood. Hernández García said that the prison doctors had said many times that they would treat Ricart Hernández "next week."[346]

Cuban authorities released Pedro Armenteros Laza, who had been condemned to six years for enemy propaganda, on July 12, 1996, when he was in a coma. He died shortly afterward.[347]

Cuba released Sebastian Arcos Bergnes, the vice-president of the Cuban Committee for Human Rights who had been serving a four-year, eight-month sentence for enemy propaganda, in May 1995. When he was examined in Miami in September 1995, his physician noted that he had a sizable rectal tumor that had been growing for well over a year that would have been detected by a standard medical exam for men his age. Due to the failure of Cuban prison doctors to treat Arcos Bergnes, his cancer only was detected in a terminal, untreatable stage. Sebastian Arcos Bergnes died on December 22, 1997.

In June and July 1998, Cuban authorities detained Martha Beatriz Roque Cabello in a prison section of the Carlos J. Finlay Hospital, where doctors examining her determined that she had a gastric ulcer. Apparently, they failed to

---

[346] Human Rights Watch interview with Marcos Antonio Hernández García, Toronto, April 13, 1998.

[347] Manuel David Orrio, "Oposición Recuerda a Opositor Fallecido," *Cooperativa de Periodistas Independientes*, October 26, 1998.

treat her initial complaint of lumps in her breasts. Her hospital stay reportedly proved particularly stressful due to the fact that she was forced to share a hospital room with another detainee who suffered from serious psychological problems. The detainee reportedly attempted suicide while confined with Roque Cabello, adding to Roque Cabello's stress.[348]

Dr. Dessy Mendoza remained in the Boniato Prison in Santiago serving an eight-year sentence for enemy propaganda until November 1998, when he was released from prison on the condition that he go into exile in Spain.[349] His wife, Dr. Carmen de la Caridad Piñón Rodríguez said that her husband suffered from severe high blood pressure and heart disease (*hipertensión y cardiopatía*) and that his condition has worsened since his imprisonment. She noted that his heart disease was often symptomatic (*se descompensa frecuentamente*), causing pain and weakness. Cuban prison authorities raised his stress levels by placing him in a cell with a man convicted of homicide in an area of the prison reserved for 119 common prisoners. Due to his worsening condition, prison authorities hospitalized him for four days in April. Yet, the government failed to provide him with appropriate medicines, and his health has slipped further due to the poor prison diet and difficult physical conditions. Like many other Cuban prisoners, Dr. Mendoza survived on the food and medicine that his wife provided him.[350]

In May 1998 Boniato prison doctors' continued refusal to treat Marcelo Diosdado Amelo Rodríguez apparently resulted in his reaching a critical state. Amelo Rodríguez, the president of the Gerardo González Ex-Political Prisoners Club serving an eight-year sentence for rebellion, suffered from high blood pressure, poor circulation, and vision loss, and apparently risked the amputation of his left leg. His wife, Raisa Lora Gaquín, reportedly said she had provided prison authorities with medications and vitamins for her husband, but they had refused to give them to him. The prison guards also insisted on Amelo Rodríguez's continued detention in a punishment cell, where they had first confined him in July 1997.[351] The same month, authorities at the Manguito Prison in Santiago refused to treat

[348] Human Rights Watch telephone interview with Magalys de Armas Chaviano, Havana, July 2, 1998.

[349] This release is discussed below, at *Political Prisoner Releases*.

[350] Human Rights Watch telephone interview with Dr. Caridad del Carmen Piñón Rodríguez, Santiago, June 25, 1998.

[351] Margarita Yero, "Preso Político en Crítico Estado de Salud," *Cuba Press*, May 8, 1998.

Orestes Rodríguez for four days, despite his complaints of severe pain in his shoulder that prevented him from sleeping.[352]

Francisco Pastor Chaviano González, who is serving a fifteen-year term in the Combinado del Este Prison in Havana for revealing secrets concerning state security, has reportedly been denied medical treatment for his high blood pressure. The hostile conditions of his confinement, where he receives minimal food and brief visits only every two months, have aggravated his illness.[353]

Dr. Omar Del Pozo Marrero suffered severe hypertension during his prison term, due to poor prison conditions and the failure to provide him with medical treatment. In response to an international outcry about his declining health, he said that Cuba minimized his ailments and misrepresented the medical treatment he received. In May 1995, a delegation led by the French organization France-Libertés and joined by Human Rights Watch examined Dr. del Pozo Marrero at the Combinado del Este prison. After that examination, Cuba promised to provide him with medical treatment. But Dr. del Pozo Marrero said that his "treatment" consisted of one month of examinations at the Carlos J. Finlay Hospital that concluded by minimizing his ailments. His health concerns included high blood pressure, kidney stones, a duodenal ulcer, and an abnormal prostate. He also had gone from 140 pounds to between 105 and 110 pounds during his confinement. Dr. del Pozo Marrero said that the doctors were treating him "politically and not medically" (*políticamente y no medicamente*). Acknowledging that some Cuban prison doctors treated their patients well, Dr. del Pozo Marrero said that most medical treatment in the prisons was only for appearance. He observed doctors only treating minor ailments, while disregarding more serious health concerns.[354]

In September 1997 Marcos Antonio Hernández García complained to the Las Tunas Provincial Prison authorities that he felt severe pain from a hernia. The prison's medical staff told him he did not feel any pain and refused him pain medication. When he continued to complain of severe pain and swelling, the prison authorities allowed him to see a urologist. He said that when the doctor learned that he was a "counterrevolutionary," he refused to treat him. Prison guards allowed his family to provide him with some pain medication. On February 2, 1998, the prison

[352] Margarita Yero, "Le Niegan Asistencia Médica a Preso de Conciencia," *Cuba Press*, May 13, 1998.

[353] Human Rights Watch interview with Omar del Pozo Marrero, Toronto, April 14, 1998.

[354] Ibid.

authorities permitted him to have the hernia surgically corrected. Hernández García said that the medical staff had an "anti-prisoner" (*anti-preso*) mindset.[355]

Guillermo Ismael Sambra Ferrándiz, who did not receive sufficient treatment for his digestive problems, vomiting, and ulcer throughout his prison term, said that the prison doctors were "more soldiers than doctors. They receive orders, they don't have ethics."[356] Raúl Ayarde Herrera recalled asking for medical assistance at the Pinar del Río Prison in 1997 for pain due to an intestinal blockage. Maj. Inocente Delgado, known as El Chino, told him that for counter-revolutionaries, there was no medical assistance.[357]

Prison Transfers

Prison authorities frequently move political prisoners to a variety of prisons throughout the duration of their sentence. The transfers penalize prisoners by forcing them to reestablish themselves at a new facility, making contact with family members more difficult, and impeding prisoners' opportunities for gathering and disseminating information about prison abuses. In the course of his four and one-half years in prison, René Portelles, who was exiled to Canada in early 1998, was confined in eleven different detention facilities. The transfers typically followed Portelles's protests over prison conditions or expressions of political dissent.

Prison Labor

Cuba's pressuring political prisoners to work while imprisoned, discussed at *Labor Rights: Prison Labor*, violates the International Labor Organization's Abolition of Forced Labor convention, which was ratified by Cuba.

Restrictions of Visits

Cuban prison authorities provide political prisoners with minimal opportunities for visits from their family members and often restrict these visits further as a punitive measure. Prison transfers also impede family contact. These practices violate the Standard Minimum Rules' provisions urging the preservation of

---

[355] Human Rights Watch interview with Marcos Antonio Hernández García, Toronto, April 13, 1998.

[356] Human Rights Watch telephone interview with Guillermo Ismael Sambra Ferrándiz, Toronto, May 8, 1998.

[357] Human Rights Watch telephone interview with Raúl Ayarde Herrera, Toronto, April 21, 1998.

community ties through regular visits.[358] As detailed above, at *Restrictions on Religious Visits*, political and common prisoners often are denied their right to meet with religious advisors as well.

Boniato Prison authorities placed Dr. Dessy Mendoza on the prison's "severe regime," only allowing him one two-hour visit every two months from no more than two immediate family members. Due to these extremely restricted opportunities for visiting, Dr. Mendoza's children only saw him a handful of times after his arrest. His wife said that their one-year-old son, who was born shortly before his father's detention, mistakenly called his thirteen-year-old brother "Daddy."[359]

On December 10, 1997, a prisoner at the Combinado de Guantánamo Prison, Alberto Joaquím Aguilera Guevara, also known as Carlos, who was serving a fifteen-year sentence for enemy propaganda, contempt for authority, and assault, went on a one-day hunger strike to honor international human rights day. In retaliation, when his mother arrived three days later for her end-of-the-year visit, the prison guards denied her entry and refused to let her leave him a fifty-pound sack of food.[360]

Prison authorities only permitted Víctor Reynaldo Infante Estrada one two-hour visit every two months with immediate family members. Infante Estrada, who was forced into exile in Canada when the Cuban government offered him no other way to avoid serving his full prison term, said, "There are several family members, my aunts and uncles and cousins, that I never saw again."[361] From June 1996 until February 1997, Micro 4 Prison authorities denied Yonaikel Baney Hernández Menéndez the right to visit her father, Marcos Antonio Hernández García.[362] When Guillermo Ismael Sambra Ferrándiz was detained in the Bahia Larga Prison in Santiago, he refused to wear a prison uniform so he would not be mistaken for "one

---

358 Articles 61 and 37.

359 Human Rights Watch telephone interview with Dr. Caridad del Carmen Piñón Rodríguez, Santiago, June 25, 1998.

360 Human Rights Watch interview with Alberto Joaquím Aguilera Guevara, Toronto, April 12, 1998.

361 Human Rights Watch interview with Víctor Reynaldo Infante Estrada, Toronto, April 14, 1998.

362 Human Rights Watch interview with Yonaikel Baney Hernández Menéndez Toronto, April 13, 1998.

more rapist." In response, on November 24, 1994, prison authorities suspended all of his visits for two years.[363]

Hardships for Family Members

Cuba's efforts to intimidate political prisoners extend to their spouses, children, and other family members. Families who have lost breadwinners struggle to make ends meet and to ensure that their imprisoned relatives have enough food and medicine. The material and emotional toll of a dissident's wrongful imprisonment is high, and government harassment creates additional difficulties for family members, raising the cost of opposition even higher.

Adriano González Marichal's mother, Adelaida Marichal Martínez, has been arrested five times. Throughout her son's imprisonment, she dealt with harassment from prison authorities. In late 1997, guards at the Valle Grande Prison in Havana strip-searched her as she was leaving the prison to try to find denunciations of human rights violations.[364] This abusive measure, designed only to squelch free expression and cover up human rights abuses, clearly did not arise from legitimate security considerations.[365]

Edelmira Matamoros Espejo, the wife of political prisoner Edelberto Del Toro Argota, was humiliated by prison guards who strip-searched her and forced her to do deep knee bends naked whenever she went for conjugal visits to the Holguín Provincial Prison. When the couple's daughter Keñia was twelve, female prison guards strip-searched her prior to one visit with her father. Capt. Héctor Hernández Escobar, a state security official who had beaten her husband in July 1995, called Matamoros Espejo into his office on two occasions. During those interviews, he revealed that he had received information that she had been traveling to Havana to visit a human rights activist. He warned her that things would get worse for her husband if she continued these trips. During her husband's imprisonment,

---

[363] Human Rights Watch telephone interview with Guillermo Ismael Sambra Ferrándiz, Toronto, May 8, 1998.

[364] Human Rights Watch interview with Adriano González Marichal, Toronto, April 12, 1998.

[365] The issue of strip-searching is discussed in detail above, at *General Prison Conditions: Visits.*

Matamoros Espejo encountered considerable difficulty maintaining a job.[366] She said, "I feel like I was a prisoner myself."[367]

Omar del Pozo Marrero's wife, Martina Guzmán Arias, said that prison visits were humiliating because guards usually forced her to strip completely. She recalled that an older aunt was strip-searched when she went to visit and felt so degraded that she never returned. Prison guards also arbitrarily delayed or denied her visits. She said that she was fortunate to have had economic assistance from outside Cuba and because her neighbors had not denounced her for being married to a political prisoner. She noted that "the machinery is so perfect, so subtle, that they can completely destroy a family."[368]

Ernesto Ferrándiz Aliat was only five and his sister Dailyn Robert Aliat fourteen when state security agents arrested their parents, Luis Alberto Ferrándiz Alfaro and Xiomara Aliat Collado in January 1993. The two young children were left to fend for themselves. Robert Aliat said that she was frightened and fainted when she first saw her mother at the Versailles detention center. She said she tried to get money to bring her parents food at the prison, but that it was "tremendously difficult," and that sometimes the guards did not give her parents what she had brought. She also had difficulty feeding and taking care of her brother. She commented that putting up anti-government flyers, as her parents had done:

> ... is no justification for sending a person to prison. They had never mistreated anyone. Having two young kids, and him only five and traumatized, they [the Cuban government] should have thought in a better way.[369]

Ferrándiz Aliat, twelve years old at this writing, said that he was very sad while his parents were away and that he and his sister went hungry most of the time. Prison guards let him visit his father occasionally, but he remembered that they usually

---

[366] Government efforts to pressure dissidents by removing them from jobs and other harassment in the labor sector are detailed below, at *Labor Rights*.

[367] Human Rights Watch interview with Edelmira Matamoros Espejo, Toronto, April 12, 1998.

[368] Human Rights Watch interview with Martina Guzmán Arias, Toronto, April 14, 1998.

[369] Human Rights Watch interview with Dailyn Robert Aliat, Toronto, April 14, 1998.

brought his father out when it was time to go. Of his exile to Canada, he said, "I feel good because I am here with my parents. ... I like it better here because now Fidel Castro cannot govern me."[370]

Hunger Strikes

Repressive measures adopted in Cuban prisons leave detainees with few avenues to express grievances. As detailed above, efforts to denounce human rights violations often result in beatings, solitary confinement, or restrictions of food or visits. Since the prison system tightly controls their liberties, political prisoners often turn to hunger strikes as a means of calling attention to prison abuses. Unfortunately, prison authorities typically respond by penalizing the prisoners for having carried out a hunger strike, failing to address the underlying problem, and refusing to provide appropriate medical treatment.

The Santa Clara Pro Human Rights Party activists undertook prolonged hunger strikes to call attention to their plight.[371] Unfortunately, their success in garnering international attention apparently contributed to heavier government repression. The hunger strikes also caused physical deterioration. Iván Lema Romero, for example, carried out a water and broth hunger strike from October 1997 until February 1998, during which he lost forty-seven pounds, and continued to suffer its effect into mid-1998, without receiving sufficient medical care.[372]

Heriberto Leiva Rodríguez went on a one-week hunger strike in May 1998 to protest Nestor Rodríguez Lobaina's continued detention. At the time, both were serving terms arising from their activities with Youth for Democracy (Jóvenes por la Democracia).[373]

Guillermo Ismael Sambra Ferrándiz undertook several short hunger strikes during his prison term. From August 13, 1994, until September 22, 1994, some 100 prisoners at the Boniato Prison in Santiago carried out a hunger strike to protest prison conditions. During this period, prison guards put Sambra Ferrándiz in an isolation cell, naked. He said that the degrading prison conditions had pushed him

---

[370] Human Rights Watch interview with Ernesto Ferrándiz Aliat, Toronto, April 14, 1998.

[371] Their prosecutions are detailed above, at *Political Prosecutions.*

[372] Marvin Hernández Monzón, "Ex-Ayunante de Santa Clara Enfermo en Prisión," *Cuba Press*, May 18, 1998.

[373] Ana Luisa López Baeza, "Fin del Ayuno de Heriberto Leiva Rodríguez," *Cuba Press*, May 13, 1998.

to take drastic action. He recalled telling prison guards that he was on hunger strike because, "you have humiliated me. I want you to realize the magnitude of the damage you are doing." On the positive side, he said that carrying out hunger strikes fortified him, "Before I was imprisoned, I felt like a rat, an insect. After I revealed myself to be a [government] opponent, I could breathe freely."[374]

Torture

Cuba's treatment of political prisoners violates its obligations under the Convention against Torture and Other Cruel, Inhuman or Degrading Treatment or Punishment, which it ratified on May 17, 1995. Prolonged periods of incommunicado pretrial and post-conviction detention, beatings, and prosecutions of previously-tried political prisoners—where those practices result in severe pain or suffering—constitute torture under the convention. Cuba's heavy reliance on incommunicado detentions rises to the level of torture in some instances and contributes to the perpetuation of torture, since isolated prisoners are not able to ask for help.[375] Moreover, the Convention against Torture clearly prohibits retaliation against individuals who denounce torture. The convention, which Cuba is bound to uphold, defines torture as:

> any act by which severe pain or suffering, whether physical or mental, is intentionally inflicted on a person for such purposes as obtaining from him or a third person information or a confession, punishing him for an act he or a third person has committed or is suspected of having committed, or intimidating or coercing him or a third person, or for any reason based on discrimination of any kind, when such pain or suffering is inflicted by or at the instigation of or with the consent or acquiescence of a public official

[374] Human Rights Watch telephone interview with Guillermo Ismael Sambra Ferrándiz, Toronto, May 8, 1998.

[375] "Detention incommunicado facilitates the act of torture or improper interrogation because the detainee has no access to individuals to notify them of his mistreatment. And, if the detainee is detained long enough, his wounds from the torture will heal and make it more difficult to prove his mistreatment." Paul R. Williams, Treatment of Detainees (Geneva: Henry Dunant Institute, 1990), pp. 73-74. The U.N. Human Rights Committee 1996 comments on Peru noted "... incommunicado detention is conducive to torture and that, consequently, this practice should be avoided." Human Rights Committee, Comments on Peru, Consideration of Reports Submitted by States Parties under Article 40 of the Covenant,U.N. CCPR/C/79/Add.67, July 25, 1996.

> or other person acting in an official capacity. It does not include pain or suffering arising only from, inherent in or incidental to lawful sanctions.[376]

The practices detailed in the discussions above, particularly those measures taken to retaliate against prisoners' attempts to report human rights abuses, fall within this definition.

The Convention against Torture requires Cuba to "take effective legislative, administrative, judicial or other measures to prevent acts of torture in any territory under its jurisdiction" and to "ensure that all acts of torture are offenses under its criminal law."[377] To date, Cuba has not made torture a crime. While Cuba has some encouraging laws that prohibit practices associated with torture, none explicitly penalize torture. This may be due in part to Cuba's denial that torture is a domestic problem. Cuba told the Committee against Torture that in Cuba, "there are no cases of persons who have been tortured or disappeared and no other grave and systematic violations of human rights."[378]

Disturbingly, Cuba's ratification of the Convention against Torture included reservations to key provisions allowing oversight by the Committee against Torture. Cuba said that the committee's authority to investigate well-founded reports of torture; to designate members to conduct confidential inquiries; and to conduct visits to the territory in cooperation with the Cuban government, must "be invoked in strict compliance with the principle of the sovereignty of States and implemented with the prior consent of the States Parties."[379] The committee's 1997 report concluded that it could not properly assess whether or not Cuba was complying with the convention because Cuba had failed to respond to allegations of torture

---

[376] Article 1, Convention against Torture and Other Cruel, Inhuman or Degrading Treatment or Punishment, G.A. Resolution 39/46, U.N. Doc. A/39/51 (1984), entered into force June 26, 1987.

[377] Arts. 2(1) and 4(1), Convention against Torture.

[378] Para. 25, Committee against Torture, Consideration of Report Submitted by States Parties under Article 19 of the Convention against Torture, Cuba, U.N. CAT/C/32/Add. 2, June 18, 1997.

[379] Convention against Torture, Declarations and Reservations, Cuba, reservations upon ratification, May 17, 1995.

and failed to provide adequate information about investigations of or reparations for torture.[380]

Despite Cuba's disdain for international oversight, it remains bound by the provisions of the Convention against Torture. The suffering endured by Cuba's political prisoners highlights the urgency for Cuba concretely to address the problem of torture, rather than deny its existence or dismiss the issue by referring to unenforced legislation. Under the convention, the government has an obligation to ensure that statements resulting from torture are not introduced as evidence in any proceeding.[381] The long-term pretrial detentions detailed above, which included severe physical and mental suffering inflicted during interrogations and resulted in convictions, violate this provision. While Cuban law bars the introduction of statements at trial obtained by coercion or violence, these cases demonstrate that Cuba has failed to guarantee this protection.[382]

The convention requires Cuba to ensure that an individual alleging torture is "protected against all ill-treatment or intimidation as a consequence of his complaint...."[383] Cuba's beatings, prosecutions, and isolation of prisoners alleging mistreatment violate this provision. Under the convention, Cuba also must conduct prompt, impartial investigations of allegations of torture and ensure that a victim of torture has an "enforceable right to fair and adequate compensation." To date, Human Rights Watch has not found information of any government prosecutions of torturers, nor of any restitutions provided to torture victims. Forcing political prisoners into exile certainly does not exempt Cuba from this requirement. The convention also bars "other acts of cruel, inhuman or degrading treatment or punishment." Cuba's denial of medical treatment to prisoners arguably constitutes cruel, inhuman, and degrading treatment, which also merits investigation and, where appropriate, punishment under the Convention against Torture.[384]

Cuba reported to the Committee against Torture that penal officials receive training in:

---

[380] Concluding Observations of the Committee against Torture, November 21, 1997.

[381] Article 15, Convention Against Torture.

[382] Article 59, Constitution of the Republic of Cuba, 1992.

[383] Article 13, Convention against Torture.

[384] Ibid., Article 16.

> the standards and rules set forth in the main international conventions and covenants, as appropriate, such as the Universal Declaration of Human Rights, the Standard Minimum Rules for the Treatment of Prisoners, the Code of Conduct for Law Enforcement Officials, the International Covenant on Civil and Political Rights, the International Covenant on Economic, Social and Cultural Rights, the Convention against Torture [and] the U.N. Declaration on the Elimination of All Forms of Racial Discrimination....[385]

If true, Cuba's provision of training on fundamental human rights and detention standards would represent an important acceptance of the primacy of these standards and satisfy, in part, the convention's requirement for educating law enforcement and prison officials.[386] However, serious rights violations in Cuban prisons, along with Cuba's continued prosecution of non-violent activists for violating the freedoms guaranteed in these instruments, show an unwillingness to comply with these norms. Even if officials received sufficient training, Cuba's failure to prosecute torturers and its lack of transparency about the prison system would undermine its effect.

Releases

When prominent international figures appeal for Cuban political prisoners' freedom, Cuba occasionally releases prisoners prior to the conclusion of their sentence, often on the condition that they leave their country forever. In an October 1998 interview, President Fidel Castro frankly discussed Cuba's approach to prisoner releases, stating:

> Cuba cannot be a country that is being pressured all the time from all directions. We are willing to accept some suggestions and requests for clemency made in another spirit; but we are not willing to collaborate with those organized and perfectly structured campaigns that follow a plan.
>
> That is where our resistence is, to all kinds of pressures; but without pressures we have freed many people.

---

[385] Cuban Report to the Committee against Torture, June 18, 1997, para. 97.

[386] Article 10, Convention against Torture.

> In relation to the pope's visit, we released...prisoners for counterrevolutionary crimes—as we call them—[and] prisoners held for common crimes, because they [the Vatican] stated that what interested them was the humanitarian action and not the type of crime.... We wanted to give special attention to the pope... keeping in mind that he did not act on anyone's behalf, even though many people sent him names.... But the pope acted on his own behalf and out of his traditional humanitarian policies....[387]

Castro's emphasis on the "spirit" in which requests for prisoner releases are made, rather than on the fairness of their prosecution and imprisonment reveals the calculated, political nature of Cuba's response to requests for prisoner releases. Castro's describes his responses to international appeals as humanitarian gestures yet avoids acknowledgement of the human rights violations that gave rise to wrongful detentions.

The government released some 100 political prisoners in early 1998, following Pope John Paul II's appeals for prisoner releases during his January visit to Cuba. Most of these had served the majority of their sentences and a few had completed their sentences. Seventeen of these prisoners were released on the condition that they be exiled to Canada, despite the pope's explicit plea for the reintegration of prisoners into their community.

Cuba repeatedly has refused to grant a general amnesty for political prisoners. Most pleas to release individual political prisoners have been refused, regardless of the character and motives of the supplicant. In his January 1998 visit, the pope specifically requested the release of the four members of the Internal Dissidents' Working Group, who had been in pretrial detention for six months. Castro took no action to release them. Months later, Canadian Prime Minister Jean Chrétien solicited their release during his April 1998 trip to Havana. Afterwards, he described President Castro's reaction. "I don't think he was very happy. He would

---

[387] "Estamos Dispuestos a Discutir en Condiciones de Igualdad, de Respeto Mutuo y de Trato Recíprico entre Cuba y los Estados Unidos: Entrevista Concedida por el Comandante en Jefe Fidel Castro Ruz, Primer Secretario del Comité Central del Partido Comunista de Cuba y Presidente de los Consejos de Estado y de Ministros, a Lucía Newman, de la CNN en el Hotel Porto Palacio, Portugal, el día 19 de Octubre de 1998, 'Año del Aniversario 40 de las Batallas Decisivas de la Guerra de Liberación,'" *Granma Diario*, October 24, 1998. Transcription by the Cuban Council of State. Translation by Human Rights Watch.

have preferred I did not mention it."[388] Cuba tried the four dissidents in March 1999, finding them guilty of inciting sedition.[389]

Dr. Omar del Pozo Marrero, a former prisoner released in 1998 on the condition that he go into exile in Canada, was the subject of international appeals for years. He remarked to us that:

> The government always wants currency to exchange. The more a prisoner is asked for, the more he's worth. They don't want to use all their currency now.... In Cuba, there's also a code of revenge. For example, there's a need to punish [political prisoner Francisco Pastor] Chaviano [González]. They want him to suffer some more. And they want to keep him off the street.[390]

In measures that appear to be purely punitive, Cuban officials continued to mistreat and harass the political prisoners destined for exile in Canada even after they had transferred them to the state security headquarters in Havana, Villa Marista, in preparation for their departure. Alberto Joaquím Aguilera spent almost sixty days in a sealed cell with twenty-four hour lighting in Villa Marista, from his arrival there on February 16, 1998, until his departure to Canada.[391] Víctor Reynaldo Infante Estrada also was held in solitary confinement. However, he recalled that during his detention at Villa Marista, several state security officials briefly took him and several other prisoners who were being forced into exile out to a field for a stroll while the guards videotaped them. Infante Estrada was

---

388 "Canadian Premier Asks Castro to Free Four Dissidents," *Agence France Presse* published in the *Miami Herald*, April 28, 1998.

389 Their case is detailed above, at *Political Prosecutions*.

390 Human Rights Watch interview with Omar del Pozo Marrero, Toronto, April 14, 1998. Dr. del Pozo Marrero was the subject of numerous international appeals for his freedom, as was Adriano González Marichal, who also was exiled to Canada in April 1998. Despite these campaigns, Cuba apparently delayed their release because both men supported the U.S. embargo on Cuba. Human Rights Watch interview with Adriano González Marichal, Toronto, April 14, 1998.

391 Human Rights Watch interview with Alberto Joaquím Aguilera, Toronto, April 12, 1998.

concerned that the guards were attempting to create "picturesque" images to cover up their abusive treatment of the prisoners.[392]

Forced Exile

Cuba routinely invokes forced exile as a condition for prisoner releases and also pressures activists to leave the country to escape future prosecution, in violation of international norms ensuring citizens' rights to remain in their own homeland.[393] In November 1998, for example, Cuba released two prominent political prisoners, Dr. Dessy Mendoza Rivero and Jesús Chamber Ramírez, who had suffered serious physical deterioration while incarcerated, on the condition that they go into exile in Spain. In a trip to Cuba, Spanish Foreign Minister Abel Matutes had requested their release along with that of several other political prisoners.[394] Armando Alonso Romero said that state security agents at Villa Marista forced him to sign papers saying that if he did not leave Cuba, he would have to complete the remainder of his sentence. He said, "this isn't liberty, it's forced exile" (*destierro*).[395]

The "choice" between continued prison terms or exile left the prisoners with no good option. The released Cuban prisoners were extremely reluctant to leave their homeland and their families. Officials at the Cerámica Roja Prison in Camagüey repeatedly called José Miranda Acosta to their offices in March and April 1998, insisting that he leave the country. But Miranda Acosta told them that he wanted to stay in Cuba. He recalled the prison's security director telling him that he could not remain in Cuba because he "had maintained a hostile attitude toward the revolution." The officials brought his brother to the prison to try and convince him to leave and stressed that exile was his "only option." Finally, Miranda Acosta acceded on the condition that he would be able to meet with some family members before leaving. But the government provided Miranda Acosta with minimal time to visit with his family prior to his exile on May 4, 1998. Although he had not seen

---

[392] Human Rights Watch interview with Víctor Reynaldo Infante Estrada, April 14, 1998.

[393] Cuban pressures on independent journalists and activists to go into exile are detailed below, at *Routine Repression*.

[394] "Prisioneros Políticos Liberados Tramitan Viaje a España," *EFE*, December 1, 1998.

[395] Human Rights Watch interview with Armando Alonso Romero, Toronto, April 12, 1998.

his daughter during his imprisonment, the state security agents at Villa Marista allowed him only five minutes with her on April 29, in the presence of a state security investigator. They did not allow him to see her again before his departure.[396]

Although Adriano González Marichal, who was exiled to Canada in April 1998, mourned the loss of his homeland and his inability to see his elderly mother, he noted that "I am proud that we panic Fidel Castro, that he is terrified of twenty people that he's had to deport."[397]

Conditional Releases and Harassment

Cuban Foreign Minister Roberto Robaina's February 1998 statement that "the pardon has not been made to stimulate acts of internal dissidence" diminished the positive impact of the prisoner releases following the pope's appeal.[398] Several released political prisoners, including the president of the Democratic Solidarity Party (Partido Democrático Solidaridad), Héctor Palacios Ruíz, expressed concern that they may face prosecutions and a return to prison if they continue to express their political viewpoints. Authorities in Santiago reportedly told several prisoners upon their release that they should not engage in opposition activities and that they must check in on a monthly basis to a local police station.[399]

Exiled prisoners expressed concern about their relatives and friends remaining in Cuba, particularly those serving prison sentences, like José Antonio Rodríguez Santana's brother José Manuel. Omar del Pozo Marrero said that government agents had harassed his brother, Miguel Jesús del Pozo Marrero, since the doctor

---

[396] Human Rights Watch telephone interview with José Miranda Acosta, Toronto, May 7, 1998.

[397] Human Rights Watch interview with Adriano González Marichal, Toronto, April 14, 1998.

[398] Frances Kerry, "Cuba: Cuban Pardons do not Mean Opening to Dissent-Minister," *Reuters News Service*, February 15, 1998.

[399] Human Rights Watch telephone interview with Mirna Riverón Guerrero, Santiago, Cuba, July 3, 1998.

had been exiled to Canada. Miguel Jesús also had been unable to find work and believed that he was under close government surveillance.[400]

[400] Human Rights Watch telephone interview with Omar del Pozo Marrero, Toronto, June 25, 1998.

VII. DEATH PENALTY

Cuba retains the death penalty for several crimes. Besides the death penalty's inherent cruelty, Human Rights Watch believes that the fallibility of criminal justice systems everywhere creates the risk that innocent persons will be executed even when full due process of law is respected. The Cuban legal system's serious procedural failings and lack of judicial independence practically guarantee miscarriages of justice. Cuban law affords convicts sentenced to death minimal opportunities to appeal their sentences. The People's Supreme Court receives death sentence appeals within five days of sentencing, leaving little opportunity to prepare an appropriate defense for a capital case, and has ten days to render a decision. If the sentence is confirmed, the court forwards the case to the Council of State.[401] Cuba's reliance on the Council of State—an entity presided over by President Castro, selected by the Cuban National Assembly, and considered the "supreme representation of the Cuban State" under Cuban law—as the ultimate arbiter in death penalty cases effectively undercuts any appearance of judicial independence. If the Council of State does not render a decision within ten days, then the Criminal Procedure Code creates a presumption that the body did not approve a commutation.[402] This procedure would allow an execution to proceed even if the Council of State never reviewed the case.

In May 1995 President Fidel Castro told the human rights delegation led by France-Libertés and joined by Human Rights Watch that he intended to introduce a bill in the National Assembly for the abolition of the death penalty. At that time, he conditioned his action on developments in the economy and the U.S. economic embargo, apparently unrelated issues. But on September 30, 1997, the Cuban delegation to the United Nations reported to the Secretary General that "given the circumstances which [Cuba] has experienced and continues to experience, the total abolition of the penalty is impracticable."[403] In March 1999, Cuba adopted the

---

[401] Article 89, Constitution of the Republic of Cuba (July 1992).

[402] Article 488, Criminal Procedure Code (1977).

[403] United Nations Commission on Human Rights, "Status of the International Covenants on Human Rights: Question of the Death Penalty, Report of the Secretary-General Submitted Pursuant to Commission Resolution 1997/12" (New York: United Nations, January 16, 1998), E/CN.4/1998/82.

death penalty for two new crimes, international drug trafficking and the corruption of minors.[404]

Cuba has not provided figures on its total prison population, much less the number of death row inmates. In March 1999, Cuba announced that a Havana court had sentenced Raúl Ernesto Cruz Leon to death for terrorism, based on his alleged involvement in bombing Cuban hotels.[405] Cuban prosecutors sentenced a second Salvadoran, Otto René Rodríguez Llerena, to death in April 1999.[406] In January 1999, a Havana court sentenced Sergio Antonio Duarte Scull and Carlos Rafael Pelaez Prieto to death for the murders of two Italian tourists in September 1998.[407]

In March 1999, the provincial court in Granma announced the executions of two men, José Luis Osorio Zamora and Francisco Javier Chávez Palacios.[408] Cuba reportedly executed two prisoners, Emilio Betancourt Bonne and Jorge Luis

---

[404] "Modificaciones al Código Penal," *Granma Diario*, March 2, 1999.

[405] Anita Snow, "Cuba Sentences Salvadoran to Death," *Associated Press*, March 23, 1999.

[406] "Cuba: Cuba Sentences Second Salvadoran Bomber to Death," *Reuters News Service*, April 1, 1999, and "Cuba: Cuba Seeks Second Death Sentence in Bombings," *Reuters News Service*, March 17, 1999.

[407] Neither the Cuban government nor the Italian embassy in Havana revealed the victims' names. Reuters reported that the victims were Fabio Usubelli and Michele Niccolai. Andrew Cawthorne, "Cuba: Cuba Hands Death Sentences to Killers of Italians," *Reuters News Service*, January 28, 1999; and Anita Snow, "Two Sentenced to Death in Cuba," *Associated Press*, January 28, 1999.

[408] The announcements did not include the dates of the executions by firing squad but noted that the sentences had been ratified on appeal by the Supreme Court and the Council of State. Tribunal Provincial Granma, "Ejecutada Pena de Muerte," *La Demajagua: Organo Informativo de la Provincia de Granma*, March 13, 1999, and Tribunal Provincial Granma, "Ejecutan Sentencia de Pena de Muerte," *La Demajagua: Organo Informativo de la Provincia de Granma*, March 6, 1999.

Chávez Palacios allegedly had slain a local official, Pedro Armando Fonseca Fernández de Castro. His lawyer expressed concern that he lacked the mental capacity to be held responsible for the crime, since he had previously been diagnosed with developmental disabilities and psychiatric conditions. Conclusiones Provisionales, Cause #511/97, Sala I de lo Penal del Tribunal Provincial Popular de Granma, Lic. David Gaston Rodríguez Mulet, October 20, 1997.

Sánchez Guilarte, in May 1998.[409] Human Rights Watch interviews with former political prisoners reveal that up until early 1998, Cuba had several death row prisoners held in at least three maximum-security prisons. The ex-prisoners, who usually were confined in cells alongside the death row inmates, also believed that Cuba carried out executions in 1997.

Human Rights Watch received credible information that a Cuban firing squad executed Daniel Reyes, an inmate in the Las Tunas Provincial Prison, on October 29, 1997. Following his death, one of the prison guards who had participated in the execution apparently told the eight other death row prisoners gruesome details about the death and threatened them with similar treatment. Las Tunas prison staff apparently carry out executions on a nearby hill where guards tie prisoners to a large wooden post. Several government vehicles reportedly shine their headlights on the prisoner as the firing squad carries out the execution.[410] Cuba reportedly executed another prisoner at the Agüica Prison in Matanzas in January 1997. A political prisoner confined there at the time recalled that the executed prisoner's first name was Gilbert, that he had been convicted of murder, and that he was blind.[411] Cuba executed Francisco Dayson Dhruyet, convicted for the murder of his wife, in December 1996.[412] We also received reports of possible executions at the Combinado del Este Prison in Havana in 1996 and 1997. The executions by firing squad reportedly take place on a hill known as Las Canteras, which is visible from some parts of the prison, from about 8:00 until 9:00 in the evening.[413] At this writing, Cuban exile Humberto Real Suárez, who was sentenced to death in 1996, remains on death row at the Cerámica Roja Prison in Camagüey. As of February 1998, five other prisoners reportedly remained on the Agüica death row, including

---

[409] Amnesty International, "Urgent Action: Death Penalty/Imminent Execution: Cuba" January 29, 1999.

[410] Human Rights Watch interview with Marcos Antonio Hernández García, Toronto, April 13, 1998.

[411] Human Rights Watch interview with Víctor Reynaldo Infante Estrada, Toronto, April 14, 1998.

[412] Amnesty International, *Amnesty International Report 1998* (London: Amnesty International Publications, 1998), p. 150.

[413] Human Rights Watch interviews with Marcos Antonio Hernández García, Toronto, April 13, 1998, and Adriano González Marichal, Toronto, April 14, 1998.

Lázaro Pino López. Erik Martínez reportedly was on the Las Tunas Provincial Prison's death row.

VIII. ROUTINE REPRESSION

In addition to imprisoning activists, Cuba employs other tactics to impede individuals and organizations from undertaking activities that are, or appear to be, in opposition to government policies or practices.[414] The range of repressive measures includes short-term arbitrary detentions, official warnings (*advertencias oficiales)*, removal from jobs and housing, surveillance, harassment, intimidation, and forced exile. Government actions against dissidents appear to occur in waves, with lulls followed by periods of intense harassment, often in response to heightened opposition activity. While the pope's January 1998 visit to Cuba marked a period of relative calm, government pressures increased as the year progressed and international attention faded. Activists faced vigorous government repression in early 1999.

Dissidents willing to criticize the government publicly risk serious consequences, from the trauma of wrongful arrests and potential prosecutions, to the loss of their homes and sources of income, as well as the significant emotional costs wrought by so-called repudiations, and the deprivation of contact with family, community, and culture through forced exile. These measures often affect activists' family members, further raising the cost of speaking out. Government intimidation, along with criminal prosecutions, has resulted in the cessation or minimizing of many dissidents' activities and the dissolution of some organizations.

Human rights activists and independent journalists are among the government's most frequent targets, along with independent labor organizers.[415] Religious leaders and their followers also face government restrictions on their activities.[416] Other members of Cuba's emerging civil society subjected to government harassment include members of independent political parties, organizations of independent academics, teachers, medical professionals, artists, environmental activists, and others. Family members of political prisoners also face government intimidation. Typically, Cuba justifies its repression by referring to the activists as counterrevolutionaries. The government's denial of legal recognition to opposition

---

[414] The government's prosecutions and imprisonment of dissidents are discussed above, at *Political Prosecutions* and *Treatment of Political Prisoners.*

[415] The situation of independent labor organizers is discussed below, at *Labor Rights.*

[416] The status of religious leaders and their followers is detailed below, at *Limits on Religious Freedom.*

groups leaves all members of unauthorized groups at risk of arrest and prosecution.[417] But independent groups that criticize the government in nonviolent ways—whether through holding meetings, distributing "Down with Fidel" signs, writing about economic conditions in Cuba, proposing open political debate, or documenting human rights abuses—are exercising fundamental rights to free expression and association.

The Cuban government also attempts to discredit the work of independent groups and justify repressing them by alleging that they are acting on behalf of or with financial support from the U.S. government, which funnels some monies to Cuban nongovernmental organizations (NGOs) under the Helms-Burton law. The U.S. has provided funding to U.S.-based organizations that channel supplies, such as books, copies of human rights treaties, and typewriters, to Cuban groups.[418] Yet, Cuban authorities have acknowledged that the government's decision to allow the formation and legal operation of Cuban NGOs (many of which are state-controlled institutions with an NGO moniker) stemmed principally from the government's interest in increasing the flow of foreign aid into Cuba.[419] Despite the problems posed by Cuba's restrictive Associations Law, which makes it difficult for foreign governments to fund Cuban groups with independent or critical political views (which cannot operate legally under Cuba's Associations Law), the European Union and Canada have provided support to legalized Cuban humanitarian aid organizations. Cuba's actions single out dissident groups, limiting their opportunities to receive aid while permitting legalized organizations to do so. And while the U.S. government, in the text of the Helms-Burton law, has endorsed the

---

[417] While Cuba has recognized approximately 2,000 putative nongovernmental organizations (NGOs) under the Associations Law, the groups include Communist Party-supported and government-controlled mass organizations, as well as groups formed by government ministries. Approximately one-fifth of the recognized groups are sports leagues. Homero Campo, "El Gobierno les Ve con Recelo y las Somete a Estrictos Controles," *Proceso*, Mexico, May 18, 1997. See also, Gillian Gunn Ph.D., "Cuba's NGOs: Government Puppets or Seeds of Civil Society?" *Cuba Briefing Paper Series: Number 7*, Georgetown University Caribbean Project, February 1995.

Cuba has consistently refused to recognize organizations critical of government policies and practices. The Associations Law is discussed above, at *Impediments to Human Rights in Cuban Law: Associations Law.*

[418] Juan O. Tamayo, "American Dollars Committed to Building Cuban Democracy," *Miami Herald*, October 25, 1998.

[419] Gillian Gunn Ph.D., "Cuba's NGOs: Government Puppets or Seeds of Civil Society?" *Cuba Briefing Paper Series: Number 7*, February 1995.

toppling of the Castro government, Cuba should not penalize dissident groups that accept U.S. funds to distribute copies of the Universal Declaration of Human Rights or report on human rights violations—activities not designed to the promote violent overthrow of the current Cuban leadership—for the exercise of their protected rights. The fact that Cuban groups have received foreign monies does not alone demonstrate that they have engaged in any improper or violent activity, nor that the groups pose a genuine threat to the security of the state.[420]

Cuba routinely denies visas to foreign journalists and human rights investigators in what appears to be an effort to avoid negative publicity. In October 1998 President Castro explained the conditions under which he would grant visas to reporters with U.S. news bureaus: "If I were certain objective reporters would come to Cuba and not be biased beforehand, we would...."[421] Cuba's restrictions on press coverage and human rights reporting are among the most severe in the Western Hemisphere.

State Organs Charged with Internal Surveillance and Repression

The Interior Ministry has principal responsibility for monitoring the Cuban population for signs of dissent. Reportedly, the ministry employs two central offices for this purpose: the General Directorate of Counter-Intelligence and the General Directorate of Internal Order. The former supervises the activities of the Department of State Security, also known as the Political Police, reportedly dividing its counter-intelligence operations into specialized units. One of the units—known as "Department Four"—reportedly focuses on the "ideological sector," which includes religious groups, writers, and artists. Three Cuban defectors who previously worked for the state security apparatus informed the *Miami Herald* that Cuba assigned between ten and fifteen intelligence officials to spy on and infiltrate the church.[422] The second Interior Ministry office monitoring

---

[420] The Law for the Protection of Cuba's National Independence and Economy, which took effect in March 1999, creates severe penalties for direct or indirect support for the U.S. embargo. The law is discussed above, at *Impediments to Human Rights in Cuban Law.* Legitimate and illegitimate justifications for state security crimes are discussed in the same chapter, at *Codifying Repression.*

[421] Doug Clifton and David Lawrence Jr., "Defiant Castro Says He'll Reign as Long as He's Needed," *Miami Herald*, October 25, 1998.

[422] Juan O. Tamayo, "Cuba has Long Spied on Church," *Miami Herald*, January 21, 1998. Department Four reportedly is based in an eleven-story building on Twenty-First Street in downtown Havana. The *Herald* also reported that Cuba's Interior Ministry

suspected dissident activity, the Directorate of Internal Order, supervises two police units with internal surveillance responsibilities, the National Revolutionary Police and the Technical Department of Investigation (Departamento Técnico de Investigaciones, DTI). Once authorities give an activist an official warning, Cuban law permits the National Revolutionary Police to monitor that person's activities.[423] But with or without official warnings, Cuban dissidents are aware that police and state security forces monitor their movements, contacts, telephones, and correspondence. Dissidents have reported that police interrogating them revealed detailed knowledge about their activities and contacts. In trials in 1992 and 1995, Cuban courts sentenced eleven citizens to lengthy prison terms because the individuals had uncovered the identities of government infiltrators in dissident groups. Remarkably, the courts sentenced the activists and government agents, five of whom remain in Cuban prisons, for the crime of "revealing secrets concerning state security."[424]

Since their creation in 1960, Cuba also has relied on the Committees for the Defense of the Revolution (Comités de Defensa de la Revolución, CDRs) to conduct intensive monitoring in every Cuban neighborhood. The CDRs are Cuba's largest organization and according to President Castro, comprise 91 percent of Cuba's population.[425] Juan Contino, a member of the Council of State, coordinates CDR activities. Castro lauded the CDRs when they were first launched as a "system of collective revolutionary vigilance so that everyone will know who everyone else is ... what they devote themselves to, who they meet with, what activities they take part in."[426] Led by block captains, the CDRs carry out numerous neighborhood activities, in which non-participation can be suspect, and maintain

---

operates an intelligence division for gathering information from outside Cuba. The office reportedly is located at the intersection of Linea and A Streets in the Vedado section of Havana.

[423] Official warnings are discussed above, at *Impediments to Human Rights in Cuban Law: Codifying Repression.*

[424] These trials are discussed above, at *Impediments to Human Rights in Cuban Law: Revealing Secrets Concerning State Security.*

[425] "Fidel en la Clausura del V Congreso de los CDR: Al Mundo no le Queda Otra Alternativa que Salvarse," *Prensa Latina*, October 27, 1998.

[426] Román Orozco, *Cuba Roja* (Buenos Aires: Información y Revista S.A. Cambio 16 - Javier Vergara Editor S.A., 1993), p. 158.

tight surveillance of suspected government opponents. In September 1998, the government called on the CDRs and state-supported vigilante groups, known as "popular revolutionary vigilance detachments" (unarmed CDR members collaborating with the police), to increase their activities in response to a worsening crime wave.[427]

In 1991 two new government-sponsored mechanisms for internal surveillance and control emerged. Communist Party leaders organized the Singular Systems of Vigilance and Protection (Sistema Unico de Vigilancia y Protección, SUVP). The SUVP membership reaches across several state institutions, including the party, the police, the CDRs, the state-controlled labor union, student groups, and members of mass organizations.[428] The government reportedly has called on the SUVPs to carry out surveillance and to intimidate opposition activists. The government also organized groups of civilian sympathizers into Rapid Action Brigades (Brigadas de Acción Rapida, also referred to as Rapid Response Brigades, or Brigadas de Respuesta Rápida) to observe and control dissidents.

The Cuban migration authorities and housing officials also have emerged as important actors in government efforts to intimidate independent activists by threatening them with forced exile or the loss of their homes, or imposing fines on them. Cuba also monitors political fielty at the workplace and in schools. The government maintains academic and labor files (*expedientes escolares y laborales*) for each citizen, in which officials record actions or statements that may bear on the person's loyalty to the regime. Before advancing to a new school or position, the individual's record must first be deemed acceptable.

Cuban universities openly profess the government's viewpoint, rather than promoting the free exchange of information and ideas. Following a tour of the government's universities, the minister of higher education, Fernando Vecino Alegret, stressed that the institutions needed to reinvigorate their political and ideological labors. The ministry backed a new Educational Project (Proyecto Educativo) in order to highlight "the necessity of leaving a profoundly political-

---

[427] "Cuba: Cubans Urged to Join Fight Against Rising Crime," *Reuters New Service*, September 27, 1998, and "Mandatorio Cubano Resalta Rol de los CDR contra el Delito," *Prensa Latina*, September 28, 1998.

[428] Orozco, *Cuba Roja*, pp. 151-152.

ideological imprint on all the substantive activities of the university" and to form "revolutionary convictions."[429]

Repressing Independent Activists

Government agents or organizations have a broad range of repressive options at their disposal to dissuade government critics from continuing their activities. Some of the most common dissuasive tactics are mentioned here and further discussed below, as they are frequently applied against independent journalists and human rights activists.

Short-term Detentions

Police and state security agents carry out short-term detentions, ranging from a few hours to two weeks, that serve to intimidate dissidents by threatening them with prosecution and a prison term and revealing how closely they are being watched. Some activists have been subjected to repeated brief detentions. Police often issue official warnings during short-term detentions. Warnings and threats of future prosecution are made while dissidents are in police custody, typically when they have not been granted contact with family members or legal counsel and are being held in very poor conditions, often with violent criminals. Migration and housing authorities also carry out some short-term detentions for the purpose of intimidating activists.

In late February 1999 Cuban police and state security agents detained over fifty independent journalists and members of opposition and human rights groups. The authorities apparently carried out the arrests to preclude the activists and journalists from being in the vicinity of the March 1 trial of the four leaders of the Internal Dissidents' Working Group.[430] The detentions ranged in length from several hours to several days and detainees were held in both police stations and residences under the control of the Interior Ministry. Many of the detained journalists and activists reportedly were threatened with criminal prosecutions. Police reportedly forced

---

[429] Vladia Rubio, "La Realidad Universitaria a Pecho Abierto," *Granma Diario*, September 18, 1998.

[430] The government closed the trial to the public, restricted the number of family members of the accused who could attend, and sealed off a two-block area around the courthouse. The trial is discussed above, at *Political Prosecutions*.

another fifty activists to remain in their homes while the trial was taking place.[431]

Throughout January 1999, Matanzas authorities required approximately twenty-five local members of the Democratic Solidarity Party (Partido Democrático Solidaridad, PSD) to report to police who briefly interrogated them about their activities.[432]

On December 16, 1998, and January 7, 1999, Miriam García Chávez of the College of Independent Teachers (Colegio de Pedagogos Independientes) planned on demonstrating outside Havana courthouse where her colleague, Lázaro Constantin Durán, was tried and convicted of dangerousness.[433] On both occasions, Cuban police detained her, holding her for seventy-two hours in December and approximately forty-eight hours in January.[434]

On November 27, 1998, Havana police reportedly detained five dissidents, holding them overnight, while beating others who also had protested the planned trial of a Cuban independent journalist Mario Julio Viera González.[435] Cuban authorities apparently arrested Dr. Oscar Elías Biscet González and Rolando Muñoz Yyobre, of the Lawton Human Rights Foundation (Fundación Lawton de Derechos Humanos), Miriam García Chávez and Lázaro Constantin Durán, and Marisela Pompa of the PSD. Police reportedly beat another member of the College of Independent Teachers, Roberto de Miranda. A government sympathizer

---

[431] Andrew Cawthorne, "Cuba: Cuba Releases Dissidents After Crackdown," *Reuters News Service*, March 2, 1999, Serge Kovaleski, "Sedition Trial in Cuba Begins Amid Skepticism," *Washington Post*, March 2, 1999, and Letter from Ann K. Cooper, executive director of the Committee to Protect Journalists, to President Fidel Castro Ruz, March 2, 1999.

[432] Human Rights Watch telephone interview with Fernando Sánchez López, president of the PSD, Havana, February 3, 1999.

[433] His case is discussed above, at *Political Prosecutions.*

[434] Human Rights Watch telephone interview with Odilia Collazo, Pro Human Rights Party, January 11, 1999.

[435] The case is discussed below, at *Independent Journalists.*

apparently shoved and punched Cable News Network (CNN) cameraman Rudy Marshall, who was attempting to film the arrests.[436]

Havana police briefly detained and questioned Jorge León Rodríguez, of the Democracy and Peace Movement (Movimiento Democracia y Paz), on September 18, 1998. León Rodríguez, a Santiago resident, said that state security officials apparently knew in advance that members of his organization would be traveling to Havana. Police interrogated him at the DTI headquarters and seized pro-democracy materials from him that they termed "counterrevolutionary."[437]

On August 28, 1998, about twenty people protested the Havana trial of activist Reynaldo Alfaro García. In early September, Havana police arrested seven of the protesters and detained them for twelve to forty-eight hours.[438] The detentions prohibited the activists from participating in a September 8, 1998, march celebrating the feast day of Cuba's patron saint, Our Lady of Charity of Cobre. Police questioned the detainees about the Alfaro García demonstration and about their plans for the march. The detainees were Nancy de Varona, a leader of the Thirteenth of July Movement (Movimiento 13 de Julio); Ofelia Nardo, of the Confederation of Democratic Workers of Cuba (Confederación de Trabajadores Democráticos de Cuba); Vicky Ruíz Labrit, of the Committee of Cubans in Peaceful Opposition (Comité Cubano de Opositores Pacíficos); Leonel Morejón Almagro, the national leader of the Cuban Council (Concilio Cubano); Miriam García Chávez, president of the College of Independent Teachers; and Dr. Oscar Elías Biscet González and Rolando Muñóz Yyobre, of the Lawton Human Rights Foundation. Foreign Ministry Spokesman Alejandro González refused to provide reporters with details about the arrests, simply stating that the government's duty was to prevent illegal activities.[439] On September 8, state security agents also

---

[436] Pascal Fletcher, "Cuba: Fights Break Out at Trial of Cuban Dissident," *Reuters News Service*, November 27, 1998; John Rice, "Protestan por Proceso de Periodista en La Habana," *Associated Press*, November 27, 1998; and Olance Nogueras, "Liberados los Detenidos en Disturbio el Viernes: Continúa Desaparecido un Joven Transeúnte Golpeado," *El Nuevo Herald*, November 29, 1998.

[437] Luis López Prendes, "Represión contra Oposicionistas Santiagueros de Visita en La Habana," *Buró de Prensa Independiente de Cuba*, September 22, 1998.

[438] Ariel Hidalgo and Tete Machado, "Nueve Disidentes Detenidos Durante una Redada," *Infoburo*, September 9, 1998.

[439] "Liberan a Disidentes Detenidos esta Semana," *Reuters News Service* published by *El Nuevo Herald*, September 11, 1998.

briefly detained thirty human rights and other activists who had gathered at the Havana home of Isabel del Pino Sotolongo, of the Christ the King Movement (Movimiento Cristo Rey). The agents barred the activists from leaving del Pino Sotolongo's residence, where they had gathered prior to joining the feast day celebrations, until the festivities had ended and the agents had ensured that the activists would not take part.[440]

Exile

Cuban police or state security agents often threaten dissidents with criminal prosecution if they do not abandon their opposition activities or go into exile. Cuba's recent prosecutions of dissidents and its significant population of political prisoners add credibility to these threats, and repeated detentions have driven many to flee Cuba. In December 1997, Héctor Peraza Linares, an independent journalist based in Pinar del Río, left Cuba for exile in Spain. On June 23, 1997, Cuban police had detained Peraza Linares and confined him in a darkened, sealed cell. He remained in detention until September 1997, when he was released on the condition that he abandon Cuba. The Cuban government forced Miguel Angel Aldana, another leader of the Cuban Council, into exile in April 1997 by threatening him with a four-year sentence for dangerousness (*estado peligroso*). Cuban authorities had arrested Aldana, also a leader of the Martiana Civic Association (Asociación Civica Martiana), on several previous occasions.[441]

Other Tactics

As described above, Cuba's regressive Associations Law leaves independent groups vulnerable to arbitrary government interference. On March 25, 1998, for example, Communist Party officials called the executive board of a humanitarian aid agency called the Group for Assistance to the Needy (Grupo de Apoyo a Necesitados, GAN) to a meeting and notified them that they were dissolving the group. Several weeks before, Orlando Bordón Gálvez, a reporter with the independent agency Cuba Press, had mentioned the group in a story, which state

---

[440] Juan O. Tamayo, "Cuban Authorities Mix Tolerance, Repression," *Miami Herald*, September 9, 1998.

[441] Armando Correa, "Expulsan a líder de Concilio Cubano por 'peligroso,'" *El Nuevo Heraldo*, April 11, 1997.

security officials acknowledged reviewing.[442] In March 1998 a group of twenty women leaders of independent organizations (including journalists, human rights activists, economists, and doctors) delivered a petition to Wilma Espín, the president of the government-controlled Federation of Cuban Women (Federación de Mujeres Cubanas, FMC) seeking permission to participate in the International Encounter of Solidarity Among Women in Havana in April 1998. The government never responded to the petition, and the women were not allowed to take part in the conference. The Solidarity and Peace Movement (Movimiento Solidaridad y Paz), one of the groups petitioning to take part in the conference, had requested government legalization under the Associations Law in 1994 without ever receiving a response.[443]

The Cuban government's near-complete monopoly on jobs allows it to exercise tight control over the nation's workforce.[444] Often, the government's first move against dissenters is to fire them from their jobs. Most of Cuba's prominent dissidents lost their jobs as they became more involved in independent organizations.

Cuba strictly controls dissidents' freedom to exit and reenter their country and to travel within Cuba. Cuban activists know that unless they obtain government permission for traveling that guarantees their right to return, any unauthorized travel may result in forced exile. But dissidents' requests for exit and reentry permits are often ignored or denied. In October 1998 Cuba reportedly denied Osvaldo Alfonso Valdés, the president of the Liberal Democratic Party (Partido Liberal Democrático), permission to attend a meeting of the Liberal Party International from November 6 to 8 in Switzerland.[445] The government reportedly denied a

---

[442] Human Rights Watch telephone interview with Raúl Rivero, Cuba Press director, Havana, July 3, 1998, and Ana Luisa López Baeza, "Periodista de Cuba Press Agredido el Sábado Ultimo," *Cuba Press*, April 22, 1998. State Security officials reportedly told the GAN leaders that Bordón Gálvez's reporting was to blame for the group's demise. In an unfortunate development, on April 18, a GAN member, Juan Carlos Figueredo, physically attacked Bordón on the basis of this information, leaving him with minor injuries.

[443] Human Rights Watch telephone interview with Marta Pargas García of the Solidarity and Peace Movement, Havana, June 25, 1998.

[444] This issue is discussed in greater detail below, at *Labor Rights: Government Control Over Employment.*

[445] Oswaldo de Céspedes, "Niega el Gobierno Cubano Permiso de Salida a Opositor," *Cooperativa de Periodistas Independientes*, October 16, 1998.

Baptist pastor, Rev. Roberto Hernández Aguiar, permission to travel outside Cuba in September 1998.[446] In May the Culture Ministry denied visas requests from the Classical Ballet of Havana (Ballet Clásico de La Habana), which was to have toured in Spain in June and July. The denial reportedly was based on the fact that the ballet, which was founded by the daughter of the director of the National Ballet of Cuba (Ballet Nacional de Cuba), "does not officially exist" and might conflict with the schedule of the previously established company.[447]

In March 1988 two leaders of the opposition Cuban Council traveled to Santiago for an organizational meeting but were not allowed to leave the airport on arrival. Cuban authorities placed Leonel Morejón Almagro, who had served a prison term based on his prior Cuban Council activities, and Oswaldo Alfonso Valdéz, on a plane back to Havana.

The government also employs so-called repudiation meetings (*mitines de repudio*), or acts of repudiation, to humiliate and intimidate dissidents publicly, sometimes violently. On September 18, Miriam García Chávez, the president of the College of Independent Teachers, and her family were subjected to an act of repudiation. Approximately fifty uniformed school children, directed by members of the local CDR and members of a Rapid Response Brigade, gathered outside García Chávez's Havana home and shouted insults about her and other dissidents.[448]

The government often enlists the support of so-called popular organizations to ratchet up pressure against independent activists. On March 15, 1998, for example, Mirna Riverón Guerrero opened the Eduardo René Chibás Independent Library (Biblioteca Independiente "Eduardo René Chibás") in Santiago. By early July, she still had received no response from various government entities to whom she had sent requests for the legalization of the library, including the provincial authorities and the Communist Party. However, in the months following the opening of the library, she received visits from members of several pro-government organizations, including the CDRs, the Federation of Cuban Women, the Union of Young Communists (Unión de Jovenes Comunistas), and an association of retired state

---

[446] Luis López Prendes, "Niegan el Partido Comunista Permisos a Pastor Bautista," *Buró de Prensa Independiente de Cuba*, September 17, 1998.

[447] Jordan Levin, "Niegan a Ballet Permiso para Viaje," *El Nuevo Herald*, May 2, 1998.

[448] Human Rights Watch telephone interview with Odilia Collazo, Pro Human Rights Party, Havana, October 23, 1998. Manuel David Orrio, "Niños Cubanos en Acto de Repudio," *Cooperativa de Periodistas Independientes*, September 21, 1998.

security agents. On each of these occasions, the visitors urged her to abandon the "illicit" activity of running the library.[449]

Independent Journalists

The Castro government maintains a firm stance against independent journalism. In June 1998 the government labelled Cuba's small group of independent reporters "self-titled 'independent journalists' dedicated to defaming our people by means of the radio stations that broadcast from Miami against Cuba."[450] Since the journalists have no means of publishing stories internally, nor access to the state-controlled radio and television, they often provide stories to international news outlets by telephone. In contrast, the government called upon the "truly free" press to serve the socialist state by "guaranteeing the continuity of socialist, patriotic, and anti-imperialist ideas and values, and the Revolution itself for future generations of Cubans."[451] In October 1998 a representative of Cuba's Interests Section in Washington stated that "We are not ashamed to admit that the national press is entirely at the service of the Communist Party and the Cuban people."[452] Noting that Communist Party efforts to "exercise adequate control over their [independent journalists'] subversive activities" had proven insufficient, the party called upon its base organizations to "drum up, in each block and community, a climate of social rejection of these elements, so that they will feel that their calumnies are repudiated and morally condemned by the people."[453]

---

[449] Human Rights Watch telephone interview with Mirna Riverón Guerrero, Santiago, July 3, 1998.

[450] From the "Introduction to the Meeting with Block Leaders and General Secretaries of the Party's Base Organizations," a document prepared by the Communist Party of Cuba and distributed in June 1998; Raúl Rivero, "Partido Insta a Combatir Periodísmo Independiente," *Cuba Press en El Nuevo Herald*, June 18, 1998; and Ana Luisa López Baeza, "Amenazante Documento que Augura Persecución Contra los Periodistas Independientes,"*Cuba Press*, June 18, 1998. Additional restrictions on Cuba's independent press are discussed above, at *Impediments to Human Rights in Cuban Law: Law for the Protection of Cuban National Independence and the Economy.*

[451] "Proyecto: El Partido de la Unidad, la Democracia y los Derechos Humanos que Defendemos," *Granma Internet*, Año 2, Número 20, June 2, 1997.

[452] Agence France Presse, "Periodista de CNN Se Queja de Labor 'Frustrante,'" *El Nuevo Herald*, October 24, 1998.

[453] López Baeza, "Amenazante Documento."

The Cuban government relies not only on mass organizations, but also on its security forces and courts to threaten, intimidate, detain, and prosecute independent journalists.[454] Cuba often uses detentions to threaten journalists with criminal prosecutions, urging them to abandon their careers or go into exile. At this writing, Manuel Antonio González Castellanos, a Cuba Press reporter in Holguín, remains in a Holguín prison, facing charges of contempt for the authority (*desacato*) of Fidel Castro. Cuban police arrested Castellanos on October 1, 1998.[455]

The Cuban government planned to try Mario Julio Viera González, the director of the Cuba Verdad press agency, for the crime of insulting someone (*injuria*) on November 27, 1998. Cuban police had not detained Viera González for the alleged crime at this writing. He reportedly committed the crime against the honor of José Peraza Chapeau, the legal director of Cuba's Ministry of Foreign Relations, when he published an article titled "Morality Wearing Underpants," (*Moral en Calzoncillos*) that questioned Cuba's commitment to an effective International Criminal Court, in light of its poor domestic judicial system. When demonstrators and police clashed outside the courthouse, resulting in several detentions, the government indefinitely postponed Viera González's trial.[456]

Cuban authorities detained at least fifteen independent journalists in late February 1999, in order to prohibit their covering the trial of the leaders of the Internal Dissidents' Working Group.[457]

On January 27, 1999, police in Ciego de Avila arrested Pedro Arguelles Morán, of Cuba Press. The authorities detained him for two days in a government-

---

[454] As detailed above, at *Political Prosecutions*, independent journalists in Cuba remain at risk of criminal prosecution for their activities.

[455] Raúl Rivero and Roberto Fabricio, "Se Intensifica Acoso a Periodistas Independientes: Sociedad Interamericana de Prensa Informe de Cuba, Segundo Ejercicio, 1998," *El Nuevo Herald*, November 16, 1998. His case is discussed above, at *Political Prosecutions*.

[456] Pascal Fletcher, "Cuba: Fights Break Out at Trial of Cuban Dissident," *Reuters News Service*, November 27, 1998; John Rice, "Protestan por Proceso de Periodista en La Habana," *Associated Press*, November 27, 1998; and Manuel David Orrio, "En 27 de Noviembre," Cooperativa de Periodistas Independientes, November 27, 1998.

[457] Letter from Ann K. Cooper, executive director of the Committee to Protect Journalists, to President Fidel Castro Ruz, March 2, 1999, and "Hubo Catorce Periodistas Detenidas," *El Nuevo Herald*, March 3, 1999.

controlled residence.[458] Earlier the same week, Havana police arrested María de los Angeles González Amaro, the director of the Union of Independent Cuban Journalists and Writers (Union de Periodistas y Escritores de Cuba Independientes, UPECI), Nancy Sotolongo, a journalist with UPECI, Santiago Martínez Trujillo, an UPECI photographer, and Angel Pablo Polanco, of the Cooperative of Independent Journalists (Cooperativa de Periodistas Independientes), holding them for three to five days before release. The arrests apparently occurred because the journalists planned to cover an event marking the first anniversary of the pope's January 1998 trip to Cuba. Police reportedly issued González Amaro with an official warning that she would face trial for criminal association and disobedience if she continued her activities.[459]

Ana Luisa López Baeza, a reporter with Cuba Press, left Cuba for exile in the United States on October 29, 1998, citing government pressure on her and her daughter.[460] On December 29, 1998, Cuban police arrested Jesús Labrador Arias, a Cuba Press reporter in Manzanillo, holding him for several hours. On December 8, Cuban state security officials went to another Cuba Press journalist's residence, warning him not to cover any events on December 10, International Human Rights Day. On December 15, 1998, and again on the next day, state security officers detained Efrén Martínez Pulgarón for several hours.[461] Previously, on August 13, 1997, Cuban police detained Martínez Pulgarón in Pinar del Río. For thirty-eight days, Cuban authorities held him in a small isolation cell, frequently urging him to abandon independent journalism. On September 10, 1998, Havana police reportedly detained Juan Antonio Sánchez Rodríguez, a reporter with Cuba Press based in Pinar del Río, transferred him to a state security detention center in his home province, and held him for at least six days. Apparently, he was not charged

---

[458] Human Rights Watch telephone interview with Ricardo González Alfonso, Cuba Press, Havana, February 1, 1999.

[459] Ibid.; Odalys Curbelo, "En Libertad Periodistas Independientes," *Cuba Press*, February 1, 1999; Letter from Ann K. Cooper, executive director of the Committee to Protect Journalists to Fidel Castro Ruz, president of Cuba, February 3, 1999; and Human Rights Watch telephone interview with Odilia Collazo, Pro Human Rights Party, Havana, February 3, 1999.

[460] Pablo Alfonso, "Anuncian Llegada de Periodista Opositora," *El Nuevo Herald*, October 30, 1998.

[461] Human Rights Watch telephone interview with Efrén Martínez Pulgarón, Cuba Press, Havana, January 13, 1999.

with any crime but was threatened with prosecution for "dangerousness."[462] State security officials in Havana arrested Luis López Prendes, the director of the Independent Press Bureau of Cuba (Buró de Prensa Independiente de Cuba, BPIC), on September 7, 1998, and detained him for over forty-eight hours. A state security captain named Ariel interrogated López Prendes about his involvement in the dissident movement, what he knew of Reynaldo Alfaro García's August 28, 1998, trial,[463] and whether he knew of any plans for the September 8 celebration of Cuba's patron saint, Our Lady of Charity of Cobre. López Prendes said the captain told him that independent journalists "weren't going to depose the government with their news." López Prendes explained that his intention was not to remove the government. As he was leaving the police station, several state security agents suggested that he join his son in the United States. The agents escorted López Prendes to his home, where they told local CDR leaders that they had detained him to avoid his contributing to problems at the celebrations for Our Lady of Charity.[464]

Often detentions last less than one day. On October 23, 1998, political police in Santa Clara detained Edel José García Díaz, a reporter with the Center-North (Centro-Norte) press agency, for several hours. A police official interrogated García Díaz and issued him an official warning (*acta de advertencia*) that he might face prosecution for enemy propaganda and spreading false news, due to his transmission on the U.S. government-operated Radio Martí.[465] On October 1, 1998, migration officials in Havana called Cuba Press journalist María de los Angeles González Amauro to a meeting, although she had no pending migration matter. The officials threatened to detain her and treat her like several dissidents who have spent long periods in pretrial detention if she did not give up her independent journalism or emigrate from Cuba.[466] Cuban state security agents in

---

[462] Raúl Rivero, "En Libertad Periodista de Esta Agencia," *Cuba Press*, September 16, 1998; and Andrew Cawthorne, "Cuba: Cuba Frees Independent Reporter Held for Six Days," *Reuters News Service*, September 16, 1998.

[463] This trial is discussed above, at *Political Prosecutions*.

[464] Luis López Prendes, "El Periodista Independiente Luis López Prendes Relata su Detención," *Buró de Prensa Independiente de Cuba,* September 10, 1998.

[465] Héctor Trujillo Pis, "Amenazan a Periodista Independiente," *Cuba Press*, October 28, 1998.

[466] Rivero and Fabricio, "Se Intensifica Acoso a Periodistas Independientes," *El Nuevo Herald,* November 16, 1998.

Caibarién required Héctor Trujillo Pis, a Cuba Press journalist, to present himself in their offices in early September 1998. The police advised him that they had sufficient evidence to prosecute him for spreading false news to counterrevolutionary foreign media, including Radio Martí.[467] In September, state security police in Manzanillo, Granma Province, detained Jesús Labrador Arias, a Cuba Press reporter, for about half an hour and threatened to prosecute him.[468] In July, the reporter was leaving a local hospital when he was subjected to an act of repudiation. Approximately thirty men surrounded him, shouting insults such as "counterrevolutionary worm" (*gusano contrarrevolucionario*).[469] Cuban police detained Luis Alberto Lazo, a reporter for the New Press Agency (Agencia Nueva Prensa) in Artemisa for approximately twenty-four hours on June 17, 1998. The agents reportedly interrogated him and issued an official warning. They accused him of having planned to report on a demonstration at the United States Interests Section by a number of former prisoners. Lazo denied having planned to cover the demonstration, which never took place.[470]

The leader of a Singular Systems of Vigilance and Protection (SUVP) in Havana reportedly attacked José Luis Rodríguez Jiménez, a photographer with the BPIC, in May 1998. The local SUVP representative, known as Eliseo, apparently beat the photographer with a stick and called him a counterrevolutionary.[471]

One of Cuba's most prominent independent journalists, Cuba Press founder and director Raúl Rivero, faced continued restrictions in 1998 of his freedom to travel. On May 25, he solicited government permission to travel to Spain on a personal visit with some friends. On June 24, an official at the Migration Office of Central Havana told him that his request had been denied. The official refused to provide Rivero with the name of the migration official responsible for the decision and

---

[467] Héctor Trujillo Pis, "Denuncia Periodista de Cuba Press Amenazas de la Policía Política," *Cuba Press*, September 11, 1998.

[468] Ana Luisa López Baeza, "Amenaza la Policía Política a Periodista Independiente," *Cuba Press*, August 12, 1998.

[469] Ricardo González Alfonso, "Hostigan a Periodista Independiente," *Cuba Press*, July 9, 1998.

[470] Human Rights Watch telephone interview with Odilia Collazo, Pro Human Rights Party, Havana, July 2, 1998.

[471] Luis López Prendes, "Agreden a Fotoreportero del Buró de Prensa Independiente de Cuba," *Buró de Prensa Independiente de Cuba*, May 28, 1998.

would not produce a written decision. Rivero noted that on several prior occasions Cuban police had informed him that he was always able to travel outside Cuba, as long as he did so in a "definitive manner," (*una manera definitiva*) meaning without an option to return. He recalled that during a three-day detention in August 1997, an official of the political police named Soroa detailed the various crimes that he had committed by operating his press agency, including illicit association and the spreading of false news (*difusión de noticias falsas*). Soroa then urged him to avoid prosecution by leaving Cuba.[472]

Santiago-based state security agents detained Margarita Sara Yero, the director of the Turquino Correspondence of the Independent Press Agency of Cuba (Agencia de Prensa Independiente de Cuba, APIC) on November 17, 1997. Her detention followed shortly after she reported on the trial of a local government opponent, Orestes Rodríguez Horruitiner, who was sentenced to four years for enemy propaganda. After questioning her at the state security headquarters known as "Versalles, " the agents released Yero later that day.

In a few cases, the government used housing regulations to harass independent reporters. In January 1999 housing authorities in Santiago notified Yero that she would be evicted from her home, where she had resided for thirty-five years. The officials apparently claimed that she had abandoned her home, but several neighbors affirmed her residency. On February 1, 1999, police and housing officials called her neighbors to a public meeting, where they reportedly stated that Yero did not belong to the local CDR and had not cast votes for Communist Party candidates. The next day, the local housing authority apparently sent Yero a written notification of her imminent eviction.[473] On September 23, 1998, officials told ANP journalist Mercedes Moreno, that according to housing regulations, she could not reside legally in her sister's Havana home and imposed heavy fines on both women. Housing inspectors returned on October 21 and advised the family that another visiting relative was not authorized to stay with them and had twenty-four hours to leave. Housing authorities went to the home of Miriam García Chávez, the president of the Independent Teachers' College, on October 3, 1998, after she had taken in Efrén Martínez Pulgarón and his mother. The officials told García Chávez that her visitors had seventy-two hours to leave her residence. Martínez Pulgarón said that for over two years he and his mother have not been able to find permanent

---

[472] Human Rights Watch telephone interview with Raúl Rivero, Cuba Press director, Havana, July 3, 1998.

[473] Adalberto Yero, "Pretenden Autoridades Desalojar de su Vivienda a Periodista de esta Agencia," *Cuba Press*, February 3, 1999.

housing, due to the government's intimidations of landlords or others who have offered them a place to stay.[474]

Human Rights Activists

Cuba maintains tight control over domestic human rights defenders. The prosecution of Reynaldo Alfaro García and the trial for sedition of the four leaders of the Internal Dissidents' Working Group mark recent heavy-handed government measures against human rights advocates.[475] Prisoners who speak out against abuses also face physical violence and other punishments in Cuba's detention centers.[476] In addition to these drastic measures, the government also persists in short-term detentions, surveillance, phone interruption, and other intimidations of human rights activists.

In late January 1999 Havana police reportedly detained seven members of the Lawton Human Rights Foundation (FLDH), including the group's leader, Dr. Oscar Elías Biscet González, for four to six days. The human rights activists had planned to participate in a celebration of the first anniversary of the pope's January 1998 visit to Cuba. The detentions prevented the FLDH members from taking part in the January 25 event, as they were not released until January 30, 1999.[477]

On December 10, 1998, Cuban authorities arrested Biscet González after he had organized a rally marking the fiftieth anniversary of the Universal Declaration of Human Rights. Cuban police arrested at least six dissidents at the event, which was held in the Butari Park in Havana.[478] Days before, on December 7, the police briefly detained Biscet González and his colleague Rolando Muñoz Yyobre.[479]

---

[474] Human Rights Watch telephone interview with Efrén Martínez Pulgarón, Cuba Press, January 13, 1999.

[475] This trial is described above, at *Political Prosecutions.*

[476] These abuses are detailed above, at *Treatment of Political Prisoners: Punitive Measures Against Political Prisoners.*

[477] Human Rights Watch telephone interview with Odilia Collazo, Pro Human Rights Party, Havana, February 3, 1999.

[478] Andrew Cawthorne, "Cuba: Cuba Detains Dissidents, Stops Rights Day Protest," *Reuters News Service*, December 10, 1998.

[479] Raúl Rivero, "Arrestan a Dos Opositores en La Habana," *El Nuevo Herald*, December 8, 1998.

On October 20, 1998, migration authorities on the Isla de la Juventud, formerly known as the Isla de Pinos, ordered Antonio Morales Torres to come to an appointment. Morales Torres, a former political prisoner who had served two years for enemy propaganda and is president of the Pinero Human Rights Committee (Comité de Derechos Humanos Pinero), had no pending migration issue. At the meeting, migration officials revealed that they had been tracking his movements and meetings with other dissidents closely, including several meetings in Havana. The officials then advised him that if he did not cease his human rights activities and abandon Cuba, he would face prosecution as a common criminal, a tactic aimed at avoiding international attention. The officials also stressed that if he decided to leave the country, they would waive his obligation to pay for costly medical exams, which are required by the Cuban government of all emigrés, and would free his son from obligatory military service.[480]

On July 9, 1998, three state security agents detained Dr. Biscet González and Muñoz Yyobre. The agents, who were assisted by several police officers, took Biscet González to his home, which they searched, and then to the DTI police station at the intersection of 100th and Aldabó Streets. Police initially held Muñoz Yyobre at a police station in Old Havana, later moving him to the DTI. The police detained both men for over two weeks, until the afternoon of July 24. During that time, the men were held in filthy, hot, poorly-lit, over-crowded cells with violent criminal suspects. Police held Muñoz Yyobre in a cell that was approximately 2.3 meters by 3.3 meters, along with three other detainees, while holding Biscet González in a slightly larger cell with about ten other detainees. After one week, the police permitted each man to visit briefly with a few family members, but warned them that the visits would end if the men discussed the reasons they were under arrest, prison conditions, or the names of any other prisoners. In keeping with Cuban laws that minimize due process protections, the police also told the men that they could not have an attorney until after their tenth day of confinement.[481] Ultimately, neither received legal assistance during his detention.[482]

---

[480] Human Rights Watch telephone interview with Odilia Collazo, Pro Human Rights Party, Havana, October 23, 1998.

[481] Due process restrictions are discussed above, at *Impediments to Human Rights in Cuban Law: Arrests and Pretrial Detentions.*

[482] Human Rights Watch telephone interviews with Dr. Elías Biscet González and Rolando Muñóz Yyobre, Havana, July 28, 1998.

Police interrogated both men several times during their confinement, accusing them of illicit activities and threatening to use criminal prosecutions to destroy them. They alleged that the men had planned a July 13 anniversary protest of the government's 1994 sinking of a boat called the 13 de Marzo, which drowned dozens of Cubans attempting to flee their country, and that they had distributed anti-government documents, including a copy of the Universal Declaration of Human Rights, letters to the domestic and international press, and a letter to the government's Council of State. Upon their release, the police warned the two that they had opened case files on them (*expedientes archivados*). The police also noted that the Lawton Human Rights Foundation was not operating legally. More than one year earlier, the men had filed a request for legalization under the Associations Law but the government never responded to their application.

On July 25, September 29, and November 3, 1997, Cuban authorities required Pedro Orlando Herrada Delgado, an engineer and member of the National Council of Civil Rights (Consejo Nacional por los Derechos Civiles) in Villa Clara, to appear at police stations. On each occasion, the police threatened Herrada Delgado with criminal prosecution for his opposition activities. At the September meeting, the police issued him an official warning of possible prosecution for enemy propaganda, spreading false news, inciting criminal activity (*incitación para delinquir*), and associating with the enemy. In November, a police official, Dennis Durán Morales, mentioned that they also could try him for "spreading news that endangers international peace."[483]

Cuba did not allow either Elizardo Sánchez Santacruz, leader of the Cuban Commission for Human Rights and National Reconciliation (Comisión Cubana para los Derechos Humanos y la Reconciliación Nacional), nor Oswaldo Paya, leader of the Christian Liberation Movement (Movimiento Cristiano de Liberación), to attend an international human rights conference in Warsaw, Poland in October 1998. After completing two issues of a human rights newsletter that was distributed on a modest scale inside and outside of Cuba, Sánchez Santacruz reportedly received word from the government in October 1998 that it would not allow his organization to produce any more issues.

International Journalists Covering Cuba

Consistent with President Castro's October 1998 comments that he would not grant foreign reporters visas unless he could guarantee their "objectivity," Cuba restricts visas for foreign journalists based on the likely or actual content of their

---

[483] Memorandum prepared by Pedro Orlando Herrada Delgado, "Denuncia de Pedro Orlando Herrada," Placetas, Cuba, November 10, 1997.

reporting. Government regulations further control reporters who do receive visas. As noted above, Cuba formalized rules governing foreign reporters' objectivity and accuracy in February 1997.[484] While Cuba permits a handful of international news bureaus to function in Cuba, *CNN* and, as of November 13, 1998, the *Associated Press* (*AP*), are the only U.S.-based media operation officially granted permission to operate in Cuba.[485] The international media operating in Havana encounter some impediments to their work. On December 10, 1998, a cameraman for *Reuters*, Alfred Tedeschi, said that he was hit and had a microphone stolen, and other journalists said that they were pushed, while covering police arresting dissidents who were celebrating International Human Rights Day.[486] As noted above, a *CNN* journalist covering a demonstration outside Cuban journalist Mario Viera's postponed trial in November 1998 also was roughed up. *CNN*'s correspondent in Havana, Lucía Newman, said that although foreign reporters can operate with some measure of freedom in Cuba, many believe that the government listens in on their phone lines.[487] Cuba's prosecutions of its own citizens for providing information to foreign reporters also limit press freedom. The case of Dr. Dessy Mendoza, who received an eight-year sentence for enemy propaganda after advising international reporters of a dengue fever epidemic, highlighted this risk.[488]

On January 28, 1999, Cuban authorities expelled a Dutch journalist, Edwin Kopmann of Radio Neederland, after accusing him of having provided funds to a "counterrevolutionary group." The radio journalist reportedly had given an independent labor organization, the Confederation of Christian Unions (Confederación de Sindicatos Cristianos), U.S. $250. Cuban officials apparently

---

[484] These regulations are discussed above, at *Impediments to Human Rights in Cuban Law: Regulations Issued for International Press.*

[485] Andrew Cawthorne, "Cuba Approves Second U.S. Media Bureau in Havana," *Reuters News Agency*, November 13, 1998.

[486] Andrew Cawthorne, "Cuba Detains Dissidents," *Reuters News Agency*, December 10, 1998.

[487] Agence France Presse, "Periodista de CNN Se Queja de Labor Frustrante," *El Nuevo Herald*, October 24, 1998.

[488] Dr. Mendoza's case is discussed above, at *Political Prosecutions.*

also fined a Cuban citizen who had housed the reporter during his stay in Havana U.S. $1,000 for violating housing regulations.[489]

The government's practice of selectively denying reporters' visas became most evident as scores of foreign journalists requested entry permits for the pope's January 1998 trip to Cuba. The government denied visas to reporters with news agencies or stations known to have been critical of the Cuban authorities, including journalists from several Miami-based news outlets, such as the *Miami Herald.* An official at the Cuban embassy in Argentina, Concepción Muñoz, reportedly denied an Argentine journalist's visa for the papal visit because the reporter, Matilde Sánchez, of the Buenos Aires newspaper *Clarín*, had written a story about Cuban hero Ché Guevara that "hurt the Cuban people."[490] In October 1998 Cuba allowed the Herald's Executive Editor Doug Clifton and Chairman David Lawrence, Jr. to enter Cuba as part of a thirty-two-member delegation from the American Society of Newspaper Editors. Castro's welcome to the group was tempered by his comments about journalists' objectivity, but his mid-November accession to the group's recommendation that *AP* be allowed to open an office in Cuba was a positive step.[491] However, Castro's January 1999 comments to an annual assembly of several thousand National Revolutionary Police about foreign journalists' writing "propaganda" and his suggestion that reporters were engaged in "repugnant" campaigns to damage Cuba's image showed little tolerance for direct or indirect criticism from international journalists.[492] Castro was referring to press references

---

[489] "France: Watchdog Says Cuba Detains Journalists, Rights Activists," *Reuters News Service*, January 29, 1999; and Human Rights Watch telephone interview with Ricardo González Alfonso, Cuba Press, Havana, February 1, 1999.

[490] Reporters Sans Frontieres, "Journalists Refused Visas," *IFEX - News from the International Freedom of Expression Community*, January 12, 1998.

[491] Pascal Fletcher, "Cuba: Feisty Castro Tells U.S. Editors 'No Surrender,'" *Reuters News Service*, October 25, 1998; and Clifton and Lawrence, Jr., "Defiant Castro Says He'll Reign as Long as He's Needed," *Miami Herald*, October 25, 1998.

[492] "Deberíamos Dejar a un Lado, en Estos Tiempos que Estamos Viviendo y por Salvar tan Hermosa Causa Como la Nuestra, que no es Siquiera ya Solo Nuestra, Ciertas Costumbres Paternalistas e Ingenuas: Discurso Pronunciado por el Comandante en Jefe Fidel Castro Ruz, Primer Secretario del Comité Central del Partido Comunista de Cuba y Presidente de los Consejos de Estado y de Ministros, en el Acto por el Aniversario 40 de la Constitución de la Policía Nacional Revolucionario, Efectuado en el Teatro 'Carlos Marx,' el Dia 5 de Enero de 1999, 'Año del 40 Aniversario del Triunfo de la Revolución,'" *Granma Diario*, January 8, 1999.

to the growing problem of prostitution in Cuba, which he himself had acknowledged to be a problem.

International Human Rights and Humanitarian Groups

The Cuban government often welcomes visits from international organizations providing humanitarian aid, particularly those that have publicly opposed the U.S. embargo on Cuba. But it provides distinct treatment to international human rights and humanitarian agencies that may be critical of its human rights record, routinely banning them from the national territory. The Cuban government has not allowed Human Rights Watch to return to Cuba since 1995. Cuba never allowed the U.N. Special Rapporteur on Human Rights in Cuba to enter the country. The U.N. High Commissioner for Human Rights José Ayala Lasso visited Cuba in November 1994, but his failure to make any public comment about the country's human rights situation represented a lost opportunity to bring public pressure on the Cubans to institute reforms.

The government last permitted the International Committee of the Red Cross (ICRC), which visits prisoners in custody for political and security offenses around the world, to conduct prison visits in Cuba in 1988 and 1989. The ICRC does not make public its evaluations of prison conditions or treatment but rather intercedes with governments on behalf of prisoners on a confidential basis.[493]

The Cuban government's refusal to allow international human rights monitors such as Human Rights Watch and Amnesty International to conduct independent investigations impedes the collection and dissemination of information about human rights abuses in Cuba. Cuba's tight restrictions—barring the kinds of investigations that Human Rights Watch routinely conducts in dozens of countries, which usually include interviews with government authorities, the press, and leaders of NGOs, as well as visits to the detention areas of prisons and police stations—mark it as the least cooperative government in the Western Hemisphere in this respect. On several occasions, Human Rights Watch telephone interviews to Cuba have been abruptly terminated or disrupted by persistent background noise that made conversation impossible.

---

[493] ICRC prison visits in Cuba are discussed in greater detail above, at *General Prison Conditions*: *Bar on Domestic and International Monitoring of Prison Conditions.*

IX. LABOR RIGHTS

Taking advantage of its position as virtually the only source of jobs in Cuba's state-controlled economy, the Cuban government exercises strict control over labor rights.[494] Cuba not only effectively bans independent labor groups and harasses persons attempting to form them, but also allows workers' political views to influence hiring and firing decisions. Cuba's firm hand over labor rights extends to its expanding foreign investment sector, where foreign companies can only hire Cuban employees through government-controlled employment agencies. And Cuba's extensive prison labor program fails to observe the basic principles of humane treatment of prisoners and violates an international ban on forced labor by requiring political prisoners to work.

These labor rights abuses contradict the Cuban government's claims of protecting the rights to association, assembly, and expression, and the right to work. The government's assertions that it guarantees these rights are further undermined by the constitutional provision that government-backed "mass and social organizations have all the facilities for carrying out [these rights], in which their members enjoy the most extensive freedom of speech and opinion."[495] Thus, Cuba only permits one confederation of state-controlled unions, the Workers' Central of Cuba (Central de Trabajadores de Cuba, CTC), which is mandated to embrace "the struggle for the defense of Socialism and its principles."[496] CTC leaders also serve among Cuba's highest political authorities. Current CTC Secretary General Pedro Ross, for example, serves on the Communist Party Political Bureau (Buró Político del Partido, *politburó*). Meanwhile, Cuba has not legalized any independent union, either in the broader national economy or in the foreign investment sector, and the

---

[494] The Cuban constitution mandates state control of the economy (Article 16) and state control and direction of foreign commerce, which is explicitly delegated to the Council of Ministers (Article 18 and Article 98 [d]). Constitution of the Republic of Cuba, 1992.

[495] Ibid., Article 54. Translation by Human Rights Watch.

[496] Silvia Martínez and Emilio del Barrio, "VIII Pleno del Comité Nacional de la CTC: Encara el Movimiento Obrero la Lucha contra el Delito y Otras Deformaciones," *Granma Diario*, May 27, 1998. Translation by Human Rights Watch.

restrictive measures of the Associations Law all but preclude such a step.[497] Independent labor activists regularly risk detentions, harassment, threats of prosecution, and pressures to go into exile.

Cuba's laws and practices fail in numerous respects to comply with international labor standards that it is bound to uphold. The Cuban government has ratified multiple international treaties protecting labor rights.[498] Cuba's obligations under the Universal Declaration of Human Rights also require that it guarantee the right to form and join trade unions.[499]

Prison Labor

Human Rights Watch interviews with former Cuban prisoners provide disturbing evidence that Cuba abuses labor rights in its prisons. The Cuban government has an extensive system of prison labor camps, and runs clothing assembly, construction, furniture, and other factories as well as agricultural camps at its maximum and minimum security prisons.[500] The Standard Minimum Rules for the Treatment of Prisoners require prisons to have physically fit convicts take part in vocational training and engage in meaningful, rehabilitative work for equitable remuneration.[501] However, Cuba's insistence that political prisoners participate in work programs and its inappropriate pressuring of inmates to work without pay in inhuman conditions violate international labor and prison rights standards.

---

[497] The Associations Law is discussed above, at *Impediments to Human Rights in Cuban Law: Associations Law.*

[498] These ratifications include the International Labor Organization's (ILO) Convention 87, guaranteeing Freedom of Association and Protection of the Right to Organize (ratified June 1952); Convention 98, which protects the Right to Organise and Collective Bargaining (April 1952); Convention 105, on the Abolition of Forced Labor (June 1958); and Convention 141, regarding Rural Workers' Organizations (April 1977).

[499] Article 23(4), Universal Declaration of Human Rights.

[500] "Lista Parcial de Prisiones y Centros Correccionales," *Comisión Cubana de Derechos Humanos y Reconciliación Nacional* (Cuban Commission of Human Rights and National Reconciliation, hereinfacter, the commission), December 31, 1996. The commission estimated that there were 200 labor camps.

[501] Articles 71, 72, and 76(1), U.N. Standard Minimum Rules for the Treatment of Prisoners, U.N. Doc E/5988 (1977), adopted August 30, 1955.

The ILO's Abolition of Forced Labor Convention of 1957, which Cuba ratified in 1958, requires states to "secure the immediate and complete abolition" of forced or compulsory labor "as a means of political coercion or education or as a punishment for holding or expressing political views or views ideologically opposed to the established political, social or economic system."[502] Thus Cuban prison authorities' requirement that individuals work while serving prison terms for holding anti-government views violates the Abolition of Forced Labor Convention.

Authorities at the Boniato prison in Santiago pressured Luis Alberto Ferrándiz Alfaro to employ the skills that led to his twelve-year sentence for enemy propaganda—he had designed anti-Castro stamps and flyers—for the benefit of the prison factory. Prison officials working for the Interior Ministry's Desa Company (Empresa Desa) reminded Ferrándiz Alfaro that since both he and his wife were imprisoned in 1993, their two young children lacked financial support.[503] Under duress, Ferrándiz Alfaro accepted a post with Desa as a designer for numerous items, including jewelry and furniture.[504] In return, the prison director sent eighty pesos per month (approximately U.S. $3.81) to the couple's children. Few prisoners receive even meager compensation. Ferrándiz Alfaro recalled the prison director commenting that other prisoners received their payment in "air and sun." Ferrándiz's work for the Desa Company ended when the Cuban government forced him into exile in Canada in February 1998.[505]

Ferrándiz Alfaro's wife, Xiomara Aliat Collado, who received a seven-year sentence for enemy propaganda, also was obligated to work. Prison guards told her that if she did not work in the prison's assembly factory she would lose her right to

---

[502] Article 1(a) and Article 2, Convention 105: Abolition of Forced Labor, ILO (1957).

[503] Their children, who were five and fourteen at the time of their parents' arrest, had great difficulty feeding themselves. Their situation is detailed above, at *Hardships for Political Prisoners' Family Members.*

[504] Ferrándiz Alfaro said that Desa Company produces furniture, crafts (*objetos de artesanía*), carpentry, shoes, clothes (*confecciones*), cookware (*fundición*), charcoal grills (*anafes*), and home decorations, including plaster figurines (*figuras de yeso*). He believed that Desa sells its products to the public and in military stores. Boniato Prison authorities also run an agricultural labor camp, selling its production to the public in the Santiago region. Human Rights Watch interview with Luis Alberto Ferrándiz Alfaro, Toronto, April 13, 1998.

[505] Ibid.

visits with her children, her right to parole, or be sent to work in the nearby agricultural camp. From her arrest in March 1993 until March 1994, she worked at the Aguadores Prison in Santiago. After she was put under a year of house arrest to care for her ill son, she was imprisoned again and worked in the Ciudamar Prison factory in Santiago from March 1995 until her release in April 1996. Prison guards forced Aliat Collado to work in clothing assembly plants, where she made undergarments, women's clothing, and costumes for carnival celebrations. The inmate-workers did not attach any brand name labels to the clothing. Aliat Collado believed that the clothes were sold in state craft stores. The prisoners also made prison uniforms, envelopes, and paper holders for ice cream, which she said were used at the Helado Coppelia ice cream store in Santiago. She said that she often felt dizzy and weak while she worked, due to malnourishment, but that prison guards accused her of pretending to be ill, failed to provide sufficient food, and required extremely long hours. The workdays often extended from 7:00 a.m. until 10:00 p.m., with a short mid-day break. The armed prison guards who patrolled the factories often required workers to labor seven days a week.[506]

At this writing, Juan Carlos Recio Martínez, a journalist with the *Cuba Press* agency, is serving a one-year sentence in a labor camp, without internment. In February 1998, a Villa Clara court found him guilty of having failed to denounce an acquaintance who had drafted a document urging abstention from local elections.[507] In June 1998, he began serving his sentence at the Abel Santamaría Cooperative, near Camajuaní in Villa Clara province, where he was forced to do agricultural work from approximately 7:00 a.m. to 5:00 p.m. each day.[508]

In October 1997, Cuban authorities arrested five members of the Pro Human Rights Party of Cuba in Cienfuegos. In March 1998, the court found the human rights activists guilty of "other acts committed against state security" (*otros actos contra la seguridad del estado*).[509] The tribunal sentenced two of the defendants,

---

[506] Human Rights Watch interview with Xiomara Aliat Collado, Toronto, April 13, 1998.

[507] The case of Recio Martínez and Cecilio Monteagudo Sánchez, the document's author, is discussed above, at *Political Prosecutions*.

[508] Human Rights Watch telephone interview with Héctor Trujillo Pis, *Cuba Press*, Havana, July 3, 1998.

[509] The trial of Israel García Hidalgo, Benito Fojaco Iser, Angel Nicolas Gonzalo, José Ramón López Filgueira, and Reynaldo Sardiñas Delgado is discussed above, at *Political Prosecutions*.

sixty-nine-year-old Angel Nicolás Gonzalo and sixty-six-year-old Reynaldo Sardiñas Delgado, to one year in a labor camp without internment. Given Gonzalo's and Sardiñas Delgado's advanced age, Cuba may be violating the Standard Minimum Rules, which recommend that only physically fit prisoners work. Forcing the human rights activists to work also violates the ILO ban on compulsory labor for political prisoners.[510]

Cuba's work programs for common prisoners failed to comply with the Standard Minimum Rules' provisions regarding prison labor in several respects. The Cuban prison labor system's reliance on malnourished prisoners, its non-existent or extremely low wages, and its insistence that prisoners work without rest periods, all violate provisions of the Standard Minimum Rules. Viewing these practices alongside the sales of prisoner-made products outside the prison walls, it appears that many Cuban prisons favor profit over prisoners' welfare, which is explicitly prohibited under the Standard Minimum Rules.[511]

Cuban prison officals provide inmates with inadequate amounts of food.[512] The malnourished prisoners, who also face poor hygiene and cramped living conditions, often are weakened and disease-prone. These prisoners most likely are not physically fit for their assigned tasks, particularly the demands of farmwork. The Standard Minimum Rules require prison medical officers to establish all inmates' physical and mental fitness to work.[513] While some prisons apparently provide inmate-workers with minor improvements in their food rations, others make no adjustments in the prisoners' diets. Some hungry prisoners reportedly seek out field work for an opportunity to eat, even though guards prohibit them from doing so. Although prisoners plant and tend vegetables and raise livestock, including dairy cows, chickens, and pigs, typically neither working prisoners nor other

---

[510] Article 71(2), Standard Minimum Rules for the Treatment of Prisoners.

[511] The rules require that "the interests of prisoners and of their vocational training... must not be subordinated to the purpose of making a financial profit from an industry in the institution." Standard Minimum Rules, Article 72(2).

[512] Malnutrition in Cuban prisons is detailed above, at *General Prison Conditions: Food.*

[513] Standard Minimum Rules, Article 71(2).

inmates benefit from this production.[514] Prison and military officials sell these products at local markets or take them for their own use. The practice of allowing military or prison officials to profit personally from prison labor creates incentives for abusing the custodial relationship with prisoners.

While failing to provide prisoners with proper nutrition, Cuban prison officials also demand that they work long hours, sometimes without any rest days all week. The Standard Minimum Rules require prison officials to grant prisoners at least one rest day per week and to comply with domestic legislation on the maximum hours worked each week.[515] The Cuban constitution mandates a maximum eight-hour work day.[516] As of early 1998, in the Boniato Prison in Santiago, the Valle Grande Prison in Havana, and the Las Tunas Provincial Prison, guards reportedly required inmates to work seven-day weeks of ten or more hours per day.[517] The prisoners in these facilities were producing cement blocks, reportedly for private homes for Interior Ministry and military officials, as well as building a cellblock on the prison grounds.

The Standard Minimum Rules require prison work programs to provide inmates with "equitable remuneration," which prisoners can spend on approved articles or send to their families, or which prisons should provide to inmates upon their release.[518] Cuba reportedly violates this provision by paying nothing to the vast majority of working inmates. Yet, the Cuban government reported to the United Nations that, "prisoners were... paid on the same basis as the rest of the population."[519] Prison authorities also arbitrarily deny promised wages, "discount"

---

[514] Human Rights Watch telephone interviews with Guillermo Ismael Sambra Ferrándiz, Toronto, May 8, 1988; and René Portelles, Toronto, April 21, 1998; and interviews with Adriano González Marichal, Toronto, April 14, 1998; and Marcos Antonio Hernández García, Toronto, April 13, 1998.

[515] Standard Minimum Rules, Article 75(1) and (2).

[516] Article 46, Constitution of the Republic of Cuba (1992).

[517] Human Rights Watch telephone interview with Guillermo Ismael Sambra Ferrándiz, May 8, 1998; and interviews with Adriano González Marichal, April 14, 1998, and Marcos Antonio Hernández García, April 13, 1998.

[518] Standard Minimum Rules, Article 76.

[519] Summary Record of the Second Part of the 310th Meeting, CAT/C/SR.310/Add.1 (March 25, 1998), para. 18.

wages with deductions for food and clothing costs, and refuse to pay prisoners their accumulated wages upon release.[520] As of early 1998 in the Agüica Prison in Matanzas, for example, officials reportedly promised prisoners a wage of twenty cents of a Cuban peso, (or U.S. 1 cent) per day to make mattresses. In contrast to Cuba's statements before the U.N., this amount is far below Cuba's minimum wage.[521] The officials discounted this wage for food and clothing costs and often refused to pay prisoners at all. On average, each prisoner reportedly could produce one mattress a day, which the prison authorities sold in local stores for approximately 1,000 pesos (or U.S.$47.62).[522]

The Cuban prison labor program's sales of prisoner-made products, such as mattresses, in conjunction with the refusal to pay inmates for their work, highlighted Cuba's apparent interest in profiting from prison labor, rather than rehabilitating prisoners. Beyond selling to domestic markets, some former prisoners told Human Rights Watch that they produced items for sale in Cuban government dollar stores or made materials for use in the Cuban tourism industry. Rosalina González Lafita worked in the Manto Negro Prison in Havana for over ten years, until February 1998. She believed that the government sold the bluejeans she sewed, which reportedly bore Jordache and Lois labels among others, in dollar stores, along with some lingerie and other clothing sewn in the prison.[523] At the Boniato Prison in Santiago, some prisoners reportedly were sent off the prison grounds to work on restaurant and cafeteria construction projects.

---

[520] Human Rights Watch telephone interviews with José Miranda Acosta, Toronto, May 7, 1998; Guillermo Ismael Sambra Ferrándiz, May 8, 1988; René Portelles, April 21, 1998; Víctor Reynaldo Infante Estrada, Toronto, April 14, 1998; Rosalina González Lafita, Toronto, April 13, 1998; Luis Alberto Ferrándiz Alfaro, April 13, 1998; Adriano González Marichal, April 14, 1998; and Marcos Antonio Hernández García, April 13, 1998.

[521] Cuba sets minimum wages according to profession, with some of the lowest paid work paying approximately 160 pesos per month. The monthly wage of a prisoner earning twenty cents per day, and working every day of a thirty-day month, would be 6 pesos (or U.S. 29 cents).

[522] Human Rights Watch interview with Víctor Reynaldo Infante Estrada, Toronto, April 14, 1998.

[523] Human Rights Watch interview with Rosalina González Lafita, Toronto, April 13, 1998.

Prison authorities apparently coerce some prisoners into working by threatening to deny prison benefits, including family visits.[524] This practice violates the Standard Minimum Rules' provision encouraging prison officials to help inmates maintain family and community ties.

Government Repression of Labor Activists

The Cuban Labor Code, Law No. 49 of December 1984, asserts workers' rights to freely associate, to form unions, and to discuss and express opinions about any matter they wish.[525] The labor code also endorses the principle that no worker should be denied a job due to his or her political opinion.[526] But the government's restrictive legal requirements on free association and expression and union formation, together with its repressive activities, form significant impediments to independent labor activism and to free expression. In practice, the government effectively bans independent labor unions. Cuba's Associations Law requires that the state play a prominent role within any legalized association.[527] If independent labor activists or union organizers wish to operate legally, they have no alternative but to subject themselves to restrictive government intervention. The members of the country's only legalized union, the state-controlled CTC, are required under the union's statutes to recognize "the superior leadership of the [Communist] Party [of Cuba] as the... maximum organization of the working class, to make it their own, and to follow its policies."[528]

---

[524] Human Rights Watch interview with Xiomara Aliat Collado, April 13, 1998, and telephone interview with Guillermo Ismael Sambra Ferrándiz, May 8, 1988.

[525] Articles 13 and 14, Law No. 49 (December 1984).

[526] Article 3(b), Law No. 49 (1984).

[527] Under Cuban law, agricultural cooperatives are considered labor entities and treated distinctly from associations. Article 19 and 20, Constitution of the Republic of Cuba and Article 7(ch), Law No. 49. The prominent state role in "independent" associations is detailed above, at *Impediments to Human Rights in Cuban Law: Associations Law.*

[528] Preamble, Statutes of the Workers' Central of Cuba (1992). See also International Confederation of Free Trade Unions (ICFTU), Cuba C87/C98, *ICFTU Annual Survey of Violations of Trade Union Rights - 1998* (July 1998). Translation by Human Rights Watch.

CTC members also should embrace "the struggle for the defense of Socialism and its principles."[529] CTC leaders double as high level government officials. The labor code recognizes the right of the CTC secretary general to participate in meetings with the government's powerful Council of Ministers and its executive committee.[530] At the union's May 1998 plenary meeting, which other politburo members attended, the CTC urged workers to "undertake a permanent, united battle against any antisocial activity that, if it were to spread, could endanger the existence of the Revolution."[531]

The government actively represses the handful of independent labor rights groups that have formed in recent years and has failed even to respond to their requests for legalization. The barriers to the formation of viable independent unions are daunting, and the number of workers willing to attempt to organize their colleagues remains relatively small.

Government Control over Employment

The Cuban government's virtual monopoly on jobs allows it to exercise tight control over the nation's workforce. Cuban authorities maintain labor files (*expedientes laborales*), which record any individual's politically suspect behavior.[532] Often, the government's first move against potential dissenters is to fire them from their job. Most of Cuba's prominent dissidents lost their jobs as they became more involved in independent organizations or rejoined society after prison terms imposed for criticizing the government. Since jobs in the non-state-controlled sector are few, and rarely include housing, job loss often spells financial disaster for workers and their families. Dissidents who cannot count on remittances

---

[529] The government-controlled *Granma Diario* reported that the CTC had adopted this goal at its eighth plenary session. Silvia Martínez and Emilio del Barrio, "VIII Pleno del Comité Nacional de la CTC: Encara el Movimiento Obrero la Lucha contra el Delito y Otras Deformaciones," *Granma Diario*, May 27, 1998. Translation by Human Rights Watch.

[530] Article 16, Law No. 49 (1984).

[531] Silvia Martínez and Emilio del Barrio, "VII Pleno del Comité Nacional de la CTC," *Granma Diario*, May 27, 1998. Translation by Human Rights Watch.

[532] The labor code defined the labor files as records of the employee's job performance that are maintained by supervisors at his or her job. However, Cuban State Security agents and others reportedly used the files to track workers' political or anti-government views, or those of their family members. Article 61, Law No. 49 (1984).

from abroad have a particularly difficult time and risk further problems with the government if economic necessity pushes them to violate regulations on individual employment. Cuba only allows limited opportunities for self-employment, such as selling produce, driving taxis, and running small restaurants, which are heavily regulated.[533]

In February 1998 the government responded aggressively to Dr. Oscar Elías Biscet González when he spoke out at his workplace, the October 10 Maternal and Children's Hospital (Hospital Maternal e Infantil 10 de Octubre) about his opposition to abortion and the death penalty, both legal in Cuba. Dr. Biscet González, who is a leader of the Lawton Human Rights Foundation, made public a written document he had authored stating his views. In early March, the Provincial Directorate of the Public Health Ministry notified Dr. Biscet González that he had been fired, and that since his apartment was a job benefit, he also would be evicted from his home. Shortly thereafter, his wife, nurse Elsa Morejón Hernández, was also fired. Local authorities also urged her to terminate her marriage because of his outspoken dissent. At this writing, some former patients had allowed the couple to live with them. In an interview with Human Rights Watch, the doctor noted ironically that, having formerly treated indigent patients, he and his wife had become dependent on their generosity.[534]

On February 19, 1997, Dr. Pedro Emilio Pacheco Pérez, a professor at the Stomach Clinic (Clínica Estomatología) in Santiago, was officially notified that he would be removed from his position due to his participation as an organizer of the Movement of Followers of Chibás (Movimiento Seguidores de Chibás).[535]

A journalist with the independent *Cuba Press* news agency, Efrén Martínez Pulgarón, said that his removal from the workforce, like that of most of his colleagues, occurred over a long period. He said that in 1992, he had been working as a professor of plastic arts, training primary school teachers and, at the same time, he was beginning to take part in dissident activities. Gradually, persistent

---

[533] While Cuba's private sector reportedly had grown to include some 208,000 people in 1996, by September 1998, it had shrunk to some 143,406 people. The decrease stemmed from heavy regulations and taxes. "Cuba: Cuba's Small Private Sector Shrinks," *Reuters News Service*, September 11, 1998.

[534] Human Rights Watch telephone interview with Dr. Biscet González, Havana, July 28, 1998. Further state actions against Dr. Biscet González are detailed aoove, at *Routine Repression*.

[535] "Expulsan a prestigioso profesor por actividades oposicionistas," *Oriente Press* and *Buró de Prensa Independiente de Cuba*, February 21, 1997.

government reports of his dissident activities resulted in a decision to terminate his contact with future teachers. He then found a job as a guard in a public park, but, after several months, was told that his counterrevolutionary views and access to children in the park were incompatible, and he was fired. Since 1993, he has been unable to find work and has faced multiple arrests.[536]

The family members of political prisoners and former political prisoners also face workplace discrimination. Most former prisoners are barred from any state-controlled job. Their close relatives also are frustrated by fruitless job hunts. Edelmira Matamoros Espejo, the wife of former political prisoner Edelberto Del Toro Argota, sought steady work for years while her husband was in prison. Cuban authorities convicted Del Toro Argota of enemy propaganda in March 1994. At that time, Matamoros Espejo had worked for twenty-six years as an operator for the national telephone company, where she had an excellent work record. In 1995, her supervisor advised her that she had been fired. She could not find a new position until 1996, when she reported for a job at the post office. She had taken a postal exam and passed with a 98 percent score. Nonetheless, her supervisor at the post office fired her after only four hours. She later learned that her supervisors had been notified that she "was not trustworthy enough to work in communications."[537]

Government Refusal to Legalize Independent Workers' Organizations

Independent labor rights groups face numerous stumbling blocks in their efforts to gain legal status in Cuba, chiefly those posed by the limitations inherent in the Associations Law. The United Council of Cuban Workers (Consejo Unitario de Trabajadores Cubanos, CUTC), for example, solicited legalization shortly after it was formed in July 1995. In October 1996, the Cuban Institute for Independent Labor Studies (Instituto Cubano de Estudios Sindicales Independientes, ICESI), which was formed in July 1996, also filed for recognition. At this writing, the government has not responded to either request. The director of the government-controlled workers' newspaper *Trabajadores* did not respond to the CUTC's request for space in the publication to reflect workers' concerns. The Confederation of Democratic Workers of Cuba (Confederación de Trabajadores Democráticos de Cuba, CTDC) has solicited government legalization on an annual basis for six years without receiving any response.

---

536 Human Rights Watch telephone interview with Efrén Martínez Pulgarón, *Cuba Press*, Havana, January 13, 1999.

537 Human Rights Watch interviews with Edilberto Del Toro Argota and Edelmira Matamoros Espejo, Toronto, April 12, 1998.

Detentions and Harassment of Labor Rights Activists

In contrast to the lack of official response to organizations' requests for legalization, the Cuban government has swiftly answered labor activism with repressive measures. Several activists have suffered brief police detentions, often accompanied by threats of future prosecution.

Havana police reportedly detained José Orlando González Bridón, of the CTDC, for brief periods in November and December 1998 and January 1999. On each occasion, González Bridón was participating in protests of dissidents' trials. Cuban officials arrested his colleague Ofelia Nardo Cruz, an attorney with the same organization, on January 6, 1999, holding her for a few hours.

Cuban officials also detained González Bridón for twenty-four hours in July and for several hours on September 8 and 23, 1998. In July, a Rapid Response Brigade composed of members of the neighborhood CDR, local workers, and others threatened González Bridón and his fifteen-year-old son. Police refused to receive his complaint about the brigade's actions.[538]

In September 1998 several state security agents reportedly told Rafael Peraza Fonte, the Havana representative for the CUTC, to appear at their office for a meeting. When he arrived, the agents apparently threatened him with prosecution, saying that they already had sufficient evidence to try him and would not warn him again. In early August, four members of a Rapid Response Brigade visited Peraza Fonte's home, criticizing his independent organizing work and threatening violence if he continued it.[539] In July, Havana police reportedly searched the home of another CUTC member, Rafael Iturralde Bello, confiscating several documents.[540]

On July 2, 1998, Havana police detained Evaristo Pérez Rodríguez, the vice-president of the Cuban Union of Independent Workers (Unión Sindical de Trabajadores Independientes de Cuba, USTIC) and the president of the Patriotic Union of Independent Christians (Unión Patriótica de Cristianos Independientes). He remained in police custody for seventy-two hours.[541]

---

[538] Human Rights Watch telephone interview with Odilia Collazo, Pro Human Rights Party, Havana, January 11, 1999.

[539] Rafael Peraza Fonte, "Represión en Artemisa," *Villa Roja*, October 23, 1998.

[540] Ibid.

[541] Florentino Ledesma Pérez, "Detenido Sindicalista No Oficial," *El Nuevo Herald*, July 7, 1998.

On November 11, 1997, Cuban police searched the homes of CUTC Secretary General Pedro Pablo Alvarez Ramos and ICESI leader Vicente Escobal Rabeiro, seizing several items that were never returned.[542] Cuban police detained several CTDC leaders for brief periods throughout 1997. In early October, police detained CTDC secretariat members Jorge Martínez and Florentino Ledesma, holding them overnight and urging them to abandon their union activities.[543] On September 24, 1997, security agents arrested union member Ramón González Fonseca and CTDC Secretary General Gustavo Toirac González, holding them for about twelve hours.[544]

In recent years, a handful of farmers have been trying to form independent agricultural cooperatives, as an alternative to the state-controlled group, the National Association of Small Farmers (Asociación Nacional de Agricultores Pequeños). On several occasions, these groups, in their efforts to raise farmers' concerns, have suffered from harassment and short-term detentions.[545]

In mid-October 1998 Cuban police in Santiago reportedly required three members of the Transition Cooperative and the National Alliance of Independent Farmers of Cuba (Alianza Nacional de Agricultores Independientes de Cuba, ANAIC), Camilo Berenguer Alonso, Juan San Emeterio Berenguer, and Raúl Ruíz Bonne, to report to local offices of the Interior Ministry. The police apparently interrogated the men about their activities and encouraged them to abandon their nongovernmental organizations.[546]

Cuban authorities prevented the First Meeting of Independent Cooperatives (Primer Encuentro Inter-Cooperativas Independientes), scheduled for May 5, 1998, from taking place in Loma del Gato, Santiago province. Several regional cooperatives had invited the official press, the police, the Communist Party, and

---

[542] Human Rights Watch telephone interview with Vicente Escobar Rabeiro, ICESI director, Havana, June 26, 1998.

[543] "Persecución a Dirigentes Sindiciales Independientes," *Agencia de Prensa Independiente de Cuba,* November 8, 1997.

[544] Cuba C87/C98, *ICFTU Annual Survey of Violations of Trade Union Rights - 1998*, July 1998.

[545] André Linard, "Down on the Farm: Trade Unions in Cuba," *ICFTU OnLine*, ICFTU, June 25, 1998.

[546] "Amenaza Policía Política a Cooperativistas Independientes," *CubaNet*, October 22, 1998.

others to discuss the problems of Cuban farmers in an "environment of national reconciliation." On May 3 police arrested Reynaldo Hernández, the president of both the ANAIC and the Progreso I agricultural and fishing cooperative in Guantánamo. Cuban authorities released Hernández on the evening of May 5.[547] A state security official had detained Hernández in March, holding him for several hours and threatening him with criminal prosecution if he did not abandon his organizing activities and specifically, his plans for the May meeting. On May 5, over one dozen police and members of a Rapid Response Brigade thwarted the meeting's occurrence by blocking access to the site. They also surrounded the home of Jorge Béjar, the president of the Transition Cooperative and host of the conference, detaining him and his wife for several hours.[548]

On May 13, 1998, a local official, Rosa Concepción Sarmiento, reportedly threatened Antonio Alonzo Pérez, the vice-president of the Transition Cooperative, saying that he would be found dead in the street. She also fined him 500 pesos (approximately US$23.81) for allegedly "having deficiently made use of or having negligently abandoned" land that was in his use.[549] Alonso Pérez challenged the accusation that he had neglected to work his land. The fine and threat appear designed to discourage him from his work with the cooperative.

Cuban authorities held Jesús Escandel, the former international relations secretary of the government-controlled CTC, in detention without trial from July 1997 until April 1998. Police reportedly beat him shortly after his arrest, while questioning him in Villa Marista. The government reportedly threatened him with prosecution for treason, but the reasons for his lengthy detention remained unclear. Escandel may have raised official ire by meeting with independent labor groups during his travels outside of Cuba.

Manuel Antonio Brito López, the secretary general for the Union of Independent Workers (Union de Trabajadores Independiente) and the human rights coordinator for the CUTC, was called to a Havana police station on July 12, 1997, and interrogated for several hours by state security agents. The agents told him to

---

[547] Santiago Santana, "Detienen a Dirigente Campesino," *Agencia de Prensa Libre Oriental en El Nuevo Herald*, May 5, 1998.

[548] Santiago Santana, "Régimen Frustra Encuentro de Cooperativas Independientes," *Agencia de Prensa Libre Oriental en El Nuevo Herald*, May 7, 1998.

[549] Alonso Pérez reportedly was fined under Decree-Law 203, Article 1, section E. Translation by Human Rights Watch. Letter from Antonio Alonso Pérez to Alfredo Jordán Morales, Minister, Ministry of Agriculture, May 25, 1998, distributed by *CubaNet*, June 4, 1998.

remain in his neighborhood until August 6th, the day that the International World Festival of Youth and Students was scheduled to conclude elsewhere in Havana.[550]

Labor Rights in the International Investment Sector

In recent years, Cuba has devoted tremendous energy at the highest levels of government to attracting foreign investment in recent years. In February 1998 Carlos Lage, the secretary of the executive committee of the Council of Ministers, which oversees all foreign investment in Cuba, described the Cuban economy's principal problem as a shortfall in foreign financing. Under the Cuban constitution, the executive committee comprises the president, the vice presidents, and "other members of the Council of Ministers determined by the President."[551] The Council of Ministers is "the top-ranking executive and administrative organ, and constitutes the Government of the Republic."[552] Lage urged the Ministry for Foreign Investment and Economic Collaboration (Ministerio para la Inversión Extranjera y la Colaboración Económica, MINVEC) to seek long-term investors and acquire new technologies and markets.[553]

MINVEC reported that by September 1998, 340 economic associations with foreign capital were operating in Cuba. Canada, Spain, and Italy were the top investors, followed by France, Holland, the United Kingdom, and Mexico. Most foreign capital was concentrated in petroleum extraction, mining (particularly of nickel), telecommunications, and tourism. Lesser amounts of capital were invested in construction materials, electronics, food products, energy, and other sectors. Minister for Foreign Investment and Economic Collaboration Ibrahim Ferradaz stated that in the 1990s, tourism grew 20 percent each year, with some one million tourist visits in 1996 and two million projected for 2000.[554] As the most important foreign investment growth area, Cuba planned to increase its tourist capacity from

---

[550] Manuel David Orrio, "Hostigado Sindicalista Independiente Cubano," *Agencia Nueva Prensa*, July 21, 1998.

[551] Article 97, Constitution of the Republic of Cuba (1992). Translation by Human Rights Watch.

[552] Ibid., Article 95. Translation by Human Rights Watch.

[553] Susana Lee, "Hay que Atraer las Inversiones Extranjeras que Garanticen los Objetivos Básicos del País," *Granma Diario*, February 19, 1998.

[554] Susana Lee, "En el País Más de 340 Asociaciones Económicas con Capital Extranjero," *Granma Diario*, September 10, 1998.

some 27,000 hotel rooms in late 1997 to 50,000 rooms by the year 2000.[555] At the November 1998 National Meeting of Tourist Entities, where Carlos Lage presided, Minister of Work and Social Security Salvador Valdés reported that Cuba has 75,940 workers in the tourist sector and plans to add some 30,000 more by 2001.[556]

To entice international investors, Cuba has adopted several laws that tightly control labor rights in businesses backed by foreign investment. Under these laws, detailed below, the government plays a prominent role in the selection, payment, and firing of workers, thus effectively barring most employees from forming unions or even from entering into independent, direct discussions of labor rights with their employers. These restrictions on labor rights—Cuba's virtual guarantee that no investor will face any independent union organizing in the workplace—were created to attract foreign investors. Cubans nonetheless find jobs in the foreign investment sector attractive. Although Cuban workers receive peso salaries from state-controlled employment agencies, the jobs often offer access to dollar tips or bonuses and scarce consumer goods, such as shampoo and soap. The Cuban government profits from this arrangement as well, not only from the long-term value of international investment, but also because the state-controlled employment agencies receive convertible foreign currency payments for all workers' wages.[557] The government has not revealed what percentage of workers' wages ultimately

---

[555] Rodolfo Casals, "Escápate al Caribe, Escápate a Cuba," *Granma Internacional*, September 16, 1997. Tourism is a lightning rod for public frustration due to a practice popularly known as "tourist apartheid," whereby security guards frequently bar Cuban nationals from entering hotels, beaches, restaurants, and other tourist facilities. The constitutional provisions that should deter such practices are detailed above, at *Impediments to Human Rights in Cuban Law: Cuban Constitution.*

[556] Iraida Calzadilla Rodríguez, "Reunión Nacional de Entidades Turísticas: El Sistema Muestra una Dinámica Mayor hasta Septiembre," *Granma Diario*, November 4, 1998.

As Cuba has sought greater opportunities for foreign investment, the Armed Forces have taken on increased responsibility for economic growth. Luis Pérez Róspide, a brigade general (*general de brigada*) and the director of the military's business operations, the Union of Military Industries (Unión de las Industrias Militares, UIM), also runs Gaviota, one of Cuba's top state-run tourist companies. Octavio La Vastida, "Industrias Militares en la Senda de la Eficiencia," *Granma Internacional*, September 3, 1997; and "Cuba: Jamaican Hotel Chain to Boost Presence in Cuba," *Reuters News Service*, September 18, 1998.

[557] Article 33 (4) and Article 34(1), Foreign Investment Law, Decree Law No. 77 (September 1995).

reach their hands—in Cuban pesos—and what portion remains in government coffers. Unfortunately, the foreign investment laws replicate the failings of labor rights practices throughout Cuba, leaving control over employees in the hands of a government that has created legal bars to free association and expression. While foreign companies reportedly insist on safety regulations beyond those typically employed in Cuban workplaces, foreign investors hoping to improve basic labor rights face daunting obstacles. Given the current regulations governing labor rights in the foreign investment sector, foreign investment carries with it a high risk that foreign companies will be complicit in the Cuban government's labor rights abuses.

Foreign governments interested in investing in Cuba face the notable challenge of reconciling investment interests with concurrent concern for human rights. The fact that Cuba's highest authorities control Cuba's human rights policies and labor rights practices, while also holding the keys to any major foreign investment project in Cuba, might dissuade foreign governments from making clear statements on human rights that would impede future investments. Thus, British Trade Minister Brian Wilson, visiting Havana in November 1998, acknowledged the European Union's common position linking future economic coooperation on on human rights improvements in Cuba, but emphasized that "I am here purely to talk about trade."[558] Distancing himself even further from human rights concerns, he added that "...Britain has no hang-ups at all about promoting trade in Cuba."[559]

Labor Rights Under the Foreign Investment Act

In recent years, the Cuban government adopted new laws to encourage foreign investment.[560] The Foreign Investment Act permits foreign investment in three

---

[558] The European Union's common position is detailed below, at *International Policy*.

[559] Andrew Cawthorne, "Cuba: British Minister Glows over 'Superb' Castro Meeting," *Reuters News Service*, November 3, 1998.

[560] Decree Law No. 77, the Foreign Investment Act of 1995, sets out the fundamental principles guiding foreign investment. The preamble states that it was "convenient to adopt new legislation to provide greater security and guarantees to the foreign investor." The preamble also notes that Cuba could benefit from foreign investment following the demise of the socialist block and in light of "the fierce blockade" imposed by the United States. Preamble, Decree Law No. 77 (September 1995). Translation by the Cuban government.

The law's labor provisions are detailed further in Resolution No. 3/96, Regulations on the Labor System in Foreign Investment (March 1996) and Decree Law No.

distinct manners, each of which leaves control over employee hiring and firing in the hands of state-controlled actors. Joint ventures bring together national (Cuban) investors and international investors, resulting in the creation of a separate legal entity that must be registered with Cuba's Chamber of Commerce.[561] Totally foreign capital companies do not include any Cuban national investors, but others must present a request to MINVEC "jointly with the corresponding Cuban entity."[562] Both joint ventures and totally foreign capital companies must rely on government "employing entit[ies]" to hire employees and negotiate employee contracts for them.[563] The foreign investment law defines "international economic association contracts" as pacts among one or more national investors and one or more international investors for joint activities, without the formation of a separate legal entity.[564] The Cuban investors, who are state-controlled since Cuba does not permit private investment, are responsible for hiring workers.[565] While international companies are granted the right to select and hire "certain top administrative positions or some posts of a technical nature" with persons who are not permanent residents of Cuba, government-controlled or approved institutions are charged with all other employment contracting.[566]

166, On Violation of the Personal [sic] Hiring System and Other Labor Regulations (July 1996). Decree Law No. 166. Translation by the Cuban government.

Law 165 on Free Zones and Industrial Parks (June 1996) sets rules for investment in Cuban duty-free zones and industrial parks. Decree Law No. 165. Translation by the Cuban government.

561 Decree Law No. 77, Article 13.

562 Ibid., Article 22.

563 Ibid., Article 33 (1) and (3). These entities are to be proposed by MINVEC and authorized by the Ministry of Labor and Social Security.

564 Ibid., Article 2 (g).

565 Ibid., Article 2(a) and (g) and Article 33 (2). If the Cuban investors wish to offer workers foreign exchange wages, they must first get approval from the Ministry of Labor. Article 18, Resolution No. 3/96 (March 1996).

566 Articles 31 and 33, Decree Law No. 77. Translation by the Cuban government.

The regulations governing worker selection, hiring, payment, and firing appear in Resolution No. 3/96, which directs foreign companies to agree to "Labor Force Supply Contract[s]" with the employing entity and with the "relevant trade union."[567] The required reliance on state-controlled employment agencies effectively leaves workers without any capacity to directly negotiate wages, benefits, the basis of promotions, and the length of the worker's trial period at the job with the employer. The state-controlled employment agencies assume each of these roles, rather than allowing the employees to contract independently with the foreign investors.[568] Since Cuba only allows one official umbrella union, the "relevant union" likely would be government-controlled.

The reliance on state employment agencies in the foreign investment sector increases the likelihood that, as in other employment sectors, dissidents would be barred from job openings. Analyzing the performance of the state's employment agencies, Salvador Valdés, Cuba's minister of work and social security, stressed the need to reassure the population that the "most revolutionary" individuals were chosen for the tens of thousands of jobs in the tourist sector.[569] The government has acknowledged through the public disciplining of several state employment agency employees that some positions were acquired with bribes. In March 1998 the government apparently uncovered fraudulent hiring practices at the state-controlled Isla Azul employment agency in the resort community of Varadero. The government sentenced three agency employees to prison terms ranging from ten to twelve years for demanding bribes of up to US $700 for jobs in tourism.[570] The job selection process apparently also is skewed by nepotism and cronyism.

In Cuba's booming tourist industry, on-the-job racism has emerged as a persistent problem. While Cuban labor laws prohibit job discrimination based on race, the vast majority of Cuban employees in tourist operations are light-skinned. As with other foreign investment sectors, government-controlled employment agencies conduct hiring for the tourist industry. One manager in a tourist corporation explained, "There is no explicit policy stating that one has to be white

---

[567] Article 7, Resolution No. 3/96. Translation by the Cuban government.

[568] Ibid., Articles 9, 12, and 14.

[569] Valdés's comments were paraphrased by the state-supported newspaper *Granma Diario*. Iraida Calzadilla Rodríguez, "Reunión Nacional de Entidades Turísticas," *Granma Diario*, November 4, 1998.

[570] "Cuba: Cuban Court Jails Three for Selling Tourism Jobs," *Reuters News Service*, March 12, 1998.

to work in tourism, but it is regulated that people must have a pleasant appearance (*aspecto agradable*), and blacks do not have it...." Alejandro de la Fuente, a university professor who researched this phenomenon, noted that increased foreign investment in tourism was worsening the job situation for Cubans with darker skin. He hypothesized that Cuban officials were conceding to the wishes of tourist operation managers who preferred lighter-skinned employees.[571]

Cuba's new laws also establish conditions for firing workers, some of which restrict free expression and association. Workers risk firing if they "incur improper conduct, criminal or not, affecting his/her prestige as a company employee and contrary to the standards of conduct... annexed" to the resolution.[572] The standards, which cover a wide range of non-job-related expression and behavior, leave workers at risk of removal for expression of political views. Among other things, the standards require workers "to maintain social conduct worthy of his/her fellow citizens' respect and trust, by not allowing any conspicuous signs or privileges, and by keeping a life-style in line with our society."[573] In addition to sharply limiting freedom of expression, a requirement that workers not speak to their employers or supervisors about payments, gifts, or preferential treatment effectively prohibits bargaining over wages, a fundamental labor right.

Workers risk harsh disciplinary measures if they fail to comply with the resolution's provisions. If a worker commits an "infringement," then she or he could face a penalty such as public censure or the loss of 25 percent of the monthly wage. Other possible sanctions include transfer to a lower-paying post or dismissal. The employing entity is charged with applying the penalty after considering factors including "the personal qualities of the wrongdoer," which potentially grant it authority to penalize workers for expression or activities completely unrelated to

---

[571] Alejandro de la Fuente cited this interview in "Recreating Racism: Racism and Discrimination in Cuba's 'Special Period,'" *Cuba Briefing Paper Series*, The Caribbean Project, Georgetown University (July 1998), pp. 6-7.

[572] Article 29, Resolution No. 3/96. Translation by the Cuban government.

[573] The law also requires workers "to act according to the best interests of our society"; "...to subordinate his/her acts and decisions to the best interests of our people"; and "to neither accept from, nor ask the persons above or around him/her for any payments, gifts or preferential treatment contrary to the adequate labor and personal behavior expected from our cadre and workers...." Ibid., Exhibit: Standards of Conduct Applicable to Cuban Staff in International Economic Associations. Translation by the Cuban government.

their jobs.[574] Under the personnel law, any Cuban who independently contracts with foreign representatives risks government fines ranging from 1,000 to 10,000 Cuban or convertible pesos.[575] If the individual cannot pay the fine in cash or property he or she could face criminal charges.[576]

Foreigners violating these regulations, such as using workers not legally hired, changing the legally authorized forms of payment, or giving non-authorized material incentives, face the same consequences (with all fines due in convertible pesos).[577]

In keeping with the Council of Minister's constitutional authority over foreign commerce, the Foreign Investment Act assigns its executive committee a close supervisory role over all foreign investment.[578] The law directs the executive committee to approve all foreign capital investments or designate a government commission with authority to do so and grants it the right to disregard the law's provisions and "establish special labor regulations" in "exceptional cases."[579] In this capacity, the highest levels of the Cuban government can directly and arbitrarily control labor rights in the foreign investment sector. The law on hiring also affords the executive committee of the Council of Ministers broad powers to include or exclude violations and to vary the amount of fines.[580]

Labor Rights in the Free Trade Zones and Industrial Parks

On November 5, 1997, Cuba opened its first duty-free zones (*zonas francas*) in Berroa, Wajay, and Mariel. Some of the first contracts in the Mariel zone included a Canadian company manufacturing wood paneling for homebuilding and

---

[574] Ibid., Articles 47 and 48. Translation by the Cuban government.

[575] Articles 10, 11, and 12, Decree Law No. 166 (July 1996). Translation by the Cuban government.

[576] Ibid., Article 34. Translation by the Cuban government.

[577] Ibid., Articles 6, 10, 11, 12, and 34.

[578] Decree Law No. 77 and Article 97, Constitution of the Republic of Cuba (1992).

[579] Article 2(b) and (e), Article 35, Decree Law No. 77. Translation by the Cuban government.

[580] Special Provision 1, Decree Law No. 165.

a Russian catamaran assembly factory.[581] Cuba has undertaken extensive promotion efforts to draw foreign investors to these zones. As with other foreign investments, Cuba maintains tight restrictions on labor rights and public order for the explicit purpose of attracting investors to the free trade zones.

In June 1996 the government adopted Law 165 on Free Zones and Industrial Parks.[582] The law creates an executive committee of state institutions—including the Ministry of the Revolutionary Armed Forces and the Ministry of the Interior—charged with granting free zone concessions and recommending measures to develop the zones and industrial parks.[583] The law provides for a special system to operate in the duty-free zones "as an incentive for investment" that included labor and public order regulations that were "more attractive and less rigid and onerous than the common or usual ones."[584] The law requires investors with completely foreign capital to hire their employees through employment agencies approved by the ministries of foreign investment and labor, thus engendering the same impediments to free association and expression discussed above. The law also allows the executive committee to disregard other labor norms and establish special labor regulations in "exceptional cases," an unchecked authority providing the potential for further abuse.[585]

Best Business Principles for Foreign Investors in Cuba

The Cuban government's broad authority over labor rights in the foreign investment sector effectively frustrates those companies that endorse "best business principles," such as respect for workers' right to organize, anti-discriminatory hiring

---

[581] "Tercera Zona Franca Inaugurada en Mariel," *Business Tips on Cuba*, Havana, January 1998, p. 8.

[582] The duty-free zones and industrial parks allow diverse types of foreign investment. Duty-free zones allow foreign investment "for the purposes of financial operations, importing, exporting, storage, productive activities or reexporting." Industrial parks allow "the development of productive activities with the participation of foreign capital." Law No. 77, Article 51(1) and (2).

[583] Article 6(2) and (4), Decree Law No. 165.

[584] Ibid., Article 31.1. Translation by the Cuban government.

[585] Ibid., Article 46. Translation by the Cuban government.

practices, and workplace safety.[586] In 1997, in order to encourage socially-responsible investing in Cuba, the North American Committee of the National Policy Association, a coalition of business leaders in Canada, Mexico, and the United States, devised "Principles for Private Sector Involvement in Cuba," urging companies, among other steps, to: "work to gain the right to recruit, contract, pay and promote workers directly, not through government intermediaries;" "respect employees' right to organize freely in the workplace;" and, "maintain a corporate culture that... does not condone political coercion in the workplace."[587] The Committee also recommends the strengthening of "legal procedure in Cuba," but this suggestion does not sufficiently take into account the impediments to labor rights that must be lifted before workers' rights will be protected under law. In 1994 the Cuban Committee for Human Rights, the International Society for Human Rights, and Solidarity of Cuban Workers prepared the Arcos Principles, honoring one of Cuba's leading human rights activists, Gustavo Arcos. The Arcos Principles also urge companies to seek to hire workers directly, to bar the review of workers' government-prepared labor files (*expedientes laborales*), and to allow workers to belong to governmental or independent unions.[588]

---

[586] Gillian McGillivray, "Trading with the 'Enemy': Canadian-Cuban Relations in the 1990s," *Cuba Briefing Paper Series,* The Caribbean Project, Georgetown University (December 1997), p. 7.

[587] "Trilateral Group Urges Private Sector to Play a Role in Promoting Human Rights in Cuba," National Policy Association Press Release, July 7, 1997.

[588] Rolando H. Castañeda and George Plinio Montalván, "The Arcos Principles," Cuban Committee for Human Rights, the International Society for Human Rights and Solidarity of Cuban Workers, 1994.

X. LIMITS ON RELIGIOUS FREEDOM

> *The Church calls all to bring their faith to life... in order to achieve true liberty, which includes the recognition of human rights and social justice.*
>
> *Pope John Paul II, Homily in Santiago, Cuba, January 24, 1998*

> *...The Cuban people cannot be deprived of links to other peoples that are necessary for their economic, social, and cultural development, especially when the isolation provokes indiscriminate repercussions in the population, exaggerating the difficulties of the most weak in basic respects, as with food, health, and education. Everyone can and should take concrete steps for a change in this respect.*
>
> *Pope John Paul II, Farewell Address at the José Martí International Airport, Havana, January 25, 1998*

Pope John Paul II's January 1998 visit to Cuba sparked hope that the government would ease its repressive tactics and would allow greater religious freedom. The papal visit provided unprecedented opportunities for public demonstrations of faith in a country that imposed tight restrictions on religious expression in 1960 and was officially atheist until 1992. Although Cuba refused visas to some foreign journalists and pressured some domestic critics, the pope's calls for freedom of religion, conscience, and expression created an unprecedented air of openness. But while Cuba permits greater opportunities for religious expression than it did in past years, and has allowed several religious-run humanitarian groups to operate, the government still maintains tight control on religious institutions, affiliated groups, and individual believers. Since the exercise of religious freedom is closely linked to other freedoms, including those of expression, association, and assembly, Cuban believers face multiple restrictions on religious expression.

Cuba's reluctance to lift additional bars on religious expression likely stems from the status of Cuban churches as among the country's few nongovernmental institutions with national scope. The Catholic church, which claims as adherents some 70 percent of Cuba's population—although only a small portion of these are practicing Catholocism—stands as the largest, best organized, national, nongovernmental institution.[589] Practicioners of Afro-Cuban faiths, including Santería and La Regla de Ocha, are believed to be second to Catholics in numbers, while Protestant churches, Jehovah's Witnesses, and Jews comprise smaller denominations.[590] Despite substantial impediments to religious expression, which are detailed below, Cuba's faithful have made progress in recent years. For example, Cuba apparently has improved its treatment of the nation's approximately 80,000 Jehovah's Witnesses, who previously encountered government harassment due to their religious opposition to military service and participation in pro-government organizations. At a December 1998 international conference of Jehovah's Witnesses in Havana, a member of the religion's governing board praised the Cuban government, saying that it "clearly sees that Jehovah's Witnesses form an integral part of the society in which we live."[591] Believers from distinct faiths are holding services, forming community groups, in some cases producing publications—albeit with limited distribution—and offering significant humanitarian assistance to the population.[592]

Yet, Cuba apparently keeps religious groups, particularly the Catholic church, under surveillance. One former Interior Ministry official who reportedly was responsible for questions of national security told the *Miami Herald*, that "The church was always seen as a danger because it is the only force inside the country capable of bringing people together and even organizing a subtle form of resistance." This official and two other high-ranking former Cuban government

---

[589] Tim Golden, "After a Lift, Cuban Church has a Letdown," *New York Times*, September 13, 1998.

[590] There is some cross-over in the numbers of Catholics and believers in Afro-Cuban rites, since the Afro-Cuban religions often require believers to be baptized as Catholics. Practitioners of Afro-Cuban rites faced serious impediments to practicing their faith in the aftermath of the revolution. However, in 1978, the government apparently began promoting several Santería priests-called babalowas-who one expert referred to as "diplo-babalowas," as a tourist draw. Juan Tamayo, "In Cuba Clash Between Religions: Afro-Cuban Creeds, Catholics at Odds," *Miami Herald*, January 12, 1998.

[591] "Se Abre Espacio para Testigos de Jehová," *Reuters New Service* printed in *El Nuevo Herald*, December 26, 1998.

[592] Human Rights Watch telephone interview with Damian Fernández, Ph.D., professor of international relations, Florida International University, Miami, July 15, 1998. Gillian Gunn, Ph.D., "Cuba's NGOs: Government Puppets or Seeds of Civil Society?" *Cuba Briefing Paper Series: Number 7*, Georgetown University Caribbean Project, February 1995.

officials said that Cuba assigned between ten and fifteen intelligence officials to spy on religious institutions.[593]

Cuban law claims to ensure religious freedom, and has allowed for broader religious expression in recent years, yet simultaneously restricts it. In 1992, reforms to the 1976 constitution decreed that Cuba was no longer an atheistic state and that religious freedoms would be guaranteed if they were "based on respect for the law."[594] But Cuba's constitution and other laws create impediments to the freedoms of association, expression, and assembly, all essential aspects of religious expression. Cuba's Criminal Code penalizes "abuse of the freedom of religion," which is broadly defined as invoking a religious basis to oppose educational objectives or the failure to take up arms in the country's defense or to show reverence for the homeland's symbols.[595] While Human Rights Watch does not know of any recent prosecutions for this crime, Cuba's failure to rescind it calls into question the government's commitment to protecting religious rights.

Cuba grants the Department of Attention to Religious Affairs of the Central Committee of the Communist Party (Departamento de Atención a los Asuntos Religiosos del Comité Central del Partido Comunista) a prominent role in overseeing religious institutions. Not surprisingly, religious leaders who support the government face fewer impediments to their activities than do believers who find themselves at odds with the ruling party. At the 1991 Communist Party Fourth Congress, the party decided that religious belief would no longer pose an obstacle

---

[593] Juan O. Tamayo, "Cuba has Long Spied on Church," *Miami Herald*, January 21, 1998. One of the defectors, Dariel Alarcón, a former army colonel, told the *Miami Herald* that he had helped frame a Catholic priest accused of assisting an anti-Castro hijacker who had killed a flight attendant in 1966. Alarcón said that Father Miguel Laredo, who served ten years in prison, was innocent. The government's intelligence-gathering methods are further discussed above, at *Routine Repression*.

[594] Constitution of the Republic of Cuba (1992), Articles 8 and 55. The constitution and Criminal Code provisions on religion and other fundamental freedoms are discussed in detail above, at *Impediments to Human Rights in Cuban Law: Cuban Constitution* and *Codifying Repression*.

[595] Criminal Code, Article 204. This provision is discussed above, at *Codifying Repression*.

to membership.[596] In the wake of this decision, some religious figures are now members of the Communist Party or even political leaders themselves, such as Pablo Odén Marichal, the president of the Cuban Council of Churches (Consejo Cubano de Iglesias), who is a deputy in Cuba's National Assembly. Baptist Minister Raúl Suárez Ramos, with the Cuban Council of Churches, also is a deputy in Cuba's National Assembly, and heads the Martin Luther King Memorial Center, a nongovernmental group with close ties to the government.[597] Suárez Ramos earned government acclaim in 1990 when he lauded the revolution as "a blessing for our poor people" and criticized U.S. policy toward Cuba as an "economic, political, radio, and television aggression."[598] Both deputies often travel internationally and participate in conferences on religion in Cuba. But the party treats distinctly those who do not share its political views. The current head of the party's religious affairs office, Caridad Diego, criticized an American Catholic priest who had worked in the Villa Clara area for supporting "counterrevolutionary groups."[599] The priest, Patrick Sullivan, had posted copies of the Universal Declaration on Human Rights in his church and had urged his parishioners to defend those rights. In April 1998, facing increasing government pressure, Sullivan chose to leave Cuba. Although Cuba and the Vatican had agreed that the pope would visit Cuba in 1989, the Catholic church's failure to condemn the U.S. embargo at that time apparently contributed to the several-year delay in finalizing the visit.[600] When the pope did travel to Cuba in early 1998, the Cuban government trumpeted his criticisms of the U.S. embargo.

---

[596] For a detailed discussion of this decision, see Roman Orozco, *Cuba Roja* (Buenos Aires: Informaci6n y Revistas S.A. Cambio 16 - Javier Vergara Editor S.A., 1993), pp. 587-590.

[597] Frances Kerry, "Spirits in Soup Tureens Await Pope in Cuba," *Reuters News Service*, January 15, 1998; and Homero Campo, "El Gobierno les Ve con Recelo y las Somete a Estrictos Controles," *Proceso*, May 18, 1997.

[598] "Pese a sus errores la Revoluci6n ha Sido una Bendici6n," *Granma*, April 15, 1990, as cited in Orozco, *Cuba Roja*, p. 599.

[599] Tim Golden, "After a Lift, Cuban Church has a Letdown," *New York Times*, September 13, 1998.

[600] Orozco, *Cuba Roja*, pp. 594-596.

Pope John Paul II's Visit to Cuba

On a positive note, the government allowed massive public demonstrations of faith during the pope's January 1998 visit to Cuba. The pope presided over four open-air Catholic masses, in Santa Clara, Camagüey, Santiago, and Havana. Tens of thousands of Cubans attended, hearing the pope's exhortations for freedom of religion and conscience, which also were broadcast on Cuban state-controlled television. In a remarkable visual display, Cuban authorities allowed a huge mural of the Sacred Heart of Jesus to rise in the Plaza of the Revolution, where it stood for the papal mass between statues of Cuban heroes Ernesto "Ché" Guevara and José Martí. The government not only allowed citizens to attend papal masses, but encouraged them to do so, calling on the Committees for the Defense of the Revolution and other mass organizations to turn out as well. However, government agents reportedly notified some dissidents that they should not attend the papal events. At the papal mass in Havana, some government supporters reportedly attempted to drown out the cries of "liberty" from the crowd. Two men and one woman who criticized the government reportedly were arrested at the same mass, one by state security agents and the other by men wearing Cuban Red Cross uniforms.[601] Cuba also had failed to grant dozens of foreign reporters and some international human rights activists permission to travel to Cuba for the papal pilgrimage.[602]

In his speeches and homilies, Pope John Paul II urged respect for human rights and called for the unconditional release of political prisoners. At the mass in Havana, the pope stated that liberation "finds its fullness in the exercise of the freedom of conscience, the base and foundation of the other human rights."[603] Of the Cuban clergy, Archbishop Pedro Meurice of Santiago received public acclaim when his welcoming remarks for the Santiago papal mass included the statement that, "our people are respectful of authority, and want order, but they need to learn to demystify false messiahs."[604] Following the papal visit, Cuba released some one

---

[601] Herald Staff Report, "Cuban Security Ever Vigilant," *Miami Herald*, January 27, 1998.

[602] "Argentina: Argentina Complains to Cuba Over Reporters' Visas," *Reuters News Service*, January 9, 1998, and Liz Balmaseda, "The Sound of Castro's Silence," *Miami Herald*, January 21, 1998.

[603] Pope John Paul II, Homily, Plaza de la Revolución, Havana, January 25, 1998.

[604] Archbiship Pedro Meurice, Welcome to Pope John Paul II, Santiago, January 24, 1998.

hundred political prisoners, but most of these had served the majority of their sentences, and police required them to agree to refrain from opposition activities. Cuba freed seventeen of these prisoners on the condition that they accept exile in Canada, violating their right to remain in their homeland and setting aside the pope's request for the reintegration of prisoners into Cuban society.[605]

Restrictions of Religious Expression

The Central Committee of the Communist Party's Department of Attention to Religious Affairs reportedly reviews religious institutions' requests to build churches, hold marches, print materials and obtain printing presses, import vehicles or other supplies, receive and deliver humanitarian aid, obtain entry or exit visas for religious workers or operate religious schools. Cuba's heavy-handed measures against religious institutions on these matters impede religious freedom. For example, the department's director, Caridad Diego, stated that her office had no intention of approving religious schools. Diego gave a vague response when asked about 130 pending visa applications for foreign clergy, saying only that they were "not a closed issue."[606] Since Cuba expelled most foreign priests and nuns shortly after the revolution, there are now some 900 Catholic clergy in Cuba, half of them Cuban. Cuba had approved some twenty entry visas for foreign clergy shortly before the papal visit. As of December 1998, Cuba had approved entry visas for forty additional foreign Catholic priests and nuns.[607] Cuba pressures Cuban religious workers by denying them exit visas. The government reportedly denied a Baptist pastor, Rev. Roberto Hernández Aguiar, permission to travel outside Cuba in September 1998.[608] Churches hoping to expand operations in Cuba also are slowed by the government's refusal to permit church construction and a ban on

---

[605] The releases are discussed above, at *Treatment of Political Prisoners: Political Prisoner Releases.*

[606] Golden, "After a Lift, Cuban Church Has a Letdown."

[607] Mark Fineman, "New Freedoms in a More Open Cuba," *Los Angeles Times*, December 27, 1998. At least five of the foreign priests granted visas will be taking the place of priests departing Cuba. "Cuba: Cuba Approves Entry of 19 More Catholic Priests," *Reuters News Service*, November 18, 1998.

[608] Luis López Prendes, "Niegan el Partido Comunista Permisos a Pastor Bautista," *Buró de Prensa Independiente de Cuba*, September 17, 1998.

services held outside of churches, in "house churches."[609] From the revolution until 1990, Cuba reportedly only allowed the construction of one church, a Protestant one in Varadero. In 1997 and early 1998, Cuba granted the Catholic church permission to build one seminary and one church.[610]

In June 1998 the Communist Party reportedly refused permits for religious processions in Arroyo Naranjo to celebrate the feast day of Saint Anthony, and in Calabazar, in the municipality of Boyeros, to celebrate the feast of Saint John the Baptist. When the priest requesting the permits tried to go to the municipal authorities for permission, as would other nongovernmental institutions, those authorities insisted that the Communist Party review the request.[611] On September 7, 1998, Cuban authorities allowed approximately 1,000 people to take part in a religious procession honoring the Virgin of Regla in Havana.[612] But on the next day, the feast of Cuba's patron saint, the Virgin of Charity of Cobre, seven activists could not attend the festivities because they were under arrest, while state security agents prevented thirty others from attending by not allowing them to leave the Havana home of Isabel del Pino Sotolongo of the Christ the King Movement church.[613]

Cuba allowed unprecedented access to its national airwaves during the papal visit, but has provided little opportunity for religious institutions to broadcast their message since that time. Cuba has no independent radio or television stations. While the government maintains tight control over the printed word, a few churches have been able to publish religious newsletters with limited circulation in recent years. Protestants and Catholics, in particular, continue to push for further access

---

[609] Douglas Farah, "Church Resurrected in a Changing Cuba: Pews Fill Amid Dialogue Initiated by Pope and Castro," *The Washington Post*, January 28, 1997.

[610] Serge Kovaleski, "Cuba Seen Ready to Issue More Work Visas to Clergy," *The Washington Post*, January 27, 1998.

[611] Oswaldo Paya Sardiñas, "Coartan Autoridades Cubanas Derecho a Procesiones," *Infoburo*, June 29, 1998.

[612] Juan O. Tamayo, "Cuban Authorities Mix Tolerance, Repression," *Miami Herald*, September 9, 1998.

[613] Ariel Hidalgo and Tete Machado, "Nueve Disidentes Detenidos Durante una Redada," *Infoburo*, September 9, 1998. These detentions are detailed above, at *Routine Repression*.

to the state-controlled airwaves.[614] On December 25, 1998, Cuba permitted Cardinal Jaime Ortega, the leader of Cuba's Catholic church, to deliver a Christmas message on the government's national music radio station, which reportedly has a small listening audience.[615]

One of Cuba's most prominent dissident organizations, the Christian Liberation Movement (MCL), under the direction of Oswaldo Payá Sardiñas, has been trying for a few years to get 10,000 signatures on a petition for political reform, in the hope that it would lead to a referendum. Payá Sardiñas has been outspoken in his calls for religious rights, such as the freedom to build churches and offer religious education, as well as related rights, such as forming independent associations and releasing political prisoners.[616] The MCL's activities have resulted in government pressures. In February 1997, a Cuban court convicted MCL member Enrique García Morejón, who had been gathering signatures for the petition, of enemy propaganda and sentenced him to four years in prison.[617] Cuban government officials have denied several requests from Payá Sardiñas to leave the country for MCL-related events, most recently in October 1998, when migration authorities refused permission for him to attend a human rights conference in Poland.[618]

Impediments to Humanitarian Aid Programs

Religious institutions such as the Catholic organization Caritas have assumed increasingly important roles in the provision of humanitarian aid to the Cuban population. The Martin Luther King Center, which maintains close government ties under the direction of Raúl Suárez, a Baptist pastor and member of Cuba's

---

[614] April Witt, "Religiosos de EU Viajarán a Cuba," *El Nuevo Herald*, May 29, 1998.

[615] "Cuba Agrees to Let Catholic Leader Broadcast Christmas Message," *Associated Press* printed in the *Miami Herald*, December 26, 1998.

[616] Oswaldo Paya Sardiñas, "Cuba Hacia El 2000," *Infoburo*, September 21, 1998.

[617] Human Rights Watch telephone interview with Odilia Collazo, Pro Human Rights Party, Havana, October 13, 1998.

[618] "Niegan Permiso de Viaje a Disidente," *El Nuevo Herald*, October 15, 1998.

National Assembly, also undertakes humanitarian aid projects.[619] In October 1997, Religious Affairs Director Caridad Diego notified religious groups carrying out humanitarian work that the Commerce Ministry had passed Resolution 149/97 (on August 4, 1997), which created restrictions on institutions' purchases from Cuban government stores.[620] The resolution bars wholesale purchases from any entity but the government's EMSUNA Corporate Group (Grupo Corporativo EMSUNA). Diego apparently told some religious leaders that the restrictions were in response to churches allegedly having acquired illegal products, having abused their right to buy from state stores, and having trafficked materials on the black market.[621]

The resolution bars religious institutions from purchasing fax machines, photocopiers, and other electronics.[622] Since Cuba criminalizes clandestine printing and enemy propaganda, and the government has seized computers, faxes, and photocopiers from dissident groups, this measure appears designed to impede religious groups freedom of expression.[623] The law also creates cumbersome notification requirements. Institutions planning purchases from the government must provide sworn statements, signed by "accredited and recognized authorit[ies]" in the institution, detailing what each product will be used for and confirming that they will be used only for that purpose and will not be given to any other church entitity.[624] Since many religious groups operate without official government recognition, such as the Catholic church's human rights group, the Justice and Peace Commission (Comisión Justicia y Paz), they would not be able to make any purchases under this provision. Humanitarian organizations cannot make any food purchases without giving the government thirty-day advance notice.[625] In order to

---

[619] Gillian Gunn, "Cuba's NGOs," *The Cuba Briefing Paper Series*, February 1995.

[620] Resolution 149/97, second section.

[621] Juan A. Tamayo, "Cuba Impone Restricciones a las Iglesias," *El Nuevo Herald*, October 18, 1997.

[622] Resolution 149/97, Annex 1.

[623] Cuban Criminal Code, Articles 210 and 103. These provisions are discussed above, at *Codifying Repression*.

[624] Resolution 149/97, fourth section.

[625] Ibid., sixth section.

buy personal hygiene products for homes for the elderly, children, and the physically handicapped, sanatoriums, and residences for those suffering from leprosy, the resolution requires the religious group to provide sworn declarations of the number of persons residing in each site.[626]

While Cuba can legitimately exercise its right to ration essential supplies, these restrictions impede free expression and create unreasonable limits on the capacity for religious institutions to carry out humanitarian efforts. One lay activist said that "'the message of the new regulations is that the churches...were doing too much, they were too active.'"[627]

Restrictions on Religious Visits to Prisons

The government's restrictions on pastoral visits to prisoners are detailed above, at *General Prison Conditions: Restrictions on Religious Visits.*

---

[626] Ibid., fifth section. The resolution also limits the hygiene products that the religious group can buy for these individuals, allowing four rolls of toilet paper, one tube of toothpaste, one container of deodorant, and one container of shampoo per resident per month. Ibid., Annex 2.

[627] Tamayo, "Cuba Impone Restricciones a las Iglesias," *El Nuevo Herald*, October 18, 1997.

XI. IMPUNITY

Despite encouraging constitutional provisions against impunity, Cuba routinely denies human rights abuses, fails to investigate or punish those who commit them, and retaliates against those who denounce them, particularly prisoners.[628] The persistence of human rights violations in Cuba is undoubtedly due, in part, to the fact that Cuban officials have faced virtually no consequences for the thousands of human rights violations committed in the past forty years. Yet, Cuba has clear obligations under international law to offer effective remedies to victims of human rights abuses, arising from the Universal Declaration of Human Rights and Cuba's ratification of the Convention Against Torture.[629]

The Cuban government has committed egregious, systematic human rights violations since the 1959 revolution. But the exact numbers of victims wrongfully killed, imprisoned, tortured, exiled, arrested, or suffering other human rights abuses by the Cuban government is impossible to know, in part due to the government's secrecy about its human rights practices. Human Rights Watch has monitored human rights practices in Cuba for over ten years. During that time, we have documented scores of cases of wrongful arrests, detentions, prosecutions, exile, and other abuses. Moreover, the human rights violations committed in the early years of the Castro government stand out as particularly severe. Historian Hugh Thomas, who acknowledged the impossibility of knowing precisely how many executions and other human rights violations had occurred, estimated that by early 1961, the Cuban government had "probably" executed some 2,000 Cubans, while by 1970, the government had, "perhaps," executed 5,000. Thomas does not specify whether these executions occurred following trials, but notes that "in the case of political crimes, there [was] no rule of law."[630] Thomas cites a Castro speech in in 1965 in which the Cuban leader admitted that Cuba had 20,000 "political prisoners"—an unclear number of whom had participated in armed actions against the

---

[628] These constitutional provisions are discussed above, at *Cuban Constitution.* Cuba's abuses of political prisoners are detailed above, at *Treatment of Political Prisoners.*

[629] Cuba's obligations to end impunity are discussed above, at *Cuba's International Human Rights Obligations: Impunity.*

[630] Hugh Thomas, *Cuba: The Pursuit of Freedom* (Harper & Row: New York, 1971), p. 1458.

government.[631] Human Rights Watch is not aware of the Cuban government providing restitution to any victim or family member for any of these human rights violations.[632]

In a report to the U.N. Committee against Torture, Cuba provided information about internal efforts to establish accountability for a broad range of rights and specifically mentioned receiving complaints of abuse in its prisons. Since Cuba permits no independent prison monitoring, and has not even released the number of prisoners currently detained in its prisons, it is impossible to confirm the veracity of this information. Without providing specific details of any cases, the government stated that in 1997 it had received thirty-seven complaints of ill-treatment in prison or in custody; had taken "administrative or disciplinary measures" in ten of those cases; and had sent ten cases to the courts, one of which resulted in an eight-year sentence.[633] If this information is true, Cuba's actions would be encouraging steps in the process of establishing accountability for human rights abuses. However, Cuba's retaliations against prisoners who denounce prison abuses and conditions and its ban on prison monitoring suggest a determination to cover up—rather than expose and punish—prison abuses.

The Cuban government has argued in international human rights fora that its laws ensure that victims can present complaints of human rights abuses. But these avenues fail to provide genuine options for redressing wrongs committed by state officials. Until Cuba's laws are purged of provisions that explicitly violate fundamental rights, such as enemy propaganda or contempt for authority, legal action against human rights violators likely will be stymied by the fact that many prosecutors who deprived individuals of their fundamental rights did so in keeping

---

[631] Ibid., pp. 1458-1461. Castro spoke at the National Forum on Internal Order, March 9-24, 1969. Ibid., p. 1460.

[632] In November 1998, the Cuban American National Foundation (CANF) presented a complaint before a Spanish court charging the Castro government with genocide, terrorism, and torture. Cuba's Foreign Ministry spokesman Alejandro González called the complaint "such a ridiculous infamy" that it merited no further comment. Andrew Cawthorne, "Cuba Scorns Exiles' Legal Bid Against Castro," *Reuters News Service*, November 5, 1998. A Spanish judge dismissed the suit later that month, on the grounds that the facts in the complaint were not sufficient to demonstrate the commission of genocide, terrorism, or torture. "Cuba: Spanish Judge Throws Out Fidel Castro 'Genocide' Suit," *El País*, November 20, 1998.

[633] Cuban report to the Committee Against Torture, March 3, 1998, para. 25.

with Cuban law. And Cuba's Criminal Code notably fails to criminalize torture, as required by the Convention against Torture.

Cuba has claimed that Article 116 of its Criminal Procedure Code provides a remedy for victims of human rights abuses, but this measure simply compels an individual to report the occurrence of any crime.[634] Ironically, in 1998 Cuba tried independent journalist Juan Carlos Recio Martínez for failing to denounce an acquaintance who allegedly had committed enemy propaganda (by encouraging abstention from elections). Cuba prosecuted Recio Martínez for a state security crime that requires the reporting of the commission of other state security crimes.[635] Article 116 provides no duty or protected right to denounce state officials for having violated fundamental rights. The Civil Code permits an individual to sue another individual for the violation of constitutionally protected rights, allowing the cessation of the violation and restitution.[636] But here, too, Cuban citizens have no specific right to take action against state officials.

Cuba's state mechanisms for reporting human rights violations also suffer from a lack of independence from political authorities. Conflicts of interest in enforcing Cuban laws, many of which violate human rights in their application, also diminish the potential usefulness of these mechanisms. Cuba's claim, for example, that its public prosecutors will "guarantee respect for the dignity of the citizen," although the same prosecutors might be responsible for that person's prosecution for the exercise of his or her fundamental rights, strains credulity.[637] Similarly, the Attorney General's allegiance to the National Assembly and his or her mandate to enforce Cuba's laws, however much they may restrict human rights, seriously compromise his or her role as a human rights advocate and undercut the likely efficacy of the Department of Citizens' Rights. Cuba has referred to this office as one with responsibility for overseeing the implementation of human rights.[638] While the government claims that the Attorney General ensures that legal standards are obeyed in prisons and pretrial detention centers, the rampant human rights abuses

---

[634] Cuban Report to the United Nations regarding International Human Rights Instruments (HRI/CORE/1/Add.84), October 13, 1997, para. 51.

[635] For further discussion of the Récio Martínez case, see *Political Prosecutions*.

[636] Cuban Report to the United Nations Regarding International Human Rights Instruments, para 50.

[637] Ibid., para. 67.

[638] Ibid., para. 69.

in both types of institutions say little for the success of this effort.[639] The complaint mechanisms reportedly available in the National Assembly or Council of State likely would be entirely compromised by the political nature of the institutions. Since the Interior Ministry directly carries out much of Cuba's repression, recourse to its complaints department would likely prove fruitless and perhaps dangerous. The state maintains such firm control over the practice of law, through its collective law firms, that even finding legal representation would pose a tremendous challenge for victims of human rights abuses.[640]

Impunity for the Sinking of the *13 de Marzo*

Without other avenues for redress, several Cuban exiles brought a historic human rights case before the Inter-American Commission of Human Rights (hereinafter the commission), the human rights body of the Organization of American States (OAS), in 1994. Although Cuba is not a member of the OAS, the commission considers the Cuban government responsible for protecting the rights enshrined in the American Declaration of the Rights and Duties of Man. On October 16, 1996, the commission approved a public report concluding that on July 13, 1994, Cuba violated the right to life of forty-one people who died when Cuban government boats rammed, flooded, and sank the *13 de Marzo*, a hijacked tugboat loaded with civilians fleeing Cuba.[641] The report also found that Cuba violated the right of personal integrity of the thirty-one survivors of the sinking, and violated the rights to transit and justice of all of the seventy-two persons who attempted to leave Cuba.[642] The report provides shocking survivors' testimony of the Cuban government's deliberate attempts to sink the boat. Statements by President Castro and the Interior Ministry regarding responsibility for the incident provide a disturbing counterpoint to the victims' experiences. Clearly, the government's effort was to exculpate itself from responsibility, rather than conduct a serious investigation and punish those responsible for this incident.

---

[639] Ibid., para. 68.

[640] The government's control over the practice of law is discussed above, at *Due Process Denied: Restrictions on the Right to a Lawyer.*

[641] Informe No. 47/96, Caso 11.436, Cuba (OEA/Ser.>/V/11.93), October 16, 1996, para. 105.

[642] Ibid., paras. 106 and 107.

Despite consistent testimonies that four Transportation Ministry boats fired water cannons onto the decks of the tugboat and later rammed and sank it, President Castro denied a government role in the sinking.[643] Although President Castro asserted that Cuba had fully investigated the incident, the commission noted that Cuba never recovered the bodies lost in the tugboat, nor the boat itself, and concluded that "there was no judicial investigation and the political organs directed by the Cuban Chief of State rushed to absolve of all responsibility the officials who went to meet the *13 de Marzo* tugboat."[644]

International Legal Actions Against Fidel Castro

In late 1998 the arrest in London of former Chilean dictator Gen. Augusto Pinochet sparked international interest in the possibility of trying former and current heads of state responsible for serious human rights abuses.

In November 1998 the Cuban American National Foundation (CANF), an anti-Castro organization of Cuban exiles based in Miami, filed a law suit against Castro in Madrid alleging that he had committed genocide, terrorism, and torture. A national high court judge in Spain dismissed the suit later that month, ruling that the facts presented in the complaint did not constitute genocide or torture and on the controversial grounds that states cannot commit terrorism. The judge, Ismael Moreno Chamarro, also ruled that as a sitting head of state Fidel Castro was immune from prosecution in Spain.[645] At this writing, CANF has appealed the ruling.[646]

Two Cuban exiles and one French citizen commenced legal actions against Castro in January 1999 in Paris, charging him with crimes against humanity, torture, illegal detention, and drug-trafficking. According to the plaintiffs' attorney, Serge Lewisch, Cuban authorities arrested French journalist Pierre Golendorf in 1971, imprisoning him until 1975 for having drafted a book that criticized the government. Cuba jailed Lázaro Jordana from 1982 until 1986, as a political

---

[643] Ibid., para. 32.

[644] Ibid., para. 87. Translation by Human Rights Watch.

[645] Order issued by Judge-Magistrate Ismael Moreno Chamarro, Central Instruction Court Number 2, Madrid, November 19, 1998.

[646] Human Rights Watch telephone interview with Javier Barrilero, CANF attorney, Madrid, February 5, 1999; and "Cuba: Spanish Judge Throws Out Fidel Castro 'Genocide' Suit," *El Pais* published by the *BBC Monitoring Summary of World Broadcasts*, November 21, 1998.

prisoner. Ileana de la Guardia filed the suit on behalf of her father, Col. Antonio de la Guardia, who was executed by a Cuban firing squad in 1989 after a Cuban court found him guilty of smuggling drugs.[647] In late February 1999, a French magistrate dismissed the complaints.[648]

[647] Lara Marlowe, "Pinochet Case Creates Precedent for Other Regimes," *Irish Times*, January 7, 1999; and Jon Henley, "France: Castro Accused of Role in Drug Trafficking," *Guardian*, January 7, 1999.

[648] "France: French Magistrate Rejects Charges Against Castro," *Reuters News Service*, February 26, 1999.

XII. INTERNATIONAL POLICY

Pope John Paul II's January 1998 call for the world to open up to Cuba and Cuba to open up to the world accelerated a process that has been under way since the end of the Cold War. No longer perceiving Cuba as a military threat, Western nations have increasingly distanced themselves from the U.S. policy of unrelenting confrontation with the Castro regime. Since the pontiff's unprecedented January visit to the island, several governments have restored normal relations with Cuba, some for the first time in decades. Eighteen heads of state visited Havana in 1998 as well as ministers from more than 100 countries. In an August 1998 tour of three Caribbean nations, the Cuban leader received a warm welcome, past animosities notwithstanding. In October, Castro was received in Madrid by Spain's King Juan Carlos in anticipation of a visit by the monarch to Cuba planned for 1999, while Spain's foreign minister, Abel Matutes, traveled to Cuba in November 1998. The number of countries opposing U.S. policy on Cuba at the United Nations General Assembly has steadily increased in recent years. In October 1998, the General Assembly approved by a record margin a nonbinding resolution calling for an end to the nearly forty-year-old U.S. embargo against Cuba, with only the U.S. and Israel objecting.

Cuba came in for criticism, however, following the March 16, 1999, sentencing of four dissidents—members of the Internal Dissidents' Working Group—to multi-year prison terms for the peaceful expression of opposition. Spanish Prime Minister José María Aznar said the terms could jeopardize the planned visit to Cuba by King Juan Carlos. In Ottawa, Canadian Prime Minister Jean Chrétien, who had pled for the dissidents' liberty during his April 1998 visit to Havana, called for a review of bilateral relations between the two countries.

Human Rights Watch welcomes the movement away from Washington's Cuba policy, which in nearly forty years has produced no softening of Fidel Castro's hard-line rejection of human rights reforms. A simple relaxation of pressure, however, will not by itself promote change in Cuba. If anything will bring about change in Cuba, it is international pressure. Washington's decades-old confrontational approach must be replaced by a principled and concerted human rights policy on the part of the international community. It is essential that the United States, the European Union, and Latin American and Caribbean nations reach agreement on a unified approach; the current situation in which Washington pushes confrontation while its partners promote conciliation renders them at cross purposes and leaves human rights victims in the lurch.

The cost of this dispute between erstwhile allies was evident at the United Nations Human Rights Commission in 1998, where international resistance to U.S.

policy toward Cuba doomed a resolution extending the mandate of Cuba's special human rights rapporteur. Since 1991, U.S.- backed resolutions had been approved each year by members of the U.N. Human Rights Commission in its annual meeting in Geneva. In addition to condemning human rights violations on the island, the U.N. resolutions had kept alive the mandate of a special rapporteur assigned to monitor and publicly report on the human rights situation in Cuba. On April 21, 1998, members of the commission for the first time defeated Washington's annual resolution on human rights in Cuba. The vote, in which African and Asian nations supported Cuba's longstanding efforts to evade the human rights commission's scrutiny, marked a stinging rebuke to U.S. policy toward Cuba. Cuba had never allowed the special rapporteur, Carl Johan Groth, to visit the island. While this U.S. failure may represent a welcome sign of international resistance to U.S. policy, it also signals an unwarranted letup of human rights scrutiny by the world body.

Nonetheless, Cuba's crackdown in early 1999, sentencing to prison prominent dissidents and enacting new repressive legislation, appears to have galvanized international support for renewed pressure. At the April 1999 commission meeting, a resolution condemning Cuban human rights practices, which did not include a provision for a rapporteur, passed by a narrow margin.

This chapter primarily analyzes the impact on the Cuban human rights situation of policies adopted by the United States, the European Union, and Canada. In addition, Latin American and Caribbean nations have taken on increasing importance as counterweights to U.S. policy toward Cuba. These nations have adopted more active diplomacy with Cuba, albeit with differing degrees of enthusiasm. Several Latin American and Caribbean nations, with the support of Canada, have openly promoted Cuba's readmission to the Organization of American States, even though the OAS member states, as recently as September 1997, amended the organization's charter to allow the hemisphere's governments to ostracize any government coming to power by coup.[649] In the 1960s, these countries not only expelled Cuba from the OAS but also adopted a region-wide embargo on trade with Cuba. Now Cuba has been invited to participate in the past three annual Ibero-American summit meetings of heads of state from Spain and Latin America, and the next summit has been scheduled to take place in Havana in 1999. In addition, most regional countries have adopted immigration accords with Havana providing for the immediate return to Cuba of fleeing refugees, a significant shift from past practices.

---

[649] The Washington Protocol, which amended the OAS charter, entered into force in September 1987. See Charter of the Organization of American States, Article 9, General Secretariat, Organization of American States, Washington, D.C.

Unfortunately, much of the increased engagement of Latin American and Caribbean nations with Cuba has come without serious pressure for human rights reforms. Although Fidel Castro was among the twenty-one heads of state to sign the Declaration of Viña del Mar at the end of the 1996 Ibero-American summit, he did not hesitate to imprison Héctor Palacios Ruíz after the dissident circulated copies of the declaration and questioned Castro's willingness to uphold his commitments to respect democracy and civil and political rights.[650] While Palacios Ruíz served more than a year in prison for defending the declaration, Latin signatories remained largely silent regarding Cuba's brazen action. Moreover, the persecution of Palacios Ruíz and other dissidents did not prevent the heads of state of the Ibero-American nations from scheduling their 1999 annual summit meeting in Havana.

During Castro's August 1998 tour of Jamaica, Barbados, and Grenada, the U.S. embargo was roundly criticized while human rights violations in Cuba were given short shrift. A notable exception to the conciliatory trend was the visit in May 1998 to Cuba of Brazilian Foreign Minister Luiz Felipe Lampreia, whose meeting in Havana with human rights defenders and statements emphasizing human rights sent an important signal of support for the human rights community in Cuba.[651]

United States Policy

The Embargo

The movement toward rapprochement since the Pope's visit to Cuba has brought unprecedented domestic and international opposition to the U.S. trade embargo. In January 1999 the Clinton administration announced several small steps to soften the impact of the embargo on the Cuban population, while rejecting a call from former Republican policy makers to empanel a bipartisan commission to review thoroughly U.S. policy toward Cuba. These measures followed a similar package of narrow measures announced in early 1998. Yet while the Clinton administration has adopted a more measured rhetoric toward the Castro government

---

[650] See above, *Impediments to Human Rights in Cuban Law: Contempt for the Authority of a Public Official.*

[651] "Cuba: Brazil's Foreign Minister Meets Dissident, Officials; Food Loan Agreed," *Folha de São Paulo* website, published by BBC Monitoring Service: Latin America, May 30, 1998.

than previous U.S. administrations,[652] U.S. policy remains frozen due to the enactment of legislation in 1996 known as the Helms-Burton Act that for the first time codified the embargo, removing from the president's authority any possibility of modifying it without passing new legislation. Washington's basic approach to Havana remains defined by the all-encompassing trade embargo.

Flaws in the Embargo Policy

Human Rights Watch opposes the embargo against Cuba for the reasons described below.

The embargo is counterproductive to human rights protections. Although it has gone through minor permutations over the decades, the embargo remains a sledgehammer approach aimed at overthrowing the Castro government. As an all-or-nothing policy that has failed to achieve its objective, the embargo has made achievement of any subsidiary objectives—such as improving human rights practices—highly unlikely. The Cuban Liberty and Democratic Solidarity Act of 1996, otherwise known as Helms-Burton after its Republican co-sponsors Sen. Jesse Helms and Rep. Dan Burton, requires the embargo to remain in place until a transition government that "does not include Fidel Castro or Raúl Castro..." takes control in Havana. A more calibrated policy would allow for a relaxation of pressure in response to measurable improvements in Havana, such as releasing political prisoners, reforming legislation that criminalizes free expression of opinions, or allowing the establishment of independent political parties or trade unions. Instead, the embargo will reward nothing short of revolutionary change on the island.[653] And since Castro has often predicated reform on an end to the

---

[652] In dispassionate comments unusual for a U.S. official, President Clinton responded to a reporter's question about Cuba in a May 6, 1998, press conference saying: "I understand the desire of the Cuban government to keep its health care system, to keep its commitment to universal literacy to even its poorest citizens. That's a commendable and laudable thing. But I do not accept, nor can I ever accept, some of the anti-democratic and, frankly, clearly anti-human rights policies of the government...." The White House, Office of the Press Secretary, "Press Conference of the President and Prime Minister Prodi of Italy," May 6, 1998.

[653] The Cuban Democracy Act of 1992, which was superseded by Helms-Burton, described itself as a calibrated policy, stating in its preamble that "It should be the policy of the United States ... (6) to maintain sanctions on the Castro regime so long as it continues to refuse to move toward democratization and greater respect for human rights; [and] (7) to be prepared to reduce the sanctions in carefully calibrated ways in response to positive developments in Cuba...." However, the statute's only specific provision for lifting sanctions allowed such action only after free and fair elections had been held and respect

embargo, a perfect stalemate has been achieved, to the detriment of victims of human rights violations and the Cuban population at large.

The embargo is indiscriminate. The Cuban population has suffered a steady deterioration in its standard of living over the course of nearly four decades, most sharply after the collapse of the Soviet Union, which had subsidized the island's economy since the 1960s. The embargo, which prohibits all trade—including food—with Cuba (excepting the sale of medicines under a complex and unwieldy licensing process), also severely limits travel to the island and punishes third countries that do business with Cuba.[654] This broad clampdown has harmed the population as a whole, while making little apparent impact on those in power. Indeed, the embargo on trade with Cuba is one of the few sanctions packages in recent years that explicitly includes food and medicine. Responding to a complaint filed by the Center for Human Rights Legal Action, the Inter-American Commission on Human Rights of the OAS in February 1995 called on the Clinton administration to "put in place mechanisms to ensure that the necessary steps are taken for exemptions from the trade embargo in respect of [sic] medicine, medical supplies and basic food items...."[655] In a study published in 1997, the American Association for World Health found that "the U.S. embargo has caused a significant rise in suffering—and even deaths—in Cuba."[656]

The embargo has alienated Washington's potential allies. The U.S. is likely to bring about change in Cuba only by adopting a common front with its allies. But almost every likely partner in such an endeavor—including the Pope, the United Nations General Assembly, and governments of every political stripe around the world—has condemned the embargo in unequivocal terms. Our own efforts to

---

for human rights restored. And while this may have represented a more flexible policy than the statutes it replaced, it was overtaken by Helms-Burton's all-or-nothing approach four years later.

[654] The Clinton administration's new measures announced, but not yet implemented in January 1999, would allow for some sales of food to nongovernment entities in Cuba. The embargo does not prohibit food donations, which must be licensed by the Treasury Department.

[655] Letter to Wallie Mason, Center for Human Rights Legal Action, from Alvaro Tirado Mejía, Chairman, Inter-American Commission on Human Rights, Organization of American States, Washington, D.C. February 17, 1995.

[656] American Association for World Health, "Denial of Food and Medicine: The Impact of the U.S. Embargo on Health & Nutrition in Cuba," March 1997, p. 6.

enlist Latin American governments to press for human rights improvements in Cuba have met with stiff resistance. The U.S. embargo has engendered international sympathy for and solidarity with the Castro government. Indeed, Washington's rout at the U.N. Human Rights Commission in 1998, in which members of the commission refused to condemn human rights violations in Cuba, despite an abundance of evidence, shows how far other governments will go to distance themselves from U.S. policy. Approval of a resolution without assigning a rapporteur in April 1999 reflected the international community's outrage at the Castro governemnt's crackdown on dissidents in the first months of the year.

The embargo itself violates human rights. A variety of regulations limit U.S. citizens' ability to travel to Cuba, in violation of Article 19 of the International Covenant on Civil and Political Rights (ICCPR), a treaty ratified by the United States.[657] In protecting freedom of expression, Article 19 includes "freedom to seek, receive and impart information and ideas of all kinds, regardless of frontiers." To the extent that travel constitutes a means of sharing information, limiting travel violates the free exchange of ideas. Moreover, under the 1975 Helsinki Final Act and successive accords reached by the Conference on Security and Cooperation in Europe (now the Organization for Security and Co-operation in Europe, OSCE), the United States agreed to protect "human contacts" and oppose any bans on travel and telephone communications. The principles set forth in the instruments would clearly favor the removal of any barrier to such contacts raised by an OSCE member state in its relations with other nations.[658] The embargo thus violates protected rights. The Clinton administration's January 1999 removal of the ban it had previously established on direct air travel to Cuba from Miami constituted a small step in the right direction.

The embargo is not working. If thirty-nine years of sanctions against Cuba has proven anything, it is that the policy is not working.

---

[657] Travel is restricted through licensing requirements and a prohibition on financial transactions with Cuba, as described below.

[658] Human Rights Watch, *World Report 1993* (New York: Human Rights Watch, 1992), p. 98. During direct talks between the United States and Cuba on migration in 1994, authorities agreed to allow U.S. long distance telephone companies to reestablish and upgrade long distance telephone service between the U.S. and Cuba. This step removed one impediment to communication between the two countries that Human Rights Watch had criticized in the past as a violation of Article 19 of the ICCPR.

History of U.S. Embargo

Imposition of the Embargo in the 1960s

Since shortly after Fidel Castro and his guerrillas overthrew the corrupt and brutal government of Gen. Fulgencio Batista on January 1, 1959, the United States has used a combination of covert and overt measures aimed at ousting him, including numerous assassination attempts. The most enduring of these measures has been the U.S. trade embargo, which has remained in place for thirty-nine years.

In October 1960, as relations between the Castro government and the Eisenhower administration became increasingly hostile, the Commerce Department established an embargo on most U.S. exports to Cuba. The regulations also prohibited the re-export from third countries of U.S. goods or technical data. A general license granted by the Commerce Department still allowed the export of a very limited number of items, such as specific foods, medicines, and medical supplies.[659]

In September 1961, Congress strengthened the measure undertaken by the executive branch, authorizing the president to establish "a total embargo on all trade between the U.S. and Cuba."[660] President Kennedy then proclaimed a comprehensive ban on trade with Cuba on February 3, 1962. The president ordered the Treasury Department to oversee the prohibition on imports from Cuba and to provide licenses for any needed exceptions. The Commerce Department was assigned authority for barring exports.[661] Additional legislation and regulations implemented over the years sought to press third countries to isolate Cuba economically. Among these, the 1962 amendment to the Foreign Assistance Act barred U.S. aid to any country assisting Cuba and denied U.S. government business to any foreign ships that had visited Cuban ports.

In January 1962, Washington succeeded in pressing the Organization of American States to expel Cuba and to adopt a region-wide embargo on weapons

---

[659] Michael Krinsky and David Golove, Eds, *United States Economic Measures Against Cuba: Proceedings in the United Nations and International Law Issues*, (Northampton: Aletheia Press, 1993), p. 110.

[660] Foreign Assistance Act of 1961, Pub. L. No. 87-195, 75 Stat. 424. Section 620 (a), 22. U.S.C. § 2370 (a). The president already had the authority to ban trade with Cuba under the Trading with the Enemy Act, 50 U.S.C. App § 5(b).

[661] Proclamation No. 3447, Feb. 3, 1962, 27 F.R. 1085, Embargo on Trade with Cuba.

trade.[662] In July 1964, the OAS went so far as to mandate a collective embargo on all trade with Cuba, a measure that stayed in effect for eleven years and reflected the anger of regional governments over Castro's support for revolutionary forces throughout the hemisphere.

The steady tightening of the squeeze on Cuba included regulations implemented by the Treasury Department in 1963, freezing all Cuban-owned assets in the United States, and the revocation by the Commerce Department in May 1964 of the general license for the export of food and medicines to Cuba, thus requiring the granting of specific licenses for any such exports. In general, the government granted licenses only for humanitarian, rather than commercial purposes.[663]

Cuban Democracy Act of 1992

The adoption in October 1992 of the Cuban Democracy Act expanded the embargo while trying to ease its effects on the population as a whole. The law extended the extraterritorial provisions of the embargo by prohibiting foreign-based subsidiaries of U.S. companies from trading with Cuba. At the same time, the law allowed food to be donated to nongovernmental organizations, including churches, and individuals. Medicines and medical supplies could be exported as long as the Cuban government allowed on-site inspection to ensure that the supplies "benefit...the Cuban people" and are not sold for export. The Cuban Democracy Act also allowed the U.S. government to provide aid "through appropriate nongovernmental organizations, for the support of individuals and organizations to promote nonviolent democratic change in Cuba."[664]

Cuban Liberty and Democratic Solidarity Act of 1996

The Cuban Liberty and Democratic Solidarity Act, commonly referred to as Helms-Burton, sought to intensify the economic strangulation of Cuba by increasing the embargo's extraterritorial reach. The Cuban downing of two unarmed civilian aircraft in February 1996 created the climate for this hardened stance. Helms-Burton, which became law in March 1996, curtails the president's authority to relax the embargo and allows for lawsuits against those "trafficking" in property expropriated from U.S. citizens in Cuba in the aftermath of the

---

[662] Krinsky, p. 112.

[663] Ibid., pp. 113-114.

[664] Executive Order No. 12854, July 4, 1993, 58 F.R. 36587, Implementation of the Cuban Democracy Act, Section 6004(g).

revolution. The law also requires the U.S. government to exclude from the U.S. any foreigners deemed to own property confiscated from U.S. citizens or to have "trafficked" in such property. The law gives the president the authority to suspend for six months the provisions allowing U.S. citizens to sue foreign investors.[665] The law has provoked a roar of protest from U.S. trading partners in Europe and Canada, who have increased their investment in Cuba in recent years. This friction has led President Clinton to waive the right of U.S. citizens to sue foreign investors in U.S. courts continuously since the bill became law. In May 1998, Clinton and leaders of the European Union reached an agreement on investments in Cuba intended to avoid sanctions against European companies. The understanding between the U.S. and the E.U. provided that Brussels would inhibit and deter investment in expropriated properties (in Cuba and elsewhere) and the Clinton administration would seek from Congress a waiver of the provision denying U.S. visas to investors holding properties that were expropriated from U.S. nationals. As of this writing, Congress had yet to pass legislation allowing such a waiver.[666]

Recent Measures (1999)

The administration lost an important opportunity to explore a new policy for Cuba in January 1999. In late 1998, a group of former high-level State Department and Pentagon officials along with Republican Senator John Warner of Virginia asked President Clinton to establish a bipartisan commission to review U.S. policy toward Cuba in light of the considerable global political changes since the embargo was first imposed. The initiative's supporters included former Secretaries of State Henry Kissinger and Lawrence Eagleburger, former Secretary of Defense Frank Carlucci, former Senate Majority Leader Howard Baker, and several current senators. This surprising initiative from conservative leaders reflected in large part the growing interest on the part of U.S. corporations in investment and trade with Cuba. After a few weeks of study, the administration rejected the proposal.

Instead, the Clinton administration adopted a more cautious approach, announcing a package of measures including broadening the allowance for remittances to Cuba, allowing sales of U.S. food and agricultural products to Cuban farmers and family restaurants, increasing U.S. charter flights to Cuba, and establishing direct mail service between the two countries. In addition, the

---

[665] Cuban Liberty and Democratic Solidarity (Libertad) Act of 1996, March 1, 1996, 104th Congress 2d Session, House of Representatives Report 104-468.

[666] Human Rights Watch interview with Michael E. Ranneberger, director, Office of Cuban Affairs, U.S. Department of State, February 1, 1999.

administration announced its intention to allow the Baltimore Orioles management to negotiate exhibition baseball games with the Cuban national baseball team.[667] The first of these games took place in Havana in March 1999 and the second in Baltimore in May 1999.

Many of these measures were themselves recommended by an "independent task force" organized by the prestigious Council on Foreign Relations in a December 1998 report. Without taking a position on the embargo, the task force—chaired by former Assistant Secretaries of State Bernard W. Aronson and William D. Rogers—called for a new goal for U.S. policy: "working to create the best possible conditions for a peaceful transition in Cuba and the emergence of a democratic, prosperous and free Cuba in the 21st century." In addition to encouraging a broadening of contacts between Cuba and the U.S., the report advocated increased U.S. support for Cuba's incipient civil society. Moreover, both the Council on Foreign Relations recommendations, as well as the Clinton administration's latest measures, grew out of an emerging consensus that the embargo's harsh effect on the Cuban population must be mitigated.[668] The administration's measures will not have the far-reaching effects that could have been produced by a bipartisan commission with a mandate to review all aspects of U.S. policy toward Cuba, including the embargo.

Effects of the Embargo on Travel

Limits on U.S. travel to Cuba date from a January 16, 1961, notice issued by the State Department that proclaimed travel to Cuba by U.S. citizens to be "contrary to the foreign policy of the United States and ...otherwise inimical to the national interest." Since that day, travel restrictions have been alternately tightened and

---

[667] Office of the Press Secretary, "Statement by the President," The White House, January 5, 1999. Tim Weiner, "U.S. Ready to Ease Some Restrictions in Policy on Cuba, *New York Times*, January 5, 1999; Norman Kempster, "U.S. Has Post-Castro Era in Mind With Latest Steps," *Los Angeles Times*, January 6, 1999; On-the-record briefing on Cuba, Amb. James Dobbins, Special Assistant to the President and Senior Director for Inter-American Affairs, NSC; Amb. Peter Romero, Acting Assistant Secretary of State for Western Hemisphere Affairs; and Michael Ranneberger, Coordinator for Cuban Affairs, Department of State, as released by the Office of the Spokesman, U.S. Department of State, Washington, DC, January 5, 1999.

[668] Bernard W. Aronson and William D. Rogers, "U.S.-Cuban Relations in the 21st Century," Independent Task Force of the Council on Foreign Relations, December 30, 1998.

eased at different moments, but never lifted. In 1999, travel to and from Cuba remains highly restricted.

Under the 1961 State Department notice, anyone traveling to Cuba was required to receive a specific endorsement in his or her passport from the State Department. U.S. efforts to prosecute citizens who ignored this ruling did not withstand legal challenge, however. After the Kennedy administration filed criminal indictments against American Levi Laub for organizing travel to Cuba of fifty-eight U.S. citizens whose passports were not endorsed by the State Department, the U.S. Supreme Court in 1967 ruled that travel without a specifically endorsed passport did not constitute a crime under the relevant statute.[669]

Following its defeat at the Supreme Court, the Kennedy State Department issued a new notice, proclaiming travel to or in Cuba "restricted" on the grounds that it "would seriously impair the conduct of U.S. foreign affairs." Similar notices, and a requirement that U.S. passports be specifically endorsed by the State Department for travel to Cuba, remained in effect until 1976, although there were no further efforts to prosecute those who defied the restrictions. However, Treasury Department regulations barring financial transactions related to travel to Cuba, promulgated in 1963 under the Trading With the Enemy Act of 1917, are criminally enforceable. These measures have endured as the principle means of restricting U.S. travel to Cuba. The Treasury Department has granted some licenses to travel, but the categories of these exceptions have been narrowed or broadened at different points over the past four decades. In 1999, the only exemption to the requirement for a specific license is for travel by diplomats, members of intergovernmental organizations such as the U.N., and full-time journalists. Those visiting close relatives in Cuba may also travel once a year without a license.[670] All

---

[669] Section 215 (b) of the Immigration and Nationality Act of 1952 gives the president the authority to prohibit U.S. citizens from traveling to and from certain countries without a valid passport. It does not, the court determined, make it a crime to travel to or from a designated country with a passport not specifically validated for that country. State Department area restrictions on the use of otherwise valid passports, the court ruled, are not criminally enforceable. Rather their purpose is to "make clear that the passport was not to be regarded by the traveler in Cuba as a voucher on the protective services normally afforded by the State Department." *United States v. Laub et al*, No. 176, Supreme Court of the United States, 385 U.S. 475; 87 S. Ct. 574; 1967 U.S. LEXIS 2575; 17 L. Ed. 2d 526; January 10, 1967, Decided.

[670] During the Carter Administration, restrictions on travel were considerably eased, only to be tightened again under President Ronald Reagan. Professional research remained exempt from the restrictions on travel-related expenditures, as did news-gathering,

others must apply for a license from the Office of Foreign Assets Control of the Treasury Department. Violators can be imprisoned for up to 10 years and fined up to $250,000; corporations are subject to $1,000,000 fines. Under the Cuban Democracy Act of 1992, the Treasury Department may impose an additional civil penalty of up to $50,000 per violation, a provision that has not been superseded by the Helms-Burton law.[671]

A presidential proclamation issued in 1985 by President Ronald Reagan restricts Cuban travel to the United States, barring issuance of visas to Cuban government officials. The U.S. government has used this proclamation to deny visas to Cubans of diverse backgrounds, including scientists, poets, dancers, and university students on the grounds that their salaries are paid by the government.[672]

---

official governmental travel, and those visiting close relatives in Cuba, but all others remained barred from spending any money or providing any services while traveling to Cuba. (Krinsky, pp. 119-120; Wayne S. Smith, "The Travel Ban to Cuba," *International Policy Report*, Center for International Policy, May, 1994; and Elisa Muñoz, *The Right to Travel: The Effect of Travel Restrictions on Scientific Collaboration Between American and Cuban Scientists* [Washington: American Association for the Advancement of Science, 1998], p. 8). While the Cuban Democracy Act slightly loosened restrictions in 1993, the Clinton administration tightened the restrictions again in August 1994, revoking the general license for family visits to Cuba by Cuban-Americans, as well as the general license for professional research in Cuba. The only categories of travelers still allowed to visit Cuba on a general license were full-time journalists, diplomats, and representatives of international organizations of which the U.S. is a member, such as the U.N. or OAS. All others, including family members and researchers, were required to apply to the Treasury Department for a specific license to travel to Cuba. Cuban-Americans were required to claim a compelling family need for travel to Cuba, such as a grave illness. In October 1995, Cuban-Americans were allowed to travel once a year in emergency situations under a general license. (Human Rights Watch interview with Clara David, licensing officer, Office of Foreign Assets Control, U.S. Department of Treasury, September 14, 1998.) In 1996, following the shootdown of civilian aircraft over Cuba, the U.S. cancelled direct charter flights between Miami and Havana, and again tightened restrictions on U.S. travel. Following the Pope's January 1998 visit to Cuba, Clinton again allowed charter flights.

[671] U.S. Department of the Treasury Office of Foreign Assets Control, "Cuba: Travel Restrictions, October 23, 1995; and Krinsky, pp. 115-116.

[672] American Association for the Advancement of Science, "The Effect of Travel Restrictions on Scientific Collaboration Between American and Cuban Scientists, April 1998; and Wayne S. Smith, "The Travel Ban to Cuba."

The U.S. and Cuban Exile Violence

In a July 1998 article, *The New York Times* quoted the reclusive Cuban exile Luis Posada Carriles saying that for years, the Miami-based Cuban American National Foundation (CANF) and its late president, Jorge Mas Canosa, had financed hotel bombings and other acts of violence in Cuba under the direction of Posada Carriles, an allegation the CANF hotly denied and Posada later disavowed.[673] The *New York Times* detailed the long lived relationship between the U.S. Central Intelligence Agency (CIA) and Posada Carriles's commandos. CIA agents trained Posada Carriles's commandos in sabotage and violence and directed their activities, the account states, only to abandon them as unsavory criminals in the 1970s.[674]

The *New York Times* indicated that, even after the U.S. government no longer sponsored his violent activities, Posada Carriles may have benefited from a tolerant attitude on the part of U.S. law enforcement. As bombs ripped through tourist hotels and restaurants in Havana, the *New York Times* reported, a Cuban-American business-partner of Posada Carriles's tried to inform first Guatemalan, then U.S. law enforcement of Posada's involvement and possible links to Cuban exiles in Union City, New Jersey.[675] In March and April 1999 Cuban judges sentenced two Salvadorans, Raúl Ernesto Cruz Leon and Otto René Rodríguez Llerena, to death for their alleged involvement in bombing Cuban hotels.[676]

The Clinton administration's reaction to the *New York Times* accounts suggests an effort to distance itself from the hardliners, even while its hands remain tied by the Helms-Burton Act. Weeks after the sensational *New York Times* series

---

[673] Ann Louise Bardach and Larry Rohter, "Key Cuba Foe Claims Exiles' Backing," *New York Times*, July 12, 1998; Bardach and Rohter, "Life in the Shadows, Trying to Bring Down Castro," *New York Times*, July 13, 1998; "It's All False, Exiles Say," *New York Times*, July 13, 1998; and "Cuban Exile Says He Lied to Times About Financial Support," *New York Times*, August 4, 1998.

[674] Bardach and Rohter, "Life in the Shadows, Trying to Bring Down Castro," *New York Times*, July 13, 1998.

[675] Bardach and Rohter, "Authorities Knew of Bombing Campaign, Says Cuban Exile," *New York Times,* July 12, 1998.

[676] Anita Snow, "Cuba Sentences Salvadoran to Death," *Associated Press*, March 23, 1999, "Cuba: Cuba Sentences Second Salvadoran Bomber to Death," *Reuters News Service*, April 1, 1999, and "Cuba: Cuba Seeks Second Death Sentence in Bombings," *Reuters News Service*, March 17, 1999.

appeared, U.S. prosecutors filed attempted murder charges against seven Cuban exiles who allegedly plotted to kill Castro, charges that could bring a life sentence. The decision to charge the seven with attempted murder under Section 1116 of the Federal Criminal Code, instead of violations of the Neutrality Act, allows for a harsher penalty and the avoidance of a defense based on debate over U.S. policy. Among those indicted by a federal grand jury was businessman José Antonio Llama, a member of the CANF executive committee. The conspiracy was apparently intended to culminate with the assassination of Castro as he joined other Latin heads of state for the annual Ibero-American summit meeting held in November 1997 on Margarita Island, off the coast of Venezuela. With the indictment, the Clinton administration for the first time charged someone with attempting to murder Castro—an activity that had allegedly been a prime objective of previous U.S. administrations.[677]

European Union Policy

The European Union outlined a distinctive human rights policy toward Cuba in its December 1996 "Common Position," conditioning full economic cooperation with Havana on important human rights reforms. In addition, the E.U. has expressed strong opposition to the U.S. trade embargo against Cuba, especially in its present Helms-Burton incarnation, while promoting dialogue with Cuba in the interests of encouraging a political and economic opening. Yet efforts to use European aid as a carrot to induce Castro to implement human rights reforms have been rebuffed by Havana, leaving European policy, like that of the U.S., at a stalemate. The European Union should redouble its efforts to bring about concrete human rights reforms in Cuba, in cooperation with Canada and Latin American and Caribbean nations. If major reforms are not immediately attainable, more modest goals should be more energetically pursued, such as the release of individual political prisoners and access of the International Committee of the Red Cross to Cuban prisons.

In June 1995 the European Commission recommended the initiation of exploratory talks with Cuba in the interests of reaching a "cooperation agreement" to establish conditions for European assistance to the island, such as the E.U. has with every other Latin American country. This initiative followed a surge of European trade and investment in Cuba. In the early 1990s, Europe moved from

---

[677] Gerardo Reyes and Juan O. Tamayo, "Seven Indicted in Plot to Kill Castro; CANF Official Named in Grand Jury Probe," *Miami Herald*, August 26, 1998; and Carol Rosenberg and Juan O. Tamayo, "Feds Take Hard Line in Castro-plot Case," *Miami Herald*, August 27, 1998.

being an insignificant player in Cuban trade and investment to becoming Cuba's largest trading partner and second largest foreign investor.[678] According to recent official figures, half of the 350 or so economic ventures in Cuba with foreign capital that have been approved are from E.U. member states.[679] During an E.U. summit meeting in Madrid in December 1995, the European Council asked the commission to continue its preliminary talks with the Castro government and to present a draft cooperation agreement to the council in 1996. Commissioner Manuel Marín of Spain traveled to Cuba several times. In his most important journey in February 1996, Marín met with Fidel Castro and members of his government in an unsuccessful effort to win approval for the human rights reforms necessary to reach an agreement.[680]

The incipient warming trend in European Union relations was put on ice, however, by the February 24, 1996, downing of two civilian aircraft in Cuban airspace, the imprisonment of leaders of the dissident Cuban Council, and the failure of Marin's efforts to win from Castro a commitment to human rights reforms. In addition to a commitment to allow more freedom for private enterprise, Marín's list of needed reforms included the removal from Cuba's criminal code of specific provisions that violate freedom of expression and association. As Marín prepared to leave the island empty-handed, Cuban security agents arrested the entire leadership of the Cuban Council, including those who had met with Marín earlier in his visit.[681] Castro's firm rejection of the European initiative made discussion of a cooperation agreement unthinkable.

The E.U.'s subsequent position was defined in December 1996, with the adoption of a "Common Position" on Cuba, which the European Council has renewed every six months since then. The document's preamble lays out a

---

[678] Ibid, p. 5; and Resolution on the Communication from the [European] Commission to the Council and the European Parliament on the Relations between the European Union and Cuba (COM(95)0306 - C4-0298/95).

[679] Patricia Grogg, "Politics-Cuba: Cuba Gaining Respect of World Leaders," *IPS*, November 18, 1998.

[680] Institute for European-Latin American Relations, "Cuba and the European Union: The Difficulties of Dialogue," June 17, 1996, pp. 1-2.

[681] Richard A. Nuccio, "Cuba: A U.S. Perspective," paper prepared for the Brookings Institution's Conference on "Translatlantic Tensions: The Challenge of Difficult Countries," March 9-10, 1998, Washington, D.C., February 16, 1998, p. 26.

principled position on human rights and carefully takes distance from Washington's policy:

> The objective of the European Union in its relations with Cuba is to encourage a process of transition to pluralist democracy and respect for human rights and fundamental freedoms, as well as a sustainable recovery and improvement in the living standards of the Cuban people. A transition would most likely be peaceful if the present regime were itself to initiate or permit such a process. It is not the European Union policy to try to bring about change by coercive measures with the effect of increasing the economic hardship of the Cuban people.[682]

Noting that the E.U. member states will continue on an *ad hoc* basis to provide economic cooperation and humanitarian aid through nongovernmental organizations, the Common Position affirms the E.U.'s conviction that "full cooperation with Cuba will depend upon improvements in human rights and political freedom...." In particular, the E.U. calls for "the reform of internal legislation concerning political and civil rights, including the Cuban criminal code, and, consequently, the abolition of all political offences, the release of all political prisoners and the ending of the harassment and punishment of dissidents...."[683] On December 6, 1998, the E.U. concluded that it had "intensified its dialogue with the Cuban authorities and all sectors of Cuban society, in particular regarding human rights..." and confirmed a strong desire to act "as Cuba's partner with a view to the progressive and irreversible opening of the Cuban economy." The E.U. "nevertheless considered that full cooperation with Cuba will depend on an improvement of the situation regarding human rights and fundamental freedoms."[684]

In an effort to continue dialogue with Cuba while insisting on human rights reforms, the European Union in June 1998 agreed to allow the Castro government to participate as an observer in the latest round of negotiations of the Lomé Treaty, which gives preferential trade status to seventy-one less developed countries in Africa, the Caribbean, and the Pacific (ACP). However, Cuba's full integration into

---

[682] Common Position of 2 December 1996 defined by the Council on the basis of Article J.2 of the Treaty on European Union, on Cuba. Official Journal No. L 322, 12/12/1996, p.1.

[683] Ibid.

[684] E.U. General Affairs Council conclusions of December 6, 1998.

the group will depend on substantial progress in human rights and political freedom. Cuban Foreign Minister Roberto Robaina was quick to reject these conditions.[685] During a visit to Cuba in November 1998, Spanish Foreign Minister Abel Matutes commented on Cuba's prospects to become a full-fledged member of the ACP group, stressing his hopes that "the process of reflection in which the Cuban government is immersed comes to a positive conclusion, so that Cuba can benefit from the exceptional instruments that the E.U. is offering to developing countries."[686]

In the meantime, the fact that Cuban workers in foreign enterprises—like their peers in the state sector—have no possibility to organize or bargain collectively, presents a dilemma for European companies to avoid being complicit in the Cuban government's human rights violations. Workers' rights are limited by the government's control over hiring and firing, regulations against petitioning for improved conditions or wages, and other laws limiting freedom of association.[687] The fact that European companies—like all foreign investors in Cuba—benefit financially from these restrictions should not interfere with the need to take steps to promote labor rights. Investors should insist that the criteria employed by the government in individual employment decisions not discriminate on political, religious, or racial grounds. Moreover, European governments should make the establishment of freedom to bargain collectively a primary objective in their bilateral relations with Cuba.

Canadian Policy

In the last four years, Canada also has undertaken initiatives to strengthen diplomatic ties with Cuba as its investments there grew significantly. The Canadian policy, like that of the European Union, is one of dialogue and major investment tempered by some criticism of human rights violations. To its credit, the Canadian government has kept up a bilateral conversation with Cuba about human rights since January 1997. The message Canada has delivered, however, remains meek.

---

[685] "UE: La Unión Europea ayuda a Cuba con su Inclusión en el Grupo de Países Pobres con Ventajas Comerciales," *El Pais Internacional*, June 30, 1998; "Europa Exige a Cuba Drásticos Cambios Políticos," *Contacto*, July 1998, pp. 38-39; and "EU: Cuba Rejects Conditions for Improving EU Ties," *Reuters News Service*, June 30, 1998.

[686] Patricia Grogg, "Politics-Cuba: Cuba gaining respects of world leaders," *IPS*, November 18, 1998.

[687] See above, *Labor Rights*.

Canada's constructive engagement policy with Cuba is based on a January 1997 accord between Ottawa and Havana addressing investment, taxation, banking, and other issues, as well as calling on Canada to hold seminars and train Cuban judges on human rights issues. Since then, several seminars have been held on women's and children's rights.[688] The Cuban government, which detained several dissidents during the negotiation of the accord, does not appear to have changed its human rights practices as a result of the program.

Canadian officials, especially Foreign Affairs Minister Lloyd Axworthy, have been outspoken in their criticism of the U.S. embargo, even as they withhold from Havana what they term full cooperation in the absence of human rights reforms. Unfortunately, Canada's policy, like that of the E.U., has little to show for itself in human rights improvements, excepting the release of a handful of prisoners on the condition that they abandon their country. Canadian policy makers believe the U.S. embargo impedes their efforts, Nonetheless a mistaken policy by the United States does not justify an ineffectual one by other governments. Canada's government has failed to give human rights the preeminent place it deserves in its relations with Cuba. Its constructive engagement policy may now come under a much-needed review as a result of the March 1999 sentencing to three- to five-year prison terms of four dissident leaders.

Canadian Prime Minister Jean Chrétien's April 1998 visit to Havana illustrated both Ottawa's low profile approach to human rights and the ineffectiveness of that approach. Although his agenda included human rights as well as trade, the prime minister avoided public comment on civil and political liberties, and eschewed meeting with Cuban dissidents, although other members of the delegation met with rights defenders. During their private meeting, Chrétien handed Castro a list of four prisoners he wanted released, the members of the Internal Dissidents' Working Group detained for urging democratic reforms in July 1997.[689] Despite Chrétien's private request, the dissidents remained behind bars and have now been sentenced to several years in prison.

Chrétien's public silence on human rights represented a wasted opportunity to build on the momentum toward political opening begun by the pope during his visit.

---

[688] Joint Declaration of the Ministers of Foreign Affairs of Canada and Cuba, Havana, January 22, 1997; and notes prepared for delivery of speech of Peter M Boehm, Ambassador of Canada and Permanent Representative to the Organization of American States, at the annual meeting of the Cuban Committee for Democracy, Miami, September 12, 1998.

[689] Anthony DePalma, "Chrétien Finds Castro Willing to Deal, Just Not on Rights," *New York Times*, April 28, 1998. See above, *Political Prosecutions.*

While Pope John Paul II has—like Canadian officials—repeatedly denounced the U.S. embargo, he did not hesitate while on the island to call publicly for respect for human rights. Chrétien's reticence on human rights suggests a desire to maximize opportunities for trade and investment, even while Cuba thumbs its nose at international human rights principles. Indeed, Canadian companies, like their European counterparts, benefit from major investments on the island in which workers have no possibility to organize. Like the European investors, Canadian companies should insist that employment decisions not be based on political, religious, or racial grounds, while the government presses Havana to establish the right of workers to form independent unions and bargain collectively.

Canadian officials have spent two years trying to build a relationship with Havana distinct from that of the United States. It is time now for Ottawa to produce results from its careful engagement of the Castro government. In addition to the most pressing and difficult issues, like an end to the criminalization of free expression and association, Canada should press for more modest goals, such as allowing the International Committee of the Red Cross access to Cuban prisons. Otherwise Canadian human rights policy will be less detrimental than U.S. policy toward Cuba, but not any more effectual.

APPENDIX I

Universal Declaration of Human Rights
Adopted and proclaimed by the General Assembly in resolution 217 A (III), 10th of December, 1948.

Preamble
Whereas recognition of the inherent dignity and of the equal and inalienable rights of all members of the human family is the foundation of freedom, justice and peace in the world,

Whereas disregard and contempt for human rights have resulted in barbarous acts which have outraged the conscience of mankind, and the advent of a world in which human beings shall enjoy freedom of speech and belief and freedom from fear and want has been proclaimed as the highest aspiration of the common people,

Whereas it is essential, if man is not to be compelled to have recourse, as a last resort, to rebellion against tyranny and oppression, that human rights should be protected by the rule of law,

Whereas it is essential to promote the development of friendly relations between nations,

Whereas the peoples of the United Nations have in the Charter reaffirmed their faith in fundamental human rights, in the dignity and worth of the human person and in the equal rights of men and women and have determined to promote social progress and better standards of life in larger freedom,

Whereas Member States have pledged themselves to achieve, in co-operation with the United Nations, the promotion of universal respect for and observance of human rights and fundamental freedoms,

Whereas a common understanding of these rights and freedoms is of the greatest importance for the full realization of this pledge,

Now, Therefore, The General Assembly proclaims

This Universal Declaration of Human Rights as a common standard of achievement for all peoples and all nations, to the end that every individual and every organ of society, keeping this Declaration constantly in mind, shall strive by teaching and education to promote respect for these rights and freedoms and by progressive measures, national and international, to secure their universal and effective recognition and observance, both among the peoples of Member States themselves and among the peoples of territories under their jurisdiction.

Article 1
All human beings are born free and equal in dignity and rights. They are endowed with reason and conscience and should act towards one another in a spirit of brotherhood.

Article 2
Everyone is entitled to all the rights and freedoms set forth in this Declaration, without distinction of any kind, such as race, color, sex, language, religion, political or other opinion, national or social origin, property, birth or other status. Furthermore, no distinction shall be made on the basis of the political, jurisdictional or international status of the country or territory to which a person belongs, whether it be independent, trust, non-self-governing or under any other limitation of sovereignty.

Article 3
Everyone has the right to life, liberty and security of person.

Article 4
No one shall be held in slavery or servitude; slavery and the slave trade shall be prohibited in all their forms.

Article 5
No one shall be subjected to torture or to cruel, inhuman or degrading treatment or punishment.

Article 6
Everyone has the right to recognition everywhere as a person before the law.

Article 7
All are equal before the law and are entitled without any discrimination to equal protection of the law. All are entitled to equal protection against any discrimination in violation of this Declaration and against any incitement to such discrimination.

Article 8
Everyone has the right to an effective remedy by the competent national tribunals for acts violating the fundamental rights granted him by the constitution or by law.

Article 9
No one shall be subjected to arbitrary arrest, detention or exile.

Article 10
Everyone is entitled in full equality to a fair and public hearing by an independent and impartial tribunal, in the determination of his rights and obligations and of any criminal charge against him.

Article 11
(1) Everyone charged with a penal offence has the right to be presumed innocent until proved guilty according to law in a public trial at which he has had all the guarantees necessary for his defense.

(2) No one shall be held guilty of any penal offence on account of any act or omission which did not constitute a penal offence, under national or international law, at the time when it was committed Nor shall a heavier penalty be imposed than the one that was applicable at the time the penal offence was committed.

Article 12
No one shall be subjected to arbitrary interference with his privacy, family, home or correspondence, nor to attacks upon his honor and reputation Everyone has the right to the protection of the law against such interference or attacks.

Article 13
(1) Everyone has the right to freedom of movement and residence within the borders of each state.

(2) Everyone has the right to leave any country, including his own, and to return to his country.

Article 14
(1) Everyone has the right to seek and to enjoy in other countries asylum from persecution.

(2) This right may not be invoked in the case of prosecutions genuinely arising from non-political crimes or from acts contrary to the purposes and principles of the United Nations.

Article 15
(1) Everyone has the right to a nationality.

(2) No one shall be arbitrarily deprived of his nationality nor denied the right to change his nationality.

Article 16
(1) Men and women of full age, without any limitation due to race, nationality or religion, have the right to marry and to found a family. They are entitled to equal rights as to marriage, during marriage and at its dissolution.

(2) Marriage shall be entered into only with the free and full consent of the intending spouses.

(3) The family is the natural and fundamental group unit of society and is entitled to protection by society and the State.

Article 17
(1) Everyone has the right to own property alone as well as in association with others.

(2) No one shall be arbitrarily deprived of his property.

Article 18
Everyone has the right to freedom of thought, conscience and religion; this right includes freedom to change his religion or belief, and freedom, either alone or in community with others and in public or private, to manifest his religion or belief in teaching, practice, worship and observance.

Article 19
Everyone has the right to freedom of opinion and expression; this right includes freedom to hold opinions without interference and to seek, receive and impart information and ideas through any media and regardless of frontiers.

Article 20
(1) Everyone has the right to freedom of peaceful assembly and association.

(2) No one may be compelled to belong to an association.

Article 21

(1) Everyone has the right to take part in the government of his country, directly or through freely chosen representatives.

(2) Everyone has the right to equal access to public service in his country.

(3) The will of the people shall be the basis of the authority of government; this shall be expressed in periodic and genuine elections which shall be by universal and equal suffrage and shall be held by secret vote or by equivalent free voting procedures.

Article 22

Everyone, as a member of society, has the right to social security and is entitled to realization, through national effort and international co-operation and in accordance with the organization and resources of each State, of the economic, social and cultural rights indispensable for his dignity and the free development of his personality.

Article 23

(1) Everyone has the right to work, to free choice of employment, to just and favorable conditions of work and to protection against unemployment.

(2) Everyone, without any discrimination, has the right to equal pay for equal work.

(3) Everyone who works has the right to just and favorable remuneration ensuring for himself and his family an existence worthy of human dignity, and supplemented, if necessary, by other means of social protection.

(4) Everyone has the right to form and to join trade unions for the protection of his interests.

Article 24

Everyone has the right to rest and leisure, including reasonable limitation of working hours and periodic holidays with pay.

Article 25

(1) Everyone has the right to a standard of living adequate for the health and well-being of himself and of his family, including food, clothing, housing and

medical care and necessary social services, and the right to security in the event of unemployment, sickness, disability, widowhood, old age or other lack of livelihood in circumstances beyond his control.

(2) Motherhood and childhood are entitled to special care and assistance. All children, whether born in or out of wedlock, shall enjoy the same social protection.

Article 26
(1) Everyone has the right to education. Education shall be free, at least in the elementary and fundamental stages. Elementary education shall be compulsory. Technical and professional education shall be made generally available and higher education shall be equally accessible to all on the basis of merit.

(2) Education shall be directed to the full development of the human personality and to the strengthening of respect for human rights and fundamental freedoms. It shall promote understanding, tolerance and friendship among all nations, racial or religious groups, and shall further the activities of the United Nations for the maintenance of peace.

(3) Parents have a prior right to choose the kind of education that shall be given to their children.

Article 27
(1) Everyone has the right freely to participate in the cultural life of the community, to enjoy the arts and to share in scientific advancement and its benefits.

(2) Everyone has the right to the protection of the moral and material interests resulting from any scientific, literary or artistic production of which he is the author.

Article 28
Everyone is entitled to a social and international order in which the rights and freedoms set forth in this Declaration can be fully realized.

Article 29
(1) Everyone has duties to the community in which alone the free and full development of his personality is possible.

(2) In the exercise of his rights and freedoms, everyone shall be subject only to such limitations as are determined by law solely for the purpose of securing due recognition and respect for the rights and freedoms of others and of meeting the

just requirements of morality, public order and the general welfare in a democratic society.

(3) These rights and freedoms may in no case be exercised contrary to the purposes and principles of the United Nations.

Article 30

Nothing in this Declaration may be interpreted as implying for any State, group or person any right to engage in any activity or to perform any act aimed at the destruction of any of the rights and freedoms set forth herein.

APPENDIX II

Convention against Torture and Other Cruel, Inhuman or Degrading Treatment or Punishment

Adopted and opened for signature, ratification and accession by General Assembly resolution 39/46 of 10 December 1984 entry into force 26 June 1987, in accordance with article 27 (1) status of ratifications.

The States Parties to this Convention, Considering that,

In accordance with the principles proclaimed in the Charter of the United Nations, recognition of the equal and inalienable rights of all members of the human family is the foundation of freedom, justice and peace in the world,

Recognizing that those rights derive from the inherent dignity of the human person,

Considering the obligation of States under the Charter, in particular Article 55, to promote universal respect for, and observance of, human rights and fundamental freedoms,

Having regard to article 5 of the Universal Declaration of Human Rights and article 7 of the International Covenant on Civil and Political Rights, both of which provide that no one shall be subjected to torture or to cruel, inhuman or degrading treatment or punishment,

Having regard also to the Declaration on the Protection of All Persons from Being Subjected to Torture and Other Cruel, Inhuman or Degrading Treatment or Punishment, adopted by the General Assembly on 9 December 1975,

Desiring to make more effective the struggle against torture and other cruel, inhuman or degrading treatment or punishment throughout the world,

Have agreed as follows:

PART I

Article 1

1. For the purposes of this Convention, the term "torture" means any act by which severe pain or suffering, whether physical or mental, is intentionally inflicted on a person for such purposes as obtaining from him or a third person information or a

confession, punishing him for an act he or a third person has committed or is suspected of having committed, or intimidating or coercing him or a third person, or for any reason based on discrimination of any kind, when such pain or suffering is inflicted by or at the instigation of or with the consent or acquiescence of a public official or other person acting in an official capacity. It does not include pain or suffering arising only from, inherent in or incidental to lawful sanctions.

2. This article is without prejudice to any international instrument or national legislation which does or may contain provisions of wider application.

Article 2

1. Each State Party shall take effective legislative, administrative, judicial or other measures to prevent acts of torture in any territory under its jurisdiction.

2. No exceptional circumstances whatsoever, whether a state of war or a threat of war, internal political in stability or any other public emergency, may be invoked as a justification of torture.

3. An order from a superior officer or a public authority may not be invoked as a justification of torture.

Article 3

1. No State Party shall expel, return ("refouler") or extradite a person to another State where there are substantial grounds for believing that he would be in danger of being subjected to torture.

2. For the purpose of determining whether there are such grounds, the competent authorities shall take into account all relevant considerations including, where applicable, the existence in the State concerned of a consistent pattern of gross, flagrant or mass violations of human rights.

Article 4

1. Each State Party shall ensure that all acts of torture are offences under its criminal law. The same shall apply to an attempt to commit torture and to an act by any person which constitutes complicity or participation in torture.

2. Each State Party shall make these offences punishable by appropriate penalties which take into account their grave nature.

Article 5
1. Each State Party shall take such measures as may be necessary to establish its jurisdiction over the offences referred to in article 4 in the following cases:

(a) When the offences are committed in any territory under its jurisdiction or on board a ship or aircraft registered in that State;

(b) When the alleged offender is a national of that State;

(c) When the victim is a national of that State if that State considers it appropriate.

2. Each State Party shall likewise take such measures as may be necessary to establish its jurisdiction over such offences in cases where the alleged offender is present in any territory under its jurisdiction and it does not extradite him pursuant to article 8 to any of the States mentioned in paragraph I of this article.

3. This Convention does not exclude any criminal jurisdiction exercised in accordance with internal law.

Article 6
1. Upon being satisfied, after an examination of information available to it, that the circumstances so warrant, any State Party in whose territory a person alleged to have `committed any offence referred to in article 4 is present shall take him into custody or take other legal measures to ensure his presence. The custody and other legal measures shall be as provided in the law of that State but may be continued only for such time as is necessary to enable any criminal or extradition proceedings to be instituted.

2. Such State shall immediately make a preliminary inquiry into the facts.

3. Any person in custody pursuant to paragraph I of this article shall be assisted in communicating immediately with the nearest appropriate representative of the State of which he is a national, or, if he is a stateless person, with the representative of the State where he usually resides.

4. When a State, pursuant to this article, has taken a person into custody, it shall immediately notify the States referred to in article 5, paragraph 1, of the fact that such person is in custody and of the circumstances which warrant his detention. The State which makes the preliminary inquiry contemplated in paragraph 2 of this

article shall promptly report its findings to the said States and shall indicate whether it intends to exercise jurisdiction.

Article 7

1. The State Party in the territory under whose jurisdiction a person alleged to have committed any offence referred to in article 4 is found shall in the cases contemplated in article 5, if it does not extradite him, submit the case to its competent authorities for the purpose of prosecution.

2. These authorities shall take their decision in the same manner as in the case of any ordinary offence of a serious nature under the law of that State. In the cases referred to in article 5, paragraph 2, the standards of evidence required for prosecution and conviction shall in no way be less stringent than those which apply in the cases referred to in article 5, paragraph 1.

3. Any person regarding whom proceedings are brought in connection with any of the offences referred to in article 4 shall be guaranteed fair treatment at all stages of the proceedings.

Article 8

1. The offences referred to in article 4 shall be deemed to be included as extraditable offences in any extradition treaty existing between States Parties. States Parties undertake to include such offences as extraditable offences in every extradition treaty to be concluded between them.

2. If a State Party which makes extradition conditional on the existence of a treaty receives a request for extradition from another. State Party with which it has no extradition treaty, it may consider this Convention as the legal basis for extradition in respect of such offences. Extradition shall be subject to the other conditions provided by the law of the requested State.

3. States Parties which do not make extradition conditional on the existence of a treaty shall recognize such offences as extraditable offences between themselves subject to the conditions provided by the law of the requested State.

4. Such offences shall be treated, for the purpose of extradition between States Parties, as if they had been committed not only in the place in which they occurred but also in the territories of the States required to establish their jurisdiction in accordance with article 5, paragraph 1.

Article 9

1. States Parties shall afford one another the greatest measure of assistance in connection with criminal proceedings brought in respect of any of the offences referred to in article 4, including the supply of all evidence at their disposal necessary for the proceedings.

2. States Parties shall carry out their obligations under paragraph I of this article in conformity with any treaties on mutual judicial assistance that may exist between them.

Article 10

1. Each State Party shall ensure that education and information regarding the prohibition against torture are fully included in the training of law enforcement personnel, civil or military, medical personnel, public officials and other persons who may be involved in the custody, interrogation or treatment of any individual subjected to any form of arrest, detention or imprisonment.

2. Each State Party shall include this prohibition in the rules or instructions issued in regard to the duties and functions of any such person.

Article 11

Each State Party shall keep under systematic review interrogation rules, instructions, methods and practices as well as arrangements for the custody and treatment of persons subjected to any form of arrest, detention or imprisonment in any territory under its jurisdiction, with a view to preventing any cases of torture.

Article 12

Each State Party shall ensure that its competent authorities proceed to a prompt and impartial investigation, wherever there is reasonable ground to believe that an act of torture has been committed in any territory under its jurisdiction.

Article 13

Each State Party shall ensure that any individual who alleges he has been subjected to torture in any territory under its jurisdiction has the right to complain to, and to have his case promptly and impartially examined by, its competent authorities. Steps shall be taken to ensure that the complainant and witnesses are protected against all ill-treatment or intimidation as a consequence of his complaint or any evidence given.

Article 14
1. Each State Party shall ensure in its legal system that the victim of an act of torture obtains redress and has an enforceable right to fair and adequate compensation, including the means for as full rehabilitation as possible. In the event of the death of the victim as a result of an act of torture, his dependants shall be entitled to compensation.

2. Nothing in this article shall affect any right of the victim or other persons to compensation which may exist under national law.

Article 15
Each State Party shall ensure that any statement which is established to have been made as a result of torture shall not be invoked as evidence in any proceedings, except against a person accused of torture as evidence that the statement was made.

Article 16
1. Each State Party shall undertake to prevent in any territory under its jurisdiction other acts of cruel, inhuman or degrading treatment or punishment which do not amount to torture as defined in article I, when such acts are committed by or at the instigation of or with the consent or acquiescence of a public official or other person acting in an official capacity. In particular, the obligations contained in articles 10, 11, 12 and 13 shall apply with the substitution for references to torture of references to other forms of cruel, inhuman or degrading treatment or punishment.

2. The provisions of this Convention are without prejudice to the provisions of any other international instrument or national law which prohibits cruel, inhuman or degrading treatment or punishment or which relates to extradition or expulsion.

PART II

Article 17
1. There shall be established a Committee against Torture (hereinafter referred to as the Committee) which shall carry out the functions hereinafter provided. The Committee shall consist of ten experts of high moral standing and recognized competence in the field of human rights, who shall serve in their personal capacity. The experts shall be elected by the States Parties, consideration being given to equitable geographical distribution and to the usefulness of the participation of some persons having legal experience.

2. The members of the Committee shall be elected by secret ballot from a list of persons nominated by States Parties. Each State Party may nominate one person from among its own nationals. States Parties shall bear in mind the usefulness of nominating persons who are also members of the Human Rights Committee established under the International Covenant on Civil and Political Rights and who are willing to serve on the Committee against Torture.

3. Elections of the members of the Committee shall be held at biennial meetings of States Parties convened by the Secretary-General of the United Nations. At those meetings, for which two thirds of the States Parties shall constitute a quorum, the persons elected to the Committee shall be those who obtain the largest number of votes and an absolute majority of the votes of the representatives of States Parties present and voting.

4. The initial election shall be held no later than six months after the date of the entry into force of this Convention. At. least four months before the date of each election, the Secretary-General of the United Nations shall address a letter to the States Parties inviting them to submit their nominations within three months. The Secretary-General shall prepare a list in alphabetical order of all persons thus nominated, indicating the States Parties which have nominated them, and shall submit it to the States Parties.

5. The members of the Committee shall be elected for a term of four years. They shall be eligible for re-election if renominated. However, the term of five of the members elected at the first election shall expire at the end of two years; immediately after the first election the names of these five members shall be chosen by lot by the chairman of the meeting referred to in paragraph 3 of this article.

6. If a member of the Committee dies or resigns or for any other cause can no longer perform his Committee duties, the State Party which nominated him shall appoint another expert from among its nationals to serve for the remainder of his term, subject to the approval of the majority of the States Parties. The approval shall be considered given unless half or more of the States Parties respond negatively within six weeks after having been informed by the Secretary-General of the United Nations of the proposed appointment.

7. States Parties shall be responsible for the expenses of the members of the Committee while they are in performance of Committee duties.

Article 18
1. The Committee shall elect its officers for a term of two years. They may be re-elected.

2. The Committee shall establish its own rules of procedure, but these rules shall provide, inter alia, that:

(a) Six members shall constitute a quorum;

(b) Decisions of the Committee shall be made by a majority vote of the members present.

3. The Secretary-General of the United Nations shall provide the necessary staff and facilities for the effective performance of the functions of the Committee under this Convention.

4. The Secretary-General of the United Nations shall convene the initial meeting of the Committee. After its initial meeting, the Committee shall meet at such times as shall be provided in its rules of procedure.

5. The States Parties shall be responsible for expenses incurred in connection with the holding of meetings of the States Parties and of the Committee, including reimbursement to the United Nations for any expenses, such as the cost of staff and facilities, incurred by the United Nations pursuant to paragraph 3 of this article.

Article 19
1. The States Parties shall submit to the Committee, through the Secretary-General of the United Nations, reports on the measures they have taken to give effect to their undertakings under this Convention, within one year after the entry into force of the Convention for the State Party concerned. Thereafter the States Parties shall submit supplementary reports every four years on any new measures taken and such other reports as the Committee may request.

2. The Secretary-General of the United Nations shall transmit the reports to all States Parties.

3. Each report shall be considered by the Committee which may make such general comments on the report as it may consider appropriate and shall forward these to the State Party concerned. That State Party may respond with any observations it chooses to the Committee.

4. The Committee may, at its discretion, decide to include any comments made by it in accordance with paragraph 3 of this article, together with the observations thereon received from the State Party concerned, in its annual report made in accordance with article 24. If so requested by the State Party concerned, the Committee may also include a copy of the report submitted under paragraph 1 of this article.

Article 20

1. If the Committee receives reliable information which appears to it to contain well-founded indications that torture is being systematically practiced in the territory of a State Party, the Committee shall invite that State Party to co-operate in the examination of the information and to this end to submit observations with regard to the information concerned.

2. Taking into account any observations which may have been submitted by the State Party concerned, as well as any other relevant information available to it, the Committee may, if it decides that this is warranted, designate one or more of its members to make a confidential inquiry and to report to the Committee urgently.

3. If an inquiry is made in accordance with paragraph 2 of this article, the Committee shall seek the co-operation of the State Party concerned. In agreement with that State Party, such an inquiry may include a visit to its territory.

4. After examining the findings of its member or members submitted in accordance with paragraph 2 of this article, the Commission shall transmit these findings to the State Party concerned together with any comments or suggestions which seem appropriate in view of the situation.

5. All the proceedings of the Committee referred to in paragraphs 1 to 4 of this article shall be confidential , and at all stages of the proceedings the co-operation of the State Party shall be sought. After such proceedings have been completed with regard to an inquiry made in accordance with paragraph 2, the Committee may, after consultations with the State Party concerned, decide to include a summary account of the results of the proceedings in its annual report made in accordance with article 24.

Article 21

1. A State Party to this Convention may at any time declare under this article that it recognizes the competence of the Committee to receive and consider communications to the effect that a State Party claims that another State Party is not

fulfilling its obligations under this Convention. Such communications may be received and considered according to the procedures laid down in this article only if submitted by a State Party which has made a declaration recognizing in regard to itself the competence of the Committee. No communication shall be dealt with by the Committee under this article if it concerns a State Party which has not made such a declaration. Communications received under this article shall be dealt with in accordance with the following procedure;

(a) If a State Party considers that another State Party is not giving effect to the provisions of this Convention, it may, by written communication, bring the matter to the attention of that State Party. Within three months after the receipt of the communication the receiving State shall afford the State which sent the communication an explanation or any other statement in writing clarifying the matter, which should include, to the extent possible and pertinent, reference to domestic procedures and remedies taken, pending or available in the matter;

(b) If the matter is not adjusted to the satisfaction of both States Parties concerned within six months after the receipt by the receiving State of the initial communication, either State shall have the right to refer the matter to the Committee, by notice given to the Committee and to the other State;

(c) The Committee shall deal with a matter referred to it under this article only after it has ascertained that all domestic remedies have been invoked and exhausted in the matter, in conformity with the generally recognized principles of international law. This shall not be the rule where the application of the remedies is unreasonably prolonged or is unlikely to bring effective relief to the person who is the victim of the violation of this Convention;

(d) The Committee shall hold closed meetings when examining communications under this article;

(e) Subject to the provisions of subparagraph (c), the Committee shall make available its good offices to the States Parties concerned with a view to a friendly solution of the matter on the basis of respect for the obligations provided for in this Convention. For this purpose, the Committee may, when appropriate, set up an ad hoc conciliation commission;

(f) In any matter referred to it under this article, the Committee may call upon the States Parties concerned, referred to in subparagraph (b), to supply any relevant information;

(g) The States Parties concerned, referred to in subparagraph (b), shall have the right to be represented when the matter is being considered by the Committee and to make submissions orally and/or in writing;

(h) The Committee shall, within twelve months after the date of receipt of notice under subparagraph (b), submit a report:

(i) If a solution within the terms of subparagraph (e) is reached, the Committee shall confine its report to a brief statement of the facts and of the solution reached;

(ii) If a solution within the terms of subparagraph (e) is not reached, the Committee shall confine its report to a brief statement of the facts; the written submissions and record of the oral submissions made by the States Parties concerned shall be attached to the report.

In every matter, the report shall be communicated to the States Parties concerned.

2. The provisions of this article shall come into force when five States Parties to this Convention have made declarations under paragraph 1 of this article. Such declarations shall be deposited by the States Parties with the Secretary-General of the United Nations, who shall transmit copies thereof to the other States Parties. A declaration may be withdrawn at any time by notification to the Secretary-General. Such a withdrawal shall not prejudice the consideration of any matter which is the subject of a communication already transmitted under this article; no further communication by any State Party shall be received under this article after the notification of withdrawal of the declaration has been received by the Secretary-General, unless the State Party concerned has made a new declaration.

Article 22

1. A State Party to this Convention may at any time declare under this article that it recognizes the competence of the Committee to receive and consider communications from or on behalf of individuals subject to its jurisdiction who claim to be victims of a violation by a State Party of the provisions of the Convention. No communication shall be received by the Committee if it concerns a State Party which has not made such a declaration.

2. The Committee shall consider inadmissible any communication under this article which is anonymous or which it considers to be an abuse of the right of submission of such communications or to be incompatible with the provisions of this Convention.

3. Subject to the provisions of paragraph 2, the Committee shall bring any communications submitted to it under this article to the attention of the State Party to this Convention which has made a declaration under paragraph I and is alleged to be violating any provisions of the Convention. Within six months, the receiving State shall submit to the Committee written explanations or statements clarifying the matter and the remedy, if any, that may have been taken by that State.

4. The Committee shall consider communications received under this article in the light of all information made available to it by or on behalf of the individual and by the State Party concerned.

5. The Committee shall not consider any communications from an individual under this article unless it has ascertained that:

(a) The same matter has not been, and is not being, examined under another procedure of international investigation or settlement;

(b) The individual has exhausted all available domestic remedies; this shall not be the rule where the application of the remedies is unreasonably prolonged or is unlikely to bring effective relief to the person who is the victim of the violation of this Convention.

6. The Committee shall hold closed meetings when examining communications under this article.

7. The Committee shall forward its views to the State Party concerned and to the individual.

8. The provisions of this article shall come into force when five States Parties to this Convention have made declarations under paragraph 1 of this article. Such declarations shall be deposited by the States Parties with the Secretary-General of the United Nations, who shall transmit copies thereof to the other States Parties. A declaration may be withdrawn at any time by notification to the Secretary-General. Such a withdrawal shall not prejudice the consideration of any matter which is the subject of a communication already transmitted under this article; no further communication by or on behalf of an individual shall be received under this article after the notification of withdrawal of the declaration has been received by the Secretary-General, unless the State Party has made a new declaration.

Article 23
The members of the Committee and of the ad hoc conciliation commissions which may be appointed under article 21, paragraph I (e), shall be entitled to the facilities, privileges and immunities of experts on mission for the United Nations as laid down in the relevant sections of the Convention on the Privileges and Immunities of the United Nations.

Article 24
The Committee shall submit an annual report on its activities under this Convention to the States Parties and to the General Assembly of the United Nations.

PART III

Article 25
1. This Convention is open for signature by all States.

2. This Convention is subject to ratification. Instruments of ratification shall be deposited with the Secretary-General of the United Nations.

Article 26
This Convention is open to accession by all States. Accession shall be effected by the deposit of an instrument of accession with the SecretaryGeneral of the United Nations.

Article 27
1. This Convention shall enter into force on the thirtieth day after the date of the deposit with the Secretary-General of the United Nations of the twentieth instrument of ratification or accession.

2. For each State ratifying this Convention or acceding to it after the deposit of the twentieth instrument of ratification or accession, the Convention shall enter into force on the thirtieth day after the date of the deposit of its own instrument of ratification or accession.

Article 28
1. Each State may, at the time of signature or ratification of this Convention or accession thereto, declare that it does not recognize the competence of the Committee provided for in article 20.

2. Any State Party having made a reservation in accordance with paragraph 1 of this article may, at any time, withdraw this reservation by notification to the Secretary-General of the United Nations.

Article 29

1 . Any State Party to this Convention may propose an amendment and file it with the Secretary-General of the United Nations. The SecretaryGeneral shall thereupon communicate the proposed amendment to the States Parties with a request that they notify him whether they favor a conference of States Parties for the purpose of considering an d voting upon the proposal. In the event that within four months from the date of such communication at least one third of the States Parties favors such a conference, the Secretary General shall convene the conference under the auspices of the United Nations. Any amendment adopted by a majority of the States Parties present and voting at the conference shall be submitted by the Secretary-General to all the States Parties for acceptance.

2. An amendment adopted in accordance with paragraph 1 of this article shall enter into force when two thirds of the States Parties to this Convention have notified the Secretary-General of the United Nations that they have accepted it in accordance with their respective constitutional processes.

3. When amendments enter into force, they shall be binding on those States which have accepted them, other States Parties still being bound by the provisions of this Convention and any earlier amendments that they have accepted.

Article 30

1. Any disputes between two or more States Parties concerning the interpretation or application of this Convention which cannot be settled through negotiation shall, at the request of one of them, be submitted to arbitration. If within six months from the date of the request for arbitration the Parties are unable to agree on the organization of the arbitration, any one of those Parties may refer the dispute to the International Court of Justice by request in conformity with the Statute of the Court.

2. Each State Party may, at the time of signature or ratification of this Convention or accession thereto, declare that it does not consider itself bound by paragraph 1 of this article. The other States Parties shall not be bound by article 1 with respect to any State Party having made such a reservation.

3. Any State Party having made a reservation in accordance with paragraph 2 of this article may at anytime withdraw the reservation by notification to the Secretary-General of the United Nations.

Article 31

1. A State Party may denounce this Convention by written notification to the Secretary-General of the United Nations. Denunciation becomes effective one year after the date of the receipt of the notification to the Secretary- General of the United Nations.

2. Such a denunciation shall not have the effect of releasing the State Party from its obligations under this Convention in regard to any act or omission which occurs prior to the date at which the denunciation becomes effective, nor shall denunciation prejudice in any way the continued consideration of any matter which is already under consideration by the Committee prior to the date at which the denunciation becomes effective.

3. Following the date at which the denunciation of a State Party becomes effective, the committee shall not commence consideration of any new matter regarding that State.

Article 32

The Secretary-General of the United Nations shall inform the States Members of the United Nations and all States which have signed this Convention or acceded to it of the following:

(a) Signatures, ratifications and accessions under articles 25 and 26.

(b) The date of entry into force of this Convention under article 27 and the date of the entry into force of any amendments under article 29;

(c) Denunciations under article 31.

Article 33

1. This Convention, of which the Arabic, Chinese, English, French, Russian and Spanish texts are equally authentic, shall be deposited with the Secretary-General of the United Nations.

2. The Secretary-General of the United Nations shall transmit certified copies of this Convention to all States.

APPENDIX III

Protection of Persons Subjected to Detention or Imprisonment: Standard Minimum Rules for the Treatment of Prisoners

Adopted by the First United Nations Congress on the Prevention of Crime and the Treatment of Offenders, held at Geneva in 1955, and approved by the Economic and Social Council by its resolutions 663 C (XXIV) of July 31, 1957 and 2076 (LXII) of May 13, 1977.

Preliminary Observations

1. The following rules are not intended to describe in detail a model system of penal institutions. They seek only, on the basis of the general consensus of contemporary thought and the essential elements of the most adequate systems of today, to set out what is generally accepted as being good principle and practice in the treatment of prisoners and the management of institutions.

2. In view of the great variety of legal, social, economic and geographical conditions of the world, it is evident that not all of the rules are capable of application in all places and at all times. They should, however, serve to stimulate a constant endeavor to overcome practical difficulties in the way of their application, in the knowledge that they represent, as a whole, the minimum conditions which are accepted as suitable by the United Nations.

3. On the other hand, the rules cover a field in which thought is constantly developing. They are not intended to preclude experiment and practices, provided these are in harmony with the principles and seek to further the purposes which derive from the text of the rules as a whole. It will always be justifiable for the central prison administration to authorize departures from the rules in this spirit.

4. (1) Part 1 of the rules covers the general management of institutions, and is applicable to all categories of prisoners, criminal or civil, untried or convicted, including prisoners subject to "security measures" or corrective measures ordered by the judge.

(2) Part II contains rules applicable only to the special categories dealt with in each section. Nevertheless, the rules under Section A, applicable to prisoners under sentence, shall be equally applicable to categories of prisoners dealt with in sections B, C and D, provided they do not conflict with the rules governing those categories and are for their benefit.

5. (1) The rules do not seek to regulate the management of institutions set aside for young
persons such as Borstal institutions or correctional schools, but in general part I would be
equally applicable in such institutions.

(2) The category of young prisoners should include at least all young persons who come within the jurisdiction of juvenile courts. As a rule, such young persons should not be sentenced to imprisonment.

PART I - RULES OF GENERAL APPLICATION

Basic Principle

6. (1) The following rules shall be applied impartially. There shall be no discrimination on grounds of race, color, sex, language, religion, political or other opinion, national or social origin, property, birth or other status.

(2) On the other hand, it is necessary to respect the religious beliefs and moral precepts of the group to which the prisoner belongs.

Register

7. (1) In every place where persons are imprisoned there shall be kept a bound registration book with numbered pages in which shall be entered in respect of each prisoner received:

(a) Information concerning his identity;

(b) The reasons for his commitment and the authority therefor;

(c) The day and hour of his admission and release.

(2) No person shall be received in an institution without a valid commitment order of which the details shall have been previously entered in the register.

Separation of Categories

8. The different categories of prisoners shall be kept in separate institutions or parts of institutions taking account of their sex, age, criminal record, the legal reason for their detention and the necessities of their treatment. Thus,

(a) Men and women shall so far as possible be detained in separate institutions; in an institution which receives both men and women the whole of the premises allocated to women shall be entirely separate;

(b) Untried prisoners shall be kept separate from convicted prisoners;

(c) Persons imprisoned for debt or other civil prisoners shall be kept separate from persons imprisoned by reason of a criminal offence;

(d) Young prisoners shall be kept separate from adults.

Accommodation

9. (1) Where sleeping accommodation is in individual cells or rooms, each prisoner shall occupy by night a cell or room by himself. If for special reasons, such as temporary overcrowding, it becomes necessary for the central prison administration to make an exception to this rule, it is not desirable to have two prisoners in a cell or room.

(2) Where dormitories are used, they shall be occupied by prisoners carefully selected as being suitable to associate with one another in those conditions. There shall be regular supervision by night, in keeping with the nature of the institution.

10. All accommodation provided for the use of prisoners and in particular all sleeping accommodation shall meet all requirements of health, due regard being paid to climatic conditions and particularly to cubic content of air, minimum floor space, lighting, heating and ventilation.

11. In all places where prisoners are required to live or work,

(a) The windows shall be large enough to enable the prisoners to read or work by natural light, and shall be so constructed that they can allow the entrance of fresh air whether or not there is artificial ventilation;

(b) Artificial light shall be provided sufficient for the prisoners to read or work without injury to eyesight.

12. The sanitary installations shall be adequate to enable every prisoner to comply with the needs of nature when necessary and in a clean and decent manner.

13. Adequate bathing and shower installations shall be provided so that every prisoner may be enabled and required to have a bath or shower, at a temperature suitable to the climate, as frequently as necessary for general hygiene according to season and geographical region, but at least once a week in a temperate climate.

14. All parts of an institution regularly used by prisoners shall be properly maintained and kept
scrupulously clean at all times.

Personal Hygiene
15. Prisoners shall be required to keep their persons clean, and to this end they shall be provided with water and with such toilet articles as are necessary for health and cleanliness.

16. In order that prisoners may maintain a good appearance compatible with their self-respect, facilities shall be provided for the proper care of the hair and beard, and men shall be enabled to shave regularly.

Clothing and Bedding
17. (1) Every prisoner who is not allowed to wear his own clothing shall be provided with an outfit of clothing suitable for the climate and adequate to keep him in good health. Such clothing shall in no manner be degrading or humiliating.

(2) All clothing shall be clean and kept in proper condition. Underclothing shall be changed and washed as often as necessary for the maintenance of hygiene.

(3) In exceptional circumstances, whenever a prisoner is removed outside the institution for an authorized purpose, he shall be allowed to wear his own clothing or other inconspicuous clothing.

18. If prisoners are allowed to wear their own clothing, arrangements shall be made on their admission to the institution to ensure that it shall be clean and fit for use.

19. Every prisoner shall, in accordance with local or national standards, be provided with a separate bed, and with separate and sufficient bedding which shall be clean when issued, kept in good order and changed often enough to ensure its cleanliness.

Food

20. (1) Every prisoner shall be provided by the administration at the usual hours with food of nutritional value adequate for health and strength, of wholesome quality and well prepared and
served.

(2) Drinking water shall be available to every prisoner whenever he needs it.

Exercise and Sport

21. (1) Every prisoner who is not employed in outdoor work shall have at least one hour of suitable exercise in the open air daily if the weather permits.

(2) Young prisoners, and others of a suitable age and physique, shall receive physical and recreational training during the period of exercise. To this end space, installations and equipment should be provided.

Medical Services

22. (1) At every institution there shall be available the services of at least one qualified medical officer who should have some knowledge of psychiatry. The medical services should be organized in close relationship to the general health administration of the community or nation. They shall include a psychiatric service for the diagnosis and, in proper cases, the treatment of states of mental abnormality.

(2) Sick prisoners who require specialist treatment shall be transferred to specialized institutions or to civil hospitals. Where hospital facilities are provided in an institution, their equipment, furnishings and pharmaceutical supplies shall be proper for the medical care and treatment of sick prisoners, and there shall be a staff of suitable trained officers.

(3) The services of a qualified dental officer shall be available to every prisoner.

23. (1) In women's institutions there shall be special accommodation for all necessary pre-natal and post-natal care and treatment. Arrangements shall be made wherever practicable for children to be born in a hospital outside the institution. If a child is born in prison, this fact shall not be mentioned in the birth certificate.

(2) Where nursing infants are allowed to remain in the institution with their mothers, provision shall be made for a nursery staffed by qualified persons, where the infants shall be placed when they are not in the care of their mothers.

24. The medical officer shall see and examine every prisoner as soon as possible after his admission and thereafter as necessary, with a view particularly to the discovery of physical or mental illness and the taking of all necessary measures; the segregation of prisoners suspected of infectious or contagious conditions; the noting of physical or mental defects which might hamper rehabilitation, and the determination of the physical capacity of every prisoner for work.

25. (1) The medical officer shall have the care of the physical and mental health of the prisoners and should daily see all sick prisoners, all who complain of illness, and any prisoner to whom his attention is specially directed.

(2) The medical officer shall report to the director whenever he considers that a prisoner's physical or mental health has been or will be injuriously affected by continued imprisonment or by any condition of imprisonment.

26. (1) The medical officer shall regularly inspect and advise the director upon:

(a) The quantity, quality, preparation and service of food;

(b) The hygiene and cleanliness of the institution and the prisoners;

(c) The sanitation, heating, lighting and ventilation of the institution;

(d) The suitability and cleanliness of the prisoners' clothing and bedding;

(e) The observance of the rules concerning physical education and sports, in cases where there is no technical personnel in charge of these activities.

(2) The director shall take into consideration the reports and advice that the medical officer submits according to rules 25 (2) and 26 and, in case he concurs with the recommendations made, shall take immediate steps to give effect to those recommendations; if they are not within his competence or if he does not concur with them, he shall immediately submit his own report and the advice of the medical officer to a higher authority.

Discipline and Punishment

27. Discipline and order shall be maintained with firmness, but with no more restriction than is necessary for safe custody and well-ordered community life.

28. (1) No prisoner shall be employed, in the service of the institution, in any disciplinary capacity.

(2) This rule shall not, however, impede the proper functioning of systems based on self-government, under which specified social, educational or sports activities or responsibilities are entrusted, under supervision, to prisoners who are formed into groups for the purposes of treatment.

29. The following shall always be determined by the law or by the regulation of the competent administrative authority:

(a) Conduct constituting a disciplinary offence;

(b) The types and duration of punishment which may be inflicted;

(c) The authority competent to impose such punishment.

30. (1) No prisoner shall be punished except in accordance with the terms of such law or regulation, and never twice for the same offence.

(2) No prisoner shall be punished unless he has been informed of the offence alleged against him and given a proper opportunity of presenting his defense. The competent authority shall conduct a thorough examination of the case. (3) Where necessary and practicable the prisoner shall be allowed to make his defense through an interpreter.

31. Corporal punishment, punishment by placing in a dark cell, and all cruel, inhuman or degrading punishments shall be completely prohibited as punishments for disciplinary offenses.

32. (1) Punishment by close confinement or reduction of diet shall never be inflicted unless the medical officer has examined the prisoner and certified in writing that he is fit to sustain it.

(2) The same shall apply to any other punishment that may be prejudicial to the physical or mental health of a prisoner. In no case may such punishment be contrary to or depart from the principle stated in rule 31.

(3) The medical officer shall visit daily prisoners undergoing such punishments and shall advise the director if he considers the termination or alteration of the punishment necessary on grounds of physical or mental health.

Instruments of Restraint

33. Instruments of restraint, such as handcuffs, chains, irons and strait-jackets shall never be applied as a punishment. Furthermore, chains or irons shall not be used as restraints. Other instruments of restraint shall not be used except in the following circumstances:

(a) As a precaution against escape during transfer, provided that they shall be removed when the prisoner appears before a judicial or administrative authority;

(b) On medical grounds by direction of the medical officer;

(c) By order of the director, if other methods of control fail, in order to prevent a prisoner from injuring himself or others or from damaging property; in such instances the director shall at once consult the medical officer and report to the higher administrative authority.

34. The patterns and manner of use of instruments of restraint shall be decided by the central prison administration. Such instruments must not be applied for any longer time than is strictly necessary.

Information to and Complaints by Prisoners

35. (1) Every prisoner on admission shall be provided with written information about the regulations governing the treatment of prisoners in his category, the disciplinary requirements of the institution, the authorized methods of seeking information and making complaints, and all such other matters as are necessary to enable him to understand both his rights and his obligations and to adapt himself to the life of the institution.

(2) If a prisoner is illiterate, the aforesaid information shall be conveyed to him orally.

36. (1) Every prisoner shall have the opportunity each week day of making requests or complaints to the director of the institution or the officer authorized to represent him.

(2) It shall be possible to make requests or complaints to the inspector of prisons during his inspection. The prisoner shall have the opportunity to talk to the inspector or to any other inspecting officer without the director or other members of the staff being present.

(3) Every prisoner shall be allowed to make a request or complaint, without censorship as to substance but in proper form, to the central prison administration, the judicial authority or other proper authorities through approved channels.

(4) Unless it is evidently frivolous or groundless, every request or complaint shall be promptly dealt with and replied to without undue delay.

Contact with the Outside World

37. Prisoners shall be allowed under necessary supervision to communicate with their family and reputable friends at regular intervals, both by correspondence and by receiving visits.

38. (1) Prisoners who are foreign nationals shall be allowed reasonable facilities to communicate with the diplomatic and consular representatives of the State to which they belong.

(2) Prisoners who are nationals of States without diplomatic or consular representation in the country and refugees or stateless persons shall be allowed similar facilities to communicate with the diplomatic representatives of the State which takes charge of their interests or any national or international body whose task it is to protect such persons.

39. Prisoners shall be kept informed regularly of the more important items of news by the reading of newspapers, periodicals or special institutional publications, by hearing wireless transmissions, by lectures or by any similar means as authorized or controlled by the administration.

Books

40. Every institution shall have a library for the use of all categories of prisoners, adequately stocked with both recreational and instructional books, and prisoners shall be encouraged to make full use of it.

Religion

41. (1) If the institution contains a sufficient number of prisoners of the same religion, a qualified representative of that religion shall be appointed or approved.

If the number of prisoners justifies it and conditions permit, the arrangement should be on a full-time basis.

(2) A qualified representative appointed or approved under paragraph (1) shall be allowed to hold regular services and to pay pastoral visits in private to prisoners of his religion at proper times.

(3) Access to a qualified representative of any religion shall not be refused to any prisoner. On the other hand, if any prisoner should object to a visit of any religious representative, his attitude shall be fully respected.

42. So far as practicable, every prisoner shall be allowed to satisfy the needs of his religious life by attending the services provided in the institution and having in his possession the books of religious observance and instruction of his denomination.

Retention of Prisoners' Property

43. (1) All money, valuables, clothing and other effects belonging to a prisoner which under the regulations of the institution he is not allowed to retain shall on his admission to the institution be placed in safe custody. An inventory thereof shall be signed by the prisoner. Steps shall be taken to keep them in good condition.

(2) On the release of the prisoner all such articles and money shall be returned to him except in so far as he has been authorized to spend money or send any such property out of the institution, or it has been found necessary on hygienic grounds to destroy any article of clothing. The prisoner shall sign a receipt for the articles and money returned to him.

(3) Any money or effects received for a prisoner from outside shall be treated in the same way.

(4) If a prisoner brings in any drugs or medicine, the medical officer shall decide what use shall be made of them.

Notification of Death, Illness, Transfer, Etc.

44. (1) Upon the death or serious illness of, or serious injury to a prisoner, or his removal to an institution for the treatment of mental affections, the director shall at once inform the spouse, if the prisoner is married, or the nearest relative and shall in any event inform any other person previously designated by the prisoner.

(2) A prisoner shall be informed at once of the death or serious illness of any near relative. In case of the critical illness of any near relative, the prisoner should be authorized, whenever circumstances allow, to go to his bedside either under escort or alone.

(3) Every prisoner shall have the right to inform at once his family of his imprisonment or his transfer to another institution.

Removal of Prisoners

45. (1) When prisoners are being removed to or from an institution, they shall be exposed to public view as little as possible, and proper safeguards shall be adopted to protect them from insult, curiosity and publicity in any form.

(2) The transport of prisoners in conveyances with inadequate ventilation or light, or in any way which would subject them to unnecessary physical hardship, shall be prohibited.

(3) The transport of prisoners shall be carried out at the expense of the administration and equal conditions shall obtain for all of them.

Institutional Personnel

46. (1) the prison administration shall provide for the careful selection of every grade of the personnel, since it is on their integrity, humanity, professional capacity and personal suitability for the work that the proper administration of the institutions depends.

(2) The prison administration shall constantly seek to awaken and maintain in the minds both of the personnel and of the public the conviction that this work is a social service of great importance, and to this end all appropriate means of informing the public should be used.

(3) To secure the foregoing ends, personnel shall be appointed on a full-time basis as professional prison officers and have civil service status with security of tenure subject only to good conduct, efficiency and physical fitness. Salaries shall be adequate to attract and retain suitable men and women; employment benefits and conditions of service shall be favorable in view of the exacting nature of the work.

47. (1) The personnel shall possess an adequate standard of education and intelligence.

(2) Before entering on duty, the personnel shall be given a course of training in their general and specific duties and be required to pass theoretical and practical tests.

(3) After entering on duty and during their career, the personnel shall maintain and improve their knowledge and professional capacity by attending courses of in-service training to be organized at suitable intervals.

48. All members of the personnel shall at all times so conduct themselves and perform their duties as to influence the prisoners for good by their example and to command their respect.

49. (1) So far as possible, the personnel shall include a sufficient number of specialists such as psychiatrists, psychologists, social workers, teachers and trade instructors.

(2) The services of social workers, teachers and trade instructors shall be secured on a permanent basis, without thereby excluding part-time or voluntary workers.

50. (1) The director of an institution should be adequately qualified for his task by character, administrative ability, suitable training and experience.

(2) He shall devote his entire time to his official duties and shall not be appointed on a part-time basis.

(3) He shall reside on the premises of the institution or in its immediate vicinity.

(4) When two or more institutions are under the authority of one director, he shall visit each of them at frequent intervals. A responsible resident official shall be in charge of each of these institutions.

51. (1) The director, his deputy, and the majority of the other personnel of the institution shall be able to speak the language of the greatest number of prisoners, or a language understood by the greatest number of them.

(2) Whenever necessary, the services of an interpreter shall be used.

52. (1) In institutions which are large enough to require the services of one or more full-time medical officers, at least one of them shall reside on the premises of the institution or in its immediate vicinity.

(2) In other institutions the medical officer shall visit daily and shall reside near enough to be able to attend without delay in cases of urgency.

53 (1) In an institution for both men and women, the part of the institution set aside for women shall be under the authority of a responsible woman officer who shall have the custody of the keys of all that part of the institution.

(2) No male member of the staff shall enter the part of the institution set aside for women unless accompanied by a woman officer.

(3) Woman prisoners shall be attended and supervised only by women officers. This does not, however, preclude male members of the staff, particularly doctors and teachers, from carrying out their professional duties in institutions or parts of institutions set aside for women.

54. (1) Officers of the institutions shall not, in their relations with the prisoners, use force except in self-defence or cases of attempted escape, or active or passive physical resistance to an order based on law or regulations. Officers who have recourse to force must use no more than is strictly necessary and must report the incident immediately to the director of the institution.

(2) Prison officers shall be given special physical training to enable them to restrain aggressive prisoners.

(3) Except in special circumstances, staff performing duties which bring them into direct contact with prisoners should not be armed. Furthermore, staff should in no circumstances be provided with arms unless they have been trained in their use.

Inspection
55. There shall be regular inspection of penal institutions and services by qualified and experienced inspectors appointed by a competent authority. their task shall be in particular to ensure that these institutions are administered in accordance with existing laws and regulations and with a view to bringing about the objectives of the penal and correctional services.

PART II -- RULES APPLICABLE TO SPECIAL CATEGORIES

A. PRISONERS UNDER SENTENCE

Guiding Principles

56. The guiding principles hereafter are intended to show the spirit in which penal institutions should be administered and the purposes at which they should aim, in accordance with the declaration made under Preliminary Observation 1 of the present text.

57. Imprisonment and other measures which result in cutting off an offender from the outside world are afflictive by the very fact of taking from the person the right to self-determination by depriving him of his liberty. Therefore the prison system shall not, except as incidental to justifiable segregation or the maintenance of discipline, aggravate the suffering inherent in such a situation.

58. The purpose and justification of a sentence of imprisonment or a similar measure deprivative of liberty is ultimately to protect society against crime. This end can only be achieved if the period of imprisonment is used to ensure, so far as possible, that upon his return to society the offender is not only willing but able to lead a law-abiding and self-supporting life.

59. To this end, the institution should utilize all the remedial, educational, moral, spiritual and other forces and forms of assistance which are appropriate and available, and should seek to apply them according to the individual treatment needs of the prisoners.

60. (1) The regime of the institution should seek to minimize any differences between prison life and life at liberty which tend to lessen the responsibility of the prisoners or the respect due to their dignity as human beings.

(2) Before the completion of the sentence, it is desirable that the necessary steps be taken to ensure for the prisoner a gradual return to life in society. This aim may be achieved, depending on the case, by a pre-release regime organized in the same institution or in another appropriate institution, or by release on trial under some kind on supervision which must not be entrusted to the police but should be combined with effective social aid.

61. The treatment of prisoners should emphasize not their exclusion from the community, but their continuing part in it. Community agencies should, therefore,

be enlisted wherever possible to assist the staff of the institution in this task of social rehabilitation of the prisoners. There should be in connexion with every institution social workers charged with the duty of maintaining and improving all desirable relations of a prisoner with his family and with valuable social agencies. Steps should be taken to safeguard, to the maximum extent compatible with the law and the sentence, the rights relating to civil interests, social security rights and other social benefits of prisoners.

62. The medical services of the institution shall seek to detect and shall treat any physical or mental illnesses or defects which may hamper a prisoner's rehabilitation. all necessary medical, surgical and psychiatric services shall be provided to that end.

63. (1) The fulfilment of these principles requires individualization of treatment and for this purpose a flexible system of classifying prisoners in groups; it is therefore desirable that such groups should be distributed in separate institutions suitable for the treatment of each group.

(2) These institutions need not provide the same degree of security for every group. It is desirable to provide varying degrees of security according to the needs of different groups. Open institutions, by the very fact that they provide no physical security against escape but rely on the self-discipline of the inmates, provide the conditions most favourable to rehabilitation for carefully selected prisoners.

(3) It is desirable that the number of prisoners in closed institutions should not be so large that the individualization of treatment is hindered. In some countries it is considered that the population of such institutions should not exceed five hundred. In open institutions the population should be as small as possible.

(4) On the other hand, it is undesirable to maintain prisons that are so small that proper facilities cannot be provided.

64. The duty of society does not end with a prisoner's release. There should, therefore, be governmental or private agencies capable of lending the released prisoner efficient after-care directed towards the lessening of prejudice against him and towards his social rehabilitation.

Treatment

65. The treatment of persons sentenced to imprisonment or a similar measure shall have as its purpose, so far as the length of the sentence permits, to lead law-abiding

and self-supporting lives after their release and to fit them to do so. The treatment shall be such as will encourage their self-respect and develop their sense of responsibility.

66. (1) To these ends, all appropriate means shall be used, including religious care in the countries where this is possible, education, vocational guidance and training, social casework, employment counselling, physical development and strengthening of moral character, in his sentence and his prospects after release.

(2) For every prisoner with a sentence of suitable length, the director shall receive, as soon as possible after his admission, full reports on all the matters referred to in the foregoing paragraph. Such reports shall always include a report by a medical officer, wherever possible qualified in psychiatry, on the physical and mental condition of the prisoner.

(3) The reports and other relevant documents shall be placed in an individual file. This file shall be kept up to date and classified in such a way that it can be consulted by the responsible personnel whenever the need arises.

Classification and Individualization

67. The purposes of classification shall be:

(a) To separate from others those prisoners who, by reason of their criminal records or bad characters, are likely to cause a bad influence;

(b) To divide the prisoners into classes in order to facilitate their treatment with a view to their social rehabilitation.

68. So far as possible after admission and after a study of the personality of each prisoner with a sentence of suitable length, a programme of treatment shall be prepared for him in the light of the knowledge obtained about his individual needs, his capacities and dispositions.

Privileges

70. Systems of privileges appropriate for the different classes of prisoners and different methods of treatment shall be established at every institution, in order to encourage good conduct, develop a sense of responsibility and secure the interest and co-operation of the prisoners in their treatment.

Work

71. (1) Prison labour must not be of an afflictive nature.

(2) All prisoners under sentence shall be required to work, subject to their physical and mental fitness as determined by the medical officer.

(3) Sufficient work of a useful nature shall be provided to keep prisoners actively employed for a normal working day.

(4) So far as possible the work provided shall be such as will maintain or increase the prisoners' ability to earn an honest living after release.

(5) Vocational training in useful trades shall be provided for prisoners able to profit thereby and especially for young prisoners.

(6) Within the limits compatible with proper vocational selection and with the requirements of institutional administration and discipline, the prisoners shall be able to choose the type of work they wish to perform.

72. (1) The organization and methods of work in the institutions shall resemble as closely as possible those of similar work outside institutions, so as to prepare prisoners for the conditions of normal occupational life.

(2) The interests of the prisoners and of their vocational training, however, must not be subordinated to the purpose of making a financial profit from an industry in the institution.

73. (1) Preferably institutional industries and farms should be operated directly by the administration and not private contractors.

(2) Where prisoners are employed in work not controlled by the administration, they shall always be under the supervision of the institution's personnel. Unless the work is for other departments of the government the full normal wages for such work shall be paid to the administration by the persons to whom the labour is supplied, account being taken of the output of the prisoners.

74. (1) The precautions laid down to protect the safety and health of free workmen shall be equally observed in institutions.

(2) Provision shall be made to indemnify prisoners against industrial injury, including occupational disease, on terms not less favourable than those extended by law to free workmen.

75. (1) The maximum daily and weekly working hours of the prisoners shall be fixed by law or by administrative regulation, taking into account local rules or custom in regard to the employment of free workmen.

(2) The hours so fixed shall leave one rest day a week and sufficient time for education and other activities required as part of the treatment and rehabilitation of the prisoners.

76. (1) There shall be a system of equitable remuneration of the work of prisoners.

(2) Under the system prisoners shall be allowed to spend at least a part of their earnings on approved articles for their own use and to send a part of their earnings to their family.

(3) The system should also provide that a part of the earnings should be set aside by the administration so as to constitute a savings fund to he handed over to the prisoner on his release.

Education and Recreation

77. (1) Provision shall be made for the further education of all prisoners capable of profiting thereby, including religious instruction in the countries where this is possible. The education of illiterates and young prisoners shall be compulsory and special attention shall be paid to it by the administration.

(2) So far as practicable, the education of prisoners shall be integrated with the educational system of the country so that after their release they may continue their education without difficulty.

78. Recreational and cultural activities shall be provided in all institutions for the benefit of the mental and physical health of prisoners.

Social Relations and After-care

79. Special attention shall be paid to the maintenance and improvement of such relations between a prisoner and his family as are desirable and in the best interests of both.

80. From the beginning of a prisoner's sentence consideration shall be given to his future after release and he shall be encouraged and assisted to maintain or establish such relations with persons or agencies outside the institution as may promote the best interests of his family and his own social rehabilitation.

81. (1) Services and agencies, governmental or otherwise, which assist released prisoners to re-establish themselves in society shall ensure, so far as it is possible and necessary, that released prisoners be provided with appropriate documents and identification papers, have suitable homes and work to go to, are suitably and adequately clothed having regard to the climate and season, and have sufficient means to reach their destination and maintain themselves for the period immediately following their release.

(2) The approved representatives of such agencies shall have all necessary access to the institution and to prisoners and shall be taken into consultation as to the future of a prisoner from the beginning of his sentence.

(3) It is desirable that the activities of such agencies shall be centralized or coordinated as far as possible in order to secure the best use of their efforts.

B. Insane and Mentally Abnormal Prisoners

82. (1) Persons who are found to be insane shall not be detained in prisons and arrangements shall be made to remove them to mental institutions as soon as possible.

(2) Prisoners who suffer from other mental diseases or abnormalities shall be observed and treated in specialized institutions under medical management.

(3) During their stay in prison, such prisoners shall be placed under the special supervision of a medical officer.

(4) The medical or psychiatric service of the penal institutions shall provide for the psychiatric treatment of all other prisoners who are in need of such treatment.

83. It is desirable that steps should be taken, by arrangement with the appropriate agencies, to ensure if necessary the continuation of psychiatric treatment after release and the provision of social- psychiatric after-care.

C. PRISONERS UNDER ARREST OR AWAITING TRIAL

84. (1) Persons arrested or imprisoned by reason of a criminal charge against them, who are detained either in police custody or in prison custody (jail) but have not yet been tried and sentenced, will be referred to as "untried prisoners" in these rules.

(2) Unconvicted prisoners are presumed to be innocent and shall be treated as such.

(3) Without prejudice to legal rules for the protection of individual liberty or prescribing the
procedure to be observed in respect of untried prisoners, these prisoners shall benefit by a special regime which is described in the following rules in its essential requirements only.

85. (1) Untried prisoners shall be kept separate from convicted prisoners.

(2) Young untried prisoners shall be kept separate from adults and shall in principle be detained in separate institutions.

86. Untried prisoners shall sleep singly in separate rooms, with the reservation of different local custom in respect of the climate.

87. Within the limits compatible with the good order of the institution, untried prisoners may, if they so desire, have their food procured at their own expense from the outside, either through the administration or through their family or friends. Otherwise, the administration shall provide their food.

88. (1) An untried prisoner shall be allowed to wear his own clothing if it is clean and suitable.

(2) If he wears prison dress, it shall be different from that supplied to convicted prisoners.

89. An untried prisoner shall always be offered opportunity to work, but shall not be required to work. If he chooses to work, he shall be paid for it.

90. An untried prisoner shall be allowed to procure at his own expense or at the expense of a third party such books, newspapers, writing materials and other means of occupation as are compatible with the interests of the administration of justice and the security and good order of the institution.

91. An untried prisoner shall be allowed to inform immediately his family of his detention and shall be given all reasonable facilities for communicating with his family and friends, and for receiving visits from them, subject only to such restrictions and supervision as are necessary in the interests of the administration of justice and of the security and good order of the institution.

93. For the purposes of his defense, an untried prisoner shall be allowed to apply for free legal aid where such aid is available, and to receive visits from his legal adviser with a view to his defense and to prepare and hand to him confidential instructions. For these purposes, he shall if he so desires be supplied with writing material. Interviews between the prisoner and his legal adviser may be within sight but not within the hearing of a police or institution official.

D. Civil Prisoners

94. In countries where the law permits imprisonment for debt, or by order of a court under any other non-criminal process, persons so imprisoned shall not be subjected to any greater restriction or severity than is necessary to ensure safe custody and good order. Their treatment shall not be less favorable than that of untried prisoners, with the reservation, however, that they may possibly be required to work.

E. Persons Arrested or Detained Without Charge

95. Without prejudice to the provisions of article 9 of the International Covenant on Civil and Political Rights, persons arrested or imprisoned without charge shall be accorded the same protection as that accorded under part I and part II, section C. Relevant provisions of part II, section A, shall likewise be applicable where their application may be conducive to the benefit of this special group of persons in custody, provided that no measures shall be taken implying that re-education or rehabilitation is in any way appropriate to persons not convicted of any criminal offence.